The Castle Lectures
in Ethics, Politics, and Economics

THE QUESTION OF INTERVENTION

John Stuart Mill and the Responsibility to Protect

MICHAEL W. DOYLE

Yale

UNIVERSITY PRESS

New Haven and London

Yale University Press books may be purchased in quantity for
educational, business, or promotional use. For information, please e-mail
sales.press@yale.edu (U.S. office) or sales@yaleup.co.uk (U.K. office).

Set in Caslon type by Integrated Publishing Solutions.
Printed in the United States of America.

Library of Congress Cataloging-in-Publication Data

Doyle, Michael W., 1948–.
The question of intervention : John Stuart Mill and the responsibility to
protect / Michael W. Doyle.
    pages   cm.—(Castle lectures in ethics, politics, and economics)
Includes bibliographical references and index.
ISBN 978-0-300-17263-8 (cloth : alkaline paper) 1. United States—
Foreign relations—Moral and ethical aspects. 2. United States—Foreign
relations—Philosophy. 3. Mill, John Stuart, 1806–1873—Political and
social views. 4. Intervention (International law) 5. Responsibility to
protect (International law) 6. United States—Foreign relations—
2001–2009. 7. United States—Foreign relations—2009–. I. Title.
JZ1480.D69 2015
172'.4—dc23   2014019554

A catalogue record for this book is available from the British Library.

This paper meets the requirements of ANSI/NISO Z39.48-1992
(Permanence of Paper).

10 9 8 7 6 5 4 3 2 1

Parts of this book were given as the Castle Lectures in Yale's Program in Ethics, Politics, and Economics, delivered by Michael W. Doyle in 2011.

The Castle Lectures were endowed by Mr. John K. Castle. They honor his ancestor the Reverend James Pierpont, one of Yale's original founders. Given by established public figures, Castle Lectures are intended to promote reflection on the moral foundations of society and government and to enhance understanding of ethical issues facing individuals in our complex modern society.

For
Konrad Doyle Jurek
and his generation

CONTENTS

Preface

Sovereignty in its traditional state-centered form is being challenged throughout the international system. The events in Libya in 2011 and Syria in 2012 severely tested the balance between an emerging global norm of protecting people from violence and a traditional norm of states insisting on absolute sovereignty. This is an extremely consequential contest, with the winners as yet undecided.

At least two great powers, Russia and China, are suffering buyer's remorse for having bought into the global principle of the "responsibility to protect" peoples from massacres. They retreated from the principle after that responsibility was invoked to authorize regime change in countries such as Libya. Their remorse occurred just a few short years after they and every other member state of the United Nations unanimously endorsed the same principle at the World Summit in 2005, and then overwhelmingly reaffirmed it in 2009.

In a seemingly related process over the past twenty years, following the end of the Cold War, new nation states have been carved from old sovereign territories. In Yugoslavia in the 1990s there were the births, midwifed by NATO, of Slovenia, Croatia, Bosnia, Macedonia, and then, taking more than a decade, Kosovo. In seeming retort encouraged by Russia, there occurred the separations of Abkhazia and South Ossetia from Georgia. Most recently, South Sudan seceded from Sudan, and other states in Africa (Somalia, Congo, and Sudan again with Darfur) are experiencing separatist strains.

On top of those trends, the United Nations has shifted from its Cold War commitment to sovereign inviolability to a new intrusiveness in settling civil wars, called peacebuilding. And, reacting to the threats of international terrorism, states claim a right to preventive intervention.

What is at stake for sovereign nations and the world in how they understand the "responsibility to protect"—known as "R2P" by the activists and, in self-conscious distinction, "RtoP" by the United Nations? What should we make of the new wave of secessions? Is the enhanced UN role a determining factor in the new willingness to intervene?

To answer these questions, it is important to recognize that both sovereign countries and the organized international community have answered the most fundamental questions of state sovereignty—*Who* rules? *What principles* rule?—in evolving ways.

In the nineteenth century, European states, the US, and a few other powerful states such as Japan constructed high walls about their sovereign domestic jurisdiction. No foreign interference was allowed. Governments treated their subjects poorly or well solely according to local whims, laws, and constitutions. Other political societies in Africa, East and South Asia, and Latin America had very low sovereign walls. The great powers ruled them as colonies or intervened at will to impose foreign rules and foreign interests, whether it was protecting foreigners, collecting debts, or enforcing Christian morality.

Two of the great global governance achievements of the twentieth century revolutionized those norms. The first great milestone was recognition of the principle of sovereign equality: self-determination for all peoples, East and West, North and South. The second was the articulation of human rights: rights that should be accorded to all human beings.

Many of these achievements were routinely disregarded in

the Cold War, when the US and USSR repeatedly and unilaterally intervened to protect their perceived national interests and promote their ideologies throughout the world. But in the 1990s, sparked by both the opportunities emerging for global cooperation at the end of the Cold War and the disgraceful failures of strong countries to protect the most vulnerable peoples from genocide and other gross violations of basic human rights in Rwanda and the Balkans—and specifically the failure of the UN to protect Kosovars from war crimes and ethnic cleansing—humanitarian activists proposed the new Responsibility to Protect doctrine. RtoP was designed to fill a doctrinal governance gap between legal national sovereignty and ethical global humanity. Related sentiments of global responsibility and the new sense of international interdependence led to the recognition of new nations, the enhanced UN role in settling civil wars, and cross-border policing against terrorists.

In order to understand RtoP and the other new claimed responsibilities, we must begin by returning to an old and still difficult question in international politics: the question of intervention. To intervene or not to intervene? This is the question that animates this inquiry.

This book builds on the classic 1859 discussion of the ethics of nonintervention and intervention, J. S. Mill's "A Few Words on Non-Intervention," which is the genuine *locus classicus* of the modern debate. Mill is the place to start, for it would be foolish to pass up the opportunity to stand on the shoulders of so eminent a philosopher, who both developed modern utilitarianism and engaged in the practical political disputes of modern liberalism, and whose thought traces through just about all later disputes on when to intervene. Indeed, no one makes the case better than he for the nonintervention norm and why it should sometimes be overridden or disregarded.

Following Mill, I thus stress, more than has been conventional, the consequentialist character of the ethics of both non-intervention and intervention. It makes a difference whether we think that an intervention will do more good than harm or vice versa, and some of the factors that determine the outcome are matters of strategy and institutional choice. I also engage in a one-sided debate with Mill as I explore the significance of the many historical examples he employs to support his argument. Do they actually support his conclusions? Could they, given what he knew or should have known? Given what we now think we know? I will try to outline what I argue are better standards for intervention and nonintervention. My conclusion will be that, persuasive as the moral logic of his argument for liberal intervention sometimes is, the facts of the particular cases he cites actually tend to favor a bias toward nonintervention— that is, against overriding or disregarding nonintervention in the many circumstances he envisaged. That said, enough of his argument survives to warrant a firm rejection of strict noninterventionism and to suggest new standards for prudent and limited intervention, including a guarded defense of the new doctrine of Responsibility to Protect.

I have many people to thank for advice and inspiration in the writing of these chapters. Nicholas Sambanis organized the lectures on which this book is based. I thank Yale University and the Castle family for establishing them. I have benefited from thoughtful research assistance and suggestions from Peter Andrews, Alicia Evangelides, Sherie Gertler, Taylor McGowan, Jan Messerschmidt, Neta Patrick, Stefanie Pleschinger, Maggie Powers, and Camille Strauss-Kahn. I received helpful comments at various stages in seminars at Columbia, Oxford, Ottawa, Princeton, the School of Oriental and African Studies (London), the University of East London School of Law, Sheffield University, and West Point. I received valuable comments from Gary Bass, Garrett Brown, Ian Fishback, John Gaddis, Marine Guillaume, Amy Gutmann, Fen Hampson, Stephen Holmes, David Malone, Jeff McMahan, Stefano Recchia, Bruce Russett, Melissa Schwartzberg, Ian Shapiro, Chandra Sriram, Nadia Urbinati, Leslie Vinjamuri, Michael Walzer, Jennifer Welsh, and Noam Zohar. Matt Waxman and Chris Blattman read the entire manuscript and offered many helpful suggestions. The curators of the Palmerston Papers at the University of Southampton graciously accommodated my visit and requests for copies of a few of the fascinating papers housed there. I thank Bill Frucht and Dan Heaton of Yale University Press for valuable suggestions and painstaking copyediting. Olena Jennings assisted with edits and helped on the footnotes. Cynthia Crippen ably prepared the index.

I thank Mrs. Julie Kidd, whose grant from the Christian Johnson Endeavor Foundation has funded my research for many years. The Columbia Global Policy Initiative, launched by President Lee Bollinger in the fall of 2013, supported the last set of revisions.

I also greatly benefited from lively discussions and uninhibited debates on this and related topics in senior seminars in Political Science and in international ethics seminars in the School of International and Public Affairs at Columbia University. Last but not least, I thank the faculty and students at Yale University for spending their Thursday afternoons in a sunny October discussing with me the topics of nonintervention and intervention.

The Question of Intervention

INTRODUCTION

There is a country in Europe . . . whose foreign policy is to let other nations alone. . . . Any attempt it makes to exert influence over them, even by persuasion, is rather in the service of others, than itself: to mediate in the quarrels which break out between foreign states, to arrest obstinate civil wars, to reconcile belligerents, to intercede for mild treatment of the vanquished, or finally, to procure the abandonment of some national crime and scandal to humanity such as the slave trade.

—J. S. Mill, "A Few Words on Non-Intervention"

The question of intervention has been a significant and disturbing issue for anyone sharing a commitment to both universal human dignity and national self-determination. This disturbing quality is evident when we compare the lengthening list of interferences with the opening description of a policy to "let other nations alone." On the one hand, liberals, who are committed to the promotion of human rights, have provided

Epigraph: Citations to the 1859 "Non-Intervention" essay are to J. S. Mill, "A Few Words on Non-Intervention," in *Essays on Equality, Law, and Education,* ed. John M. Robson, 111–124 (Toronto: University of Toronto Press; London: Routledge and Kegan Paul, 1984), vol. 21 of *Collected Works of John Stuart Mill,* 33 vols. (1963–1991). I cite the essay, which is reprinted in Appendix 1, parenthetically by page number in the text. Other citations of the *Collected Works* are cited by volume title, with a parenthetical reference to the volume number (*CW* 21).

some of the strongest reasons to abide by a strict form of the nonintervention doctrine. It was only with the security of national borders, liberals such as Immanuel Kant and John Stuart Mill thought, that peoples could work out the capacity to govern themselves as free citizens. On the other hand, when applied in different contexts, those very same principles of universal human dignity have provided justifications for overriding or disregarding the principle of nonintervention.

In explaining this dual logic, I present an interpretive summary of Mill's famous argument for and against intervention, presented most clearly in his "A Few Words on Non-Intervention." Here, Mill illustrates what makes his "few words" both so attractive yet so alarming. We should be drawn to Mill's arguments because he was among the first to address the conundrums of modern intervention. The modern conscience simultaneously tries to adhere to three contradictory principles: first, the cosmopolitan, humanitarian commitment to assistance that protects basic human dignity and welfare, irrespective of international borders; second, respect for the significance of communitarian, national self-determination; and, third, accommodation to the reality of international anarchy, or the absence of reliable world government, that puts a premium on the pursuit of national security. Understanding yet rejecting ideal solutions, Mill's practical balancing of these three principles is what makes his arguments so distinctive, so attractive, and so disturbing.

We need to begin with a working definition of intervention in international politics. In international law, "intervention" is not just any interference. Foreign ideas, foreign culture, and foreign commerce can interfere in otherwise purely domestic social relations. According to Lassa Oppenheim, the influential late–nineteenth-century international legal scholar, intervention is the "dictatorial interference" in the political independence and territorial integrity of a sovereign state.[1] No single treaty has codified principles underlying this prohibition, and customary international law, while condemning intervention, contains numerous but contested exceptions.[2] Relevant principles in the "just war" tradition have been proposed by scholars, by politicians, and by citizens who have sought to provide good reasons why one should generally abide by these conventional principles of classic international law and good reasons why one should, on some occasions, breach those principles.[3]

1. Lassa Oppenheim, *International Law: A Treatise*, 2 vols. (London: Longmans, 1920), 1: 221.

2. Article 2(4) of the UN Charter prohibits the use of force in general and GA Res 2131 (UN Doc. A/RES/20/2131) (1965) provides partial evidence for customary law norms when it outlines potential violations and declares the "Inadmissibility of Intervention into the Domestic Affairs of States." For the complicated legal record see Lori Damrosch et al., *International Law: Cases and Materials* (St. Paul, MN: West Group, 2001), chapter 12.

3. As surveys of a large literature, I have found especially valuable John Vincent, *Nonintervention and International Order* (Princeton: Princeton University Press, 1974); Charles Beitz, *Political Theory and International Relations* (Princeton: Princeton University Press, 1979); Stanley Hoffmann, *Duties Beyond Borders* (Syracuse: Syracuse University Press, 1981); Anthony Ellis, "Utilitarianism and International Ethics," in *Traditions of International Ethics*, ed. Terry Nardin and David Mapel (Cambridge: Cambridge University Press, 1992), 158–179; Fernando Teson, *Humanitarian Intervention: An Inquiry into Law and Morality* (Irvington-on-Hudson, NY: Transnational, 1997); Edward Mortimer, "Under What Circumstances Should the UN Intervene Militarily in a 'Domestic' Crisis," in *Peacemaking and Peacekeeping for the New Century*, ed. Olara Otunnu and Michael Doyle (Lanham, MD: Rowman and Littlefield, 1998), 111–144; Nicholas Wheeler, *Saving Strangers* (Oxford: Oxford University Press, 2000); Ruti Teitel, *Humanity's Law* (New York: Oxford University Press, 2011); David Scheffer, ed., *Might v. Right* (New York: Council on Foreign Relations, 1989); Simon Chesterman, *Just War or Just Peace* (Oxford: Oxford University Press, 2003); Dean Chatterjee and Don Scheid, eds., *Ethics and Foreign Intervention* (Cambridge: Cambridge University Press, 2003); J. L. Holzgrefe and Robert Keohane, eds., *Humanitarian Intervention: Ethical, Legal,*

Traditionally, intervention is "dictatorial interference" or "forcible intrusion in domestic affairs" by deployment of military forces to coercively intervene between the domestic authority of a foreign state and some or all of its population.[4] Foreign ideas, foreign culture, and foreign commerce can interfere in otherwise purely domestic social relations; most do not "intervene."[5] But some nonmilitary, nonforcible interferences rise to the level of forcible coercion amounting to "dictatorial interference." I adopt the standard legal threshold for illegal coercion: aggression, invasion, supporting a rebellion by force, bombing, or a blockade (or, its legal equivalent, Security Council–mandated, compulsory economic sanctions).

It is also important to include in "intervention" new technologies such as cyberwarfare, and close cousins like compre-

---

and Political Dimensions (Cambridge: Cambridge University Press, 2003); Martha Finnemore, *The Purpose of Intervention* (Ithaca, NY: Cornell University Press, 2003); Jennifer Welsh, ed., *Humanitarian Intervention and International Relations* (Oxford: Oxford University Press, 2006); Thomas Weiss, *Humanitarian Intervention: Ideas in Action* (Malden: Polity, 2007); Gary Bass, *Freedom's Battle* (New York: Knopf, 2008).

4. Oppenheim, 1: 221; John Vincent, *Nonintervention and International Order* (Princeton: Princeton University Press, 1974), 13. "Intervention," for Oppenheim, "is dictatorial interference by a State in the affairs of another State for the purpose of maintaining or altering the actual condition of things." He divides the topic into external and internal intervention (for the second, meaning "into the territorial or personal supremacy of the State"); and he distinguishes between interventions by "right or without a right." I will focus on the internal, leaving aside the many interventions designed to pressure a state's foreign policy. I also take into account that nineteenth-century standards of right (collecting international debts, preserving the balance of power, etc.) have changed with the ratification of the UN Charter's prohibitions against the use of force (Art. 2[4]).

5. For a discussion, see Lori Damrosch, "Politics Across Borders: Nonintervention and Nonforcible Interference over Domestic Affairs," *American Journal of International Law* 83 (1989), 1–50.

hensive economic sanctions, which have the same effects on "territorial integrity and political independence" as invasion or blockade. If, for example, a cyberattack crashes a country's transport or banking system, an "attack" should be understood as having taken place. And this is the way the US Defense Department portrays possible cyberattacks on the US today. Or, if all of a country's suppliers or all of its foreign consumers choose to embargo the country, the effect is economically equivalent to a blockade. In a classic 1970s advocacy article, Richard Ullman made a case for the effectiveness of economic sanctions against Idi Amin's abuse of his own Ugandan population, noting that with 80 percent of Uganda's export revenues in coffee and the vast majority of that exported to the US and western Europe, the West had a powerful and legitimate tool for effective, nonmilitary, humanitarian intervention (legitimate and effective because the government coffee board controlled and benefited from coffee sales and the farmers were in any case already at subsistence).[6]

Interventions also need to be distinguished from ordinary wars between two states. With an intervention, a foreign military seeks to come between armed parties at war in a state, or between the state and its citizens (for example, to topple a regime or stop a genocide).[7] Interventions, therefore, do not include every act of aggression. For example, it is not an intervention when one state seeks to conquer another state's army, annex or

6. Richard Ullman, "Human Rights and Economic Power: The United States versus Idi Amin," *Foreign Affairs* 56 (1978), 529–543.

7. Webster defines "intervene" (whose Latin source means "coming between"), in the geopolitical sense, as "to interfere usually by force or threat of force in another nation's internal affairs, especially to compel or prevent an action or to maintain or alter a condition"; *Webster's Ninth New Collegiate Dictionary* (Springfield, MA: Merriam-Webster, 1986), 633.

seize a province, or change behavior. The attack on Pearl Harbor in 1941 was not an intervention in Hawaii or the US; it was an attempt to destroy the US Pacific Fleet and prevent the US from countering Japanese expansion in the Far East. However, some interstate wars turn into interventions, as when a conqueror occupies a territory and promotes regime change. For example, the US war effort against Japan in World War II transitioned into an intervention when the US occupation of Japan began in 1945, overturning the imperial order. Indeed, interventions often involve attempts to change or preserve regimes. They are often attempts at revolutions or counterrevolutions from abroad.

I focus on when intervention is permissible, not necessarily when it is desirable from the point of view of the intervener. Desirability depends on many other considerations, including a balancing of international against domestic priorities. Many Americans reasonably wonder why the US has been doing so much expensive nation building around the world while US unemployment has soared, the national deficit has been spiraling out of control, and our own cities, poor rural areas, public education, energy conservation and development, and infrastructure all need investment.

The first and foremost question still remains salient in international politics: when is it permissible to intervene in the politics of another country? International law offers answers to this question. States, and other entities such as international organizations, should intervene in the affairs of other states or regions only when it is lawful to do so. This is traditionally limited to three cases: in response to an invitation from the host state, in a situation of individual or collective self-defense, and in cases when the UN Security Council authorizes an intervention to prevent a threat to international peace and security or to stop an international armed conflict. All other interventions are illegal aggressions.

But established law is not sufficient as a guide to justifiable public policy. The law itself changes with evolving public norms. The Responsibility to Protect is a relatively new international norm that asserts a state's responsibility to protect its population from genocide, war crimes, crimes against humanity, and ethnic cleansing. Should a state fail to meet this responsibility, the United Nations General Assembly has recommended that the Security Council should step in to provide protection, including by military measures if necessary. The norm and its practice over the past decade (as I will describe in Chapter 4) are beginning to broaden the interpretation of the UN Charter's definition of international peace and security and, complementarily, narrow its interpretation of domestic sovereignty. Depending on how RtoP is interpreted, new just causes for intervention may be added. What counts as "self-defense" may be modified, and the best understanding of when the Security Council has authorized, or should authorize, force is likely to change as well.

Somewhat independently of the law, international ethics addresses the moral and practical questions about intervention. For shouldn't citizens also ask whether states should ever break the law and intervene because it is the right thing to do? Ethics recommends against intervention unless (1) it is for a just cause, (2) it can be done using justifiable means that do not exact disproportionate damage and that respect the principle of noncombatant immunity, and (3) it is reasonable to anticipate achieving a just outcome. These are the traditional just war criteria of *jus ad bellum* (just cause) and *jus in bello* (just means), plus the new but relevant complement of *jus post bellum* (just occupation and outcome).

In this book I focus on what just cause and just outcome have meant and what they should mean today. Although also important, just means—avoiding unnecessary harm to noncombatant civilians or unnecessarily cruel weapons—do not distinguish interventions from any other uses of force. The themes of this book include what is and is not a lawful intervention, and even more important, what is a just cause and how to encourage just outcomes.

The ethics of *jus ad bellum* is further distinguished by right intentions (just cause), right authority (traditionally a state, precluding private wars), last resort (encouraging peaceful settlement, prohibiting unnecessary wars), and proportionality (ensuring that wars are started only for causes that justify the likely harms they will inflict).[8] All these are in flux. Today just causes have narrowed from nineteenth-century permissiveness but broadened from twentieth-century self-defense to include (with the emergence of RtoP) humanitarian causes, such as stopping genocide. Right authority, as we shall see in the discussion of RtoP, has also expanded to include the UN Security Council for those wider humanitarian causes, while reserving state authorization to self-defense.

There is no comprehensive, authoritative, and universal answer to these questions. Clearly, much depends on what you consider to be just and what influences the prospects of justice. We know that in practice, standards have varied. Standards have varied based not only, or even primarily, on known facts, but on prevailing attitudes. In 1739, a staggering 20 percent of the Irish population died in a famine. There was scarcely an appreciable outcry from anywhere, except in Ireland. In 1847, another

8. A valuable survey can be found in Brian Orend, *The Morality of War* (Orchard Park, NY: Broadview, 2006).

3.5 percent of the Irish population died in the Great Famine. This produced an international outcry across Europe and North America.[9] We can find similar discriminations today across the globe over much shorter periods of time. While the killing of 10,000 Kosovars in 1999 resulted in intervention, the deaths of 800,000 Rwandans in 1994 yielded merely a belated relief effort, and in 1975–1978, the killing of 1.9 million Cambodians produced only ineffectual protests.

We see greater sensitivity to the conduct of war over time, but also much greater sacrifice. In the Napoleonic Wars, British sailors were drafted (impressed) but soldiers were volunteers, and few felt embarrassed not to volunteer.[10] Casualties were much lower. In all the Napoleonic Wars (1792–1815), the deaths in battle of British forces totaled 950 army officers, 15,214 from all other ranks, and 3,662 from the navy. All totaled, the casualties amounted to but one-third the number of British dead on one day at the battle of the Somme in 1916.[11]

In short, my interest is to explore both the philosophic ethics and the legitimacy of various arguments for interventions and noninterventions. Ethics touches on fundamental questions of right and utility. Legitimacy explores what groups, including the community of states, find authoritative or normative, whether by tradition or expressed agreement.[12] Needless to say,

9. Jasper Ridley, *Lord Palmerston* (London: Panther, 1972), 4.

10. We need only recall Jane Austen's Sir Walter Elliot in *Persuasion,* who felt free to disdain naval officers for their burnt complexions, acquired by years of service at sea.

11. Ridley, *Lord Palmerston,* 52.

12. For a good discussion of international legitimacy see Christian Reus-Smit, "International Crises of Legitimacy," *International Politics* 44 (2007), 157–174; Ian Hurd, *After Anarchy* (Princeton: Princeton University Press, 2007); and Hilary Charlesworth and Jean-Marc Coicaud, eds., *Fault Lines of International Legitimacy* (London: Cambridge University Press, 2012).

the two can be in tension; the right and good and the popular do not always overlap.

I am far from the first to explore these questions of legal and ethical intervention. Building on John Stuart Mill's modestly entitled "A Few Words on Non-Intervention" ("Non-Intervention," for short), published in 1859 in *Fraser's Magazine*, I will comment on Mill's arguments, defend some, condemn some, and refine others. I will share a more nuanced understanding of his widely appreciated but also strongly criticized arguments.

I ask the reader to imagine with Mill and me that, although we may differ on many details, we share a common moral universe in its broadest strokes. Imagine that we share a commitment to the rule of law and that we also share three broad ethical principles that we would prefer to integrate, maximizing their joint realization whenever possible.

First, we share a *humanitarian protection* principle.[13] We have a genuine concern for humanitarian protection, meaning that we care to respect the equal dignity of human beings around the world. This moral concern predates the official international recognition of fundamental human rights after World War II and goes back to classical times in the West. It can be found in many global religions and was secularized in the American and French revolutions.

Gladstone described this principle well in both 1876 and 1879, twenty years after Mill. In his famous denunciation of the Bulgarian Horrors in 1876, he said:

---

13. For a discussion and argument for the weight that should be given to humanitarian protection, domestically and internationally, see Robert Goodin, *Protecting the Vulnerable* (Chicago: University of Chicago Press, 1985). For modern human rights see Samuel Moyn, *The Last Utopia: Human Rights in History* (Cambridge: Harvard University Press, 2010).

Now there are states of affairs in which human sympathy refuses to be confined by the [old] rules, necessarily limited and conventional, of international law. . . . Let us cast aside our narrow and ill-conceived construction of the ideas of a former period . . . in order to protect humanity and defend justice.[14]

And in a later speech on Afghanistan he added—in purple, British Victorian, evangelical prose:

Remember that the sanctity of life in the hill villages of Afghanistan, among the winter snows, is as inviolable in the eye of Almighty God as can be your own. Remember that He who has united you as human beings in the same flesh and blood, has bound you by the law of mutual love; that that mutual love is not limited by the shores of this island, is not limited by the bounds of Christian civilization; that it passes over the whole surface of the earth, and embraces the meanest along with the greatest in its unmeasured scope.[15]

Articulating this principle is not the same as honoring it in practice. Like many other demanding principles, humanitarian protection is often honored in the breach. And not everyone even honors it in principle.

14. W. E. Gladstone, *Bulgarian Horrors and the Question of the East* (London: Murray, 1876), 57. This speech is quoted in Paul Gordon Lauren, *The Evolution of International Human Rights Visions Seen* (Philadelphia: University of Pennsylvania Press, 1998), which offers a valuable survey of humanitarian campaigns in the nineteenth century.

15. John Morley, *The Life of William Ewart Gladstone*, 3 vols. (London: Macmillan, 1903), 2: 595.

Second, Mill, you, and I appreciate the principle of *national self-determination.* We value the importance of collective self-determination and sovereignty, and the idea that people have a right beyond their individual rights to express, defend, and have respected their collective identity against foreign interference. The roots of this principle lie in basic human needs to find collective expression of group identities and to have those identities protected from attack by those who seek to undermine or destroy them.

Third, we share a *national security* principle. We appreciate the importance of national self-defense: national security is a responsibility that no government can fully cede to an international organization. The international community lacks a world government that could provide national security for all. For that reason, national self-help is an important value.

For most readers, accepting these three ethical principles is not an act of wild imagining, and it is not for me either. I will elaborate on each in an effort to answer a critically important question in contemporary world politics: what should we think about international intervention, given these commitments to humanitarian protection, national self-determination, and national security?

Building on Mill's arguments in "Non-Intervention" and armed with our three principles, I suggest that lessons can be gained by revisiting the examples Mill used to illustrate and defend his judgments. I also consider contemporary examples of related instances of intervention. Like Shakespeare's judge in Jaques's lament, I will be exploring "wise saws" (the three principles) and raising "modern instances" (from his and our times).[16]

Mill's first insight is to see those three principles as interre-

16. William Shakespeare, *As You Like It,* act 2, scene 7.

lated and continually relevant. Mill wrote "Non-Intervention" to counter Lord Palmerston's claim that only interests should guide British policy. Palmerston, former foreign secretary and prime minister, had famously said a decade earlier that England had no perpetual enemies and no perpetual allies. Only "our interests are eternal and perpetual, and those it is our duty to follow."[17] Mill learned that Palmerston had just attempted to defeat an international project to build a Suez Canal on the grounds that it might harm British commercial and strategic interests in the East. Mill rejected the view that England should consider only its own selfish aims. Doing so was wrong and harmful to England's moral reputation. Taking his rejection of Palmerston's policy as an occasion to reflect more broadly, drawing on his experiences in India and his longer and wider view of international questions, Mill tried to express "the true principles of international morality and the legitimate modifications made in it by differences of times and circumstances" in order to show that, like individuals, "nations have duties towards the weal of the human race."[18]

17. Palmerston's reply to his critics in House of Commons, March 1, 1848, Hansard (UK Parliament Official Report), 3rd Series, xcvii, pp. 121–123. Palmerston, a politician and not a philosopher, did not reject ideals and moral duties and may not have been as far from Mill as Mill portrayed. The difference was that Palmerston saw ideals as subordinate to interests. In the same speech, Palmerston also added that, where British interests do not dictate otherwise, "the real policy of England . . . is to be the champion of justice and right; pursuing that course with moderation and prudence, not becoming the Quixote of the world, but giving the weight of her moral sanction and support wherever she thinks that justice is, and wherever she thinks that wrong has been done. And acting this way will ensure that other states will join her, leaving her never dangerously alone and thus never dependent on permanent allies."

18. J. S. Mill, *Autobiography*, in *Autobiography and Literary Essays*, ed. John M. Robson and Jack Stillinger (Toronto: University of Toronto Press; London: Routledge and Kegan Paul, 1981), 263–264 (*CW* 1), and see the discussion in

It is now widely recognized that a basic problem with national interests and even security is that they are "ambiguous concepts" that lack both clear meaning and exclusive moral hegemony as guides to policy.[19] Only survival is unambiguous in content; other lesser interests—trade, investments, raw materials, prestige, and predominance—are often sectoral (not shared by all) and thus legitimately contestable on public interest and democratic grounds.

Equally important, Mill also rejects such moral Quixoticism as enforcing abstract rules or past international treaty commitments as if states were delinquents to be hauled into court.[20] The abstract principle of humanitarian protection, valuable as it is, must give way to a respect for national self-determination. As Mill so eloquently argues in "Non-Intervention," not every oppressive abuse that justifies a rebellion by locals justifies an intervention by foreigners. Humanitarian duties are contextual, and self-determination constrains humanitarian concern.

In its turn, the worthy principle of self-determination must be constrained by deeper principles, including humanitarian concern for individual well-being. Although Mill claimed to

---

Stefan Collini, Introduction to *Essays on Equality, Law, and Education,* vii–lvi (*CW* 21).

19. See Arnold Wolfers, "National Security as an Ambiguous Concept," *Political Science Quarterly* 67 (1952), 481–502; and Michael Walzer, "Against Realism," in *Just and Unjust Wars* (New York: Basic, 1977), 3–20. Regarding the limited predictive power of balances of material power, see Brian Healy and Arthur Stein, "The Balance of Power in International History" (33–61); and Jack Levy, "Causes of War" (209–333), in *Behavior, Society, and Nuclear War,* ed. Philip E. Tetlock, Jo L. Husbands, Robert Jervis, Paul Stern, and Charles Tilly, 3 vols., vol. 1 (New York: Oxford University Press, 1989); and Michael Doyle, *Ways of War and Peace* (New York: Norton, 1997), 173.

20. In a later essay, "Treaty Obligations" (1870), Mill criticizes those who think that Russia has to be held to the terms of the peace settlement that followed the Crimean War simply because Russia once accepted them.

have "sympathized more or less ardently with most of the rebellions, successful and unsuccessful, which have taken place in
my time," the Southern secession from the United States was
not one of them. Those who rebel for "the power of oppressing
others" had not the same "sacred right as those who do the
same thing to resist oppression practiced upon themselves."[21]
We, too, must now judge rebellions and secessions by their likely
consequences for all, not just for leaders and adherents.

To come full circle, genuine national security also deserves
weight and can override principles of nonintervention favored
by those who place exclusive weight on self-determining national sovereignty (as did some of Mill's contemporary liberals)
or international law with its strict adherence to national sovereignty and noninterference, as in some interpretations of the
UN Charter protections of territorial integrity and political independence (Article 2[4]).

The three principles, Mill cogently argues, need to be considered together. They are in some tension with one another,
and each demands consideration, but no single principle deserves exclusive dominance.

In Chapter 1 I address a puzzle—nonintervention itself. As
a liberal, Mill believed in equal rights, republican government,
and beneficent administration for all. Why, then, did he (should
we) oppose intervention to enforce equal rights, republican government, and beneficent administration globally? I will show
that he thinks interventions undermine national self-determination and tend to do more harm than good, stimulating new
civil wars, renewed autocracies, or colonial dependence.

21. Mill, "The Contest in America," *Fraser's Magazine* 65 (February 1862),
258–262. Stefan Collini discusses this issue as well when he introduces Mill's
"The Contest in America" and Mill's review of John Cairnes's *The Slave Power*
in *Essays on Equality, Law, and Education* (*CW* 21).

Mill then presents us with two additional puzzles. Given Mill's and our commitment to nonintervention, why should one ever intervene? For Mill that means answering when the arguments for nonintervention should be "overridden," and then when they should be "disregarded" (see Table 1).

In Chapter 2 I will focus on when to "override," by which I mean when other moral considerations overbalance nonintervention, such as national security (including rescuing your citizens) or humanitarian protection of any fellow human beings from massacres that shock the conscience of mankind. Here I discuss citizen rescue operations like Israel's raid at Entebbe in Uganda and such humanitarian interventions as the intervention that should have protected the Rwandans in 1994, but did not.

In Chapter 3 I will tackle the question of when to "disregard." When do the Millian considerations not to intervene not apply, because the principles of self-determination at the root of nonintervention literally do not fit the case? For one example, one disregards the nonintervention principle when self-determination does not have a single self to be determined: if some parts of a country want to secede, for example, or if the country is a "failed state" incapable of ruling itself. Here we will look at secession, including such examples as declarations of independence and the case of Kosovo; the case for counter-intervention to make sure the actual local struggle prevails, not another intervention; and the problematic Millian case for benign imperialism.

In Chapter 4 I will respond to the dangers and limitations revealed by arguments to override and disregard nonintervention. They tend to produce exploitative overintervention or neglectful underintervention that leaves vulnerable populations as prey or peoples in oppression. We need multilateral deliber-

Table 1

Mill's Cases for Intervention: Justifications for and Examples

	OVERRIDING				DISREGARDING		
	Self-defense and international civil war	Postwar standing menace	Mediation of protracted civil war	Humanitarian intervention	Self-determination secession	Counter-intervention	Benign imperialism
Justifications							
Mill's Examples	16th-c. Protestant–Catholic wars; 19th-c. "Liberals vs. Despots"	Napoleon; Reconstruction in US South	Portuguese midcentury	"severities repugnant to humanity"	Greece-Turkey; Belgium-Holland	Austria-Hungary, 1848–1849	Oude/Awadh
Contemporary Examples Considered	Citizen rescues, Entebbe; Cold War Brezhnev and Reagan doctrines	Occupations of Germany and Japan; postwar peacebuilding	UN peace enforcement and peacekeeping	Rwanda 1994; RtoP Doctrine and Libya, 2011	Somaliland, East Timor; Liechtenstein draft convention	Vietnam	Chapter VII mandates in peace enforcement

ation and decision on when to intervene and on how to manage the intervention in a way that fairly distributes burdens,
avoids exploitation, and provides plans to rebuild societies so
that intervention contributes to legitimate sustainable governments. Here I explore the new doctrine of the Responsibility
to Protect and the all-important test case: Libya, which in turn
had implications for the ongoing civil war in Syria.

In Chapter 5, on postbellum peacebuilding, I will explore
the rights and duties that both the intervened and the interveners have toward each other. I begin with an account of the
rights that defenders in a just war have against former aggressors,
including the right to ensure that aggression does not recom-
mence. I explore the Hague and Geneva Conventions on occupation law and the rights interveners sometimes have to transform the intervened while recognizing duties to protect human
rights and enhance the prospects for genuine self-determination.
The chapter's cases range from Germany and Japan after World
War II to the occupation of Iraq and the norms that should
govern UN peacebuilding.

In the conclusion I summarize the argument and point to
challenges that lie ahead. Throughout the book, I will engage
arguments against and for intervention in a one-sided but sympathetic debate with Mill as well as with contemporary scholars,
such as Michael Walzer, who have made major contributions to
the ongoing dialogue on the ethics of sovereignty and intervention. My conclusions center on the judgment that, persuasive
as the moral logic of Mill's views on intervention sometimes is,
the facts of the particular cases he cited and the examples we
now experience tend to favor a stronger bias toward nonintervention to be overridden or disregarded only in grave cases and
with multilateral deliberation.

I

Nonintervention

Nonintervention is the norm of modern international law, international ethics, and the just war tradition. There is an obvious reason why this is so: states make the law; they shape the just war tradition; and from the standpoint of international ethics, wars are inevitably harmful and need to be justified as a necessary resort. But the nonintervention norm is more problematic than it may seem. Mill rendered that norm problematic at the same time as he more thoroughly justified it. Recent developments in international law and the emerging record of actual interventions have sustained and refined that central norm of nonintervention, making it still the default position today; it can be overridden or disregarded only with good reasons.

MILL'S PUZZLE

We share many of John Stuart Mill's values. He deeply engages the first principle of international humanitarian protection, but balances it with concerns for self-determination and national security. Mill developed the core of a modern understanding of human dignity, conceived as autonomy, and its implications for political decision making. He saw human beings as fundamentally equal, and therefore equally capable of experiencing pleasure and pain.

Our natural sympathy, Mill believed, should lead us to choose acts and rules that maximize pleasure and minimize pain for

the greatest number. But Mill imposed an important qualifica-
tion on this goal that is too often overlooked. Mill wanted to
constrain this maximization of utility by prioritizing both the
freedom to lead unrestricted lives, as long as those life plans
did not harm the freedom of others, and the realization that
not all pleasures and pains were equal. Some were higher,
some lower; some expressed human creativity, others did not.
Poetry was better than "pushpin."[1]

Mill defends two ideal principles for a political constitution.
The first is maximum equal liberty, allowing each adult to develop his or her own potential on the view that each individual
is the best judge of what is and is not in his or her interest,
so long, however, as no one interferes with the equal liberty of
others. When public regulation is necessary, the second principle of representative government should govern. To maximize
effective consent and the utility of collective decisions, decisive
weight should be given to the preferences of the majority, as
represented by knowledgeable politicians.[2]

This leads to Mill's puzzle: One might think that these
principles would give rise to a global commitment to enforce
an international version of the US Constitution's "Guarantee
Clause" (Article 4, Section 4), under which each state would be
required to guarantee its citizens a republican representative
form of government and a Fourteenth Amendment that provides equal protection of the laws to all persons. But Mill does

1. Pushpin was a popular but mindless game in which boys stuck pins in
each other's hats and then took turns knocking them off. Good discussions of
the wider aspects of Mill's ethical theory are in Alan Ryan, *J. S. Mill* (London:
Routledge and Kegan Paul, 1975); and Nicholas Capaldi, *John Stuart Mill: A
Biography* (New York: Cambridge University Press, 2004), 249–265.

2. For analysis of Mill's politics, see Dennis Thompson, *John Stuart Mill
and Representative Government* (Princeton: Princeton University Press, 1976).

not draw this globalizing implication, arguing instead that there is an important distinction between domestic and international justice.

Instead, he argues for nonintervention as the general rule among civilized, modern countries. Why? He does so for a variety of reasons.

Starting with the simplest and most *direct* reason not to intervene: intervention can be dangerous to national security. Mill advised us to be wary of the dangers of intervention for national security and self-defense. For Mill, national security cautioned against an otherwise justifiable British counterintervention in the Austro-Hungarian war (Hungary's rebellion against Austria) in 1848–1849. Mill warned: "It might not have been consistent with the regard every nation is bound to pay to its own safety for England to have taken up this position single-handed" ("Non-Intervention," 124).

Then there are also *indirect* reasons for nonintervention, those bearing on other valued ends, which constitute important constraints on nonintervention for Mill. Key among the indirect considerations are rules of international law among sovereign civilized states that prohibit intervention. Following the eminent British jurist John Austin, Mill distinguished between law (commands of the sovereign) and positive morality (opinions widely held). International law was the prime example of the latter.[3] These laws, though unenforceable and legally

3. See John Stuart Mill, "Austin on Jurisprudence," *Newspaper Writings,* ed. Ann Robson and John M. Robson (Toronto: Toronto University Press; London: Routledge and Kegan Paul, 1986), 177 (*CW* 22). International law is "law" only insofar as "effect is given to its maxims by the tribunals of any particular country; and in that capacity it is not international law, but a part of the particular law of that country."

discretionary as most states then saw them, had moral value
for Mill, as they do today. Peace should not be broken without
good cause. These laws might have been unenforceable, but for
Mill, they were not morally discretionary.

The rules of law embody the values of coordination and
consensual legitimacy. They help, as Mill argues, to proclaim
international equality and protect the weakest states.[4] Rules—
almost any rules—have value in themselves by helping to avoid
unintended clashes with severe consequences to human life.
Today, it is widely recognized that they serve as focal points
for coordination or rules of the road, such as "driving on the
right." Without some rules of the road, unsought strife—
including death and anarchy—would ensue. International law,
moreover, built on the foundation of sovereign equality of states,
was developed through consent and painstakingly achieved
compromises among diverse moralities. This mere process of
achieving consent made them legitimate. The process also reflected the development of an institutional infrastructure that
both mitigated the anarchy of world politics and reflected a
negotiated set of norms that constituted a kind of international
social contract.[5] They were agreed upon and the principle of
pacta sunt servanda required their validity.[6]

Some also have suggested that an expectation of intervention would be systemically harmful by creating a moral haz-

4. See "Treaty Obligations" (1870) in *Essays on Equality, Law, and Education,* ed. John M. Robson, 341–348 (*CW* 21).

5. Raising these arguments, see Joshua Cohen, *The Arc of the Moral Universe*
(Cambridge: Harvard University Press, 2011).

6. *Pacta sunt servanda* is Latin for "agreements must be upheld." For discussions of this fundamental principle, see Terry Nardin, *Law, Morality, and the
Relations of States* (Princeton: Princeton University Press, 1983), and Thomas
Franck, *Fairness in International Law and Institutions* (Oxford: Clarendon,
1995).

ard.[7] Imagine there is a norm holding that any government
that inflicts more than one thousand civilian deaths on its population will be subject to armed intervention and toppled by a
multilateral force. At first sight, this appears to be a valuable
norm of protection. But now also imagine this situation: There
is a disaffected group in the country that wants to overthrow
the government but is incapable of doing this on its own.
Hiding amid crowds, it then attacks the police in order to pro-
voke retaliation, relying on the police's inability adequately to
discriminate between ordinary civilians and terrorist attackers.
Such a group, absent the rule, might have worked peacefully
for change or have been deterred from violence. With the
eventual cost born by the foreign interveners, it now provokes
a thousand or more casualties that would not have otherwise
occurred in order to achieve a revolution it could not have otherwise won. The lower and the more certain the threshold of
deaths or casualties needed to justify an intervention, the more
likely the "moral hazard" for unnecessary armed rebellions is
likely to be.

But the moral hazard of excess intervention is not the only
moral consideration. For, conversely, the higher the threshold
and the more certain it is, the greater the license the government has to forcibly repress its population without fear of foreign intervention. With no constraint, the international cost of
violent domestic oppression is zero. Add to this the sovereign
privilege of foreign military assistance and sovereign credit for
borrowing, and international constraints on state action reduce

7. This problem was raised at the Castle Lectures by my host, Nicholas
Sambanis. One source of the argument is Alan Kuperman's criticism of intervention to stop the Rwandan genocide, discussed further in "Mitigating the
Moral Hazard of Humanitarian Intervention," *Global Governance* 14 (2008),
219–240.

even further.[8] In Syria in 2014, President Assad was importing arms and military assistance from Russia and Iran and relying on the military assistance of Hezbollah fighters. All this, as President Putin of Russia claimed, was legal. It was the privilege accorded President Assad as the government of a sovereign state, while assistance to the rebels was illegal.[9] Some threshold sufficiently high and subject to international discretion looks least likely to succumb to the dangers of unnecessary rebellion or unconstrained repression, and the consequent violence that flows from them.

To these important reasons for a rule of nonintervention, we can add the fact that outside interventions that start well can still easily become corrupted. The unavoidable "dirty hands" of the violent means of intervention often become unduly "dangerous hands" in international interventions.[10] International history is rife with interventions justified by high-sounding principles—ending the slave trade or suttee, or introducing law and order and civilized behavior, or bringing democracy to an autocratic state—that readily turn into self-serving, imperialist "rescues" in which the intervener stays to profit and control without coming close to achieving the original justifying prin-

8. Thomas Pogge, *World Poverty and Human Rights* (Cambridge: Polity, 2008), see chapter 6.3. See also Andrew Kydd and Scott Strauss's "The Road to Hell? Third Party Intervention to Prevent Atrocities," *American Journal of Political Science,* http://onlinelibrary.wiley.com/store/10.1111/ajps.12009/asset/ajps/1. The authors develop a model showing how multilateral impartiality and cost imposition can mitigate the negative effects of intervention.

9. James Blitz et al., "Putin Warns West over Arms for Rebels," *Financial Times,* June 17, 2013.

10. For discussion, see Jennifer Welsh, "Taking Consequences Seriously: Objections to Humanitarian Intervention," in *Humanitarian Intervention and International Relations,* ed. Jennifer Welsh (Oxford: Oxford University Press, 2006), 56–68.

ciples of intervention. So Mill, referencing French sympathy for the Polish rebellion against Russia, warns that even if liberal France undertakes a war "for no selfish object," in less than a year "the national character would again be perverted, as it was by Napoleon—the rage for victory and conquest would again become the dominant passion in the breasts of Frenchmen."[11] Mill therefore argues for a requirement that the intervener govern its actions according to the interests of the intervened, looking for something more than a unilateral decision, and respecting the multilateral processes of international law. These are important procedural considerations in weighing the justice of an intervention.

Mill adds yet another indirect argument against intervention, which points to the difficulties of transparency or uncertainty in understanding what self-determination might mean for a people abroad. Historically, authentic "freedom fighters" have been difficult to identify. Particular national regimes of liberty and oppression are difficult for foreigners to "unpack." They often reflect complicated historical compromises made today or long before—contracts of a Burkean sort among the dead, the living, and the yet to be born. "Every civilized country," Mill notes, "is entitled to settle its internal affairs in its own way, and no other country ought to interfere with its discretion, because one country even with best intentions, has no chance of properly understanding the internal affairs of another."[12] This is an argument against the sort of intervention

11. One wonders whether the British and other national characters are similarly subject to this. Mill, *French News Examiner,* December 19, 1830, in Newspaper Writings, 809 (*CW* 22).

12. Letter to James Beal, April 19, 1865, quoted in Kenneth Miller, "John Stuart Mill's Theory of International Relations," *Journal of the History of Ideas* 22 (1961), 509.

that assumes one country can understand another's conflicts and, secondarily, in favor of not making a decision to intervene (if necessary) easily or early, but instead after much consideration and deliberation, as just war requires, as a "last resort."

Mill acknowledges that sovereignty and the legitimacy of intervention ultimately depend upon consent of those intervened against. The legitimacy of intervention, as Mill says, is subject to "their own spontaneous election" ("Nonintervention," 121). If the people welcome an intervention, then, the contemporary just war theorist Michael Walzer adds in a Millian vein, "it would be odd to accuse [the interveners] of any crime at all."[13] But as Mill and Walzer also argue, we cannot make these judgments reliably in advance, either because our information is incomplete or because the case is complicated by competing reasonable claims to justice that foreigners do not have a reasonable basis to adjudicate.

Mill's two most powerful arguments against intervention are based *directly* on considerations of self-determination and individual harm, the collective value of sovereignty and the humanitarian protection principle. Intervention for freedom and democracy, Mill argues, will not be authentic—and neither will it do to the individual people who are subject to the intervention in their country any real good. Quite the contrary, Mill contends that the war that accompanies intervention always does harm to the resident people.

The collective value of self-determination means that outside intervention for self-determination is not "real." It is "not real" insofar as imposing a free democratic government *by force* cannot be truly authentic; it cannot be *self-determining*. It is

13. Michael Walzer, "The Moral Standing of States," in *International Ethics,* ed. Charles Beitz et al. (Princeton: Princeton University Press, 1985), 221–27.

not free self-determination, because an imposed regime is literally not the people's government—they have not struggled for it, and they have not defined its specific content in the process. Nonintervention, by its very nature and its inherent value, enables citizens to determine their own way of life without outside interference. If democratic rights and liberal freedoms are to mean something, they have to be worked out among those who share them and are realizing them through their own participation.

Kant's "Perpetual Peace" (1795) had earlier made a strong case for respecting the right of nonintervention because it afforded a polity the necessary territorial space and political independence in which free and equal citizens could work out what their own way of life would be.[14] For Mill, intervention avowedly to help others actually undermines the authenticity of domestic struggles for liberty.

A free government achieved by means of intervention would not be authentic or self-determining because the interveners— not the citizens of that state through their own actions—would determine the government. "[The] evil [of intervention]," Mill declares, "is, that if they have not sufficient love of liberty to be able to wrest it from merely domestic oppressors, the liberty

14. Kant's fifth preliminary article of perpetual peace prohibits forcible interference in "the constitution and government of another state," for to do so would violate "the right of people dependent on no other and only struggling with its internal illness"; Immanuel Kant, "Perpetual Peace," in *Kant's Political Writings*, ed. Hans Reiss, trans. H. B. Nisbet (Cambridge: Cambridge University Press, 1970), 93–130. See also the chapters by Pierre Hassner and Andrew Hurrell in *Just and Unjust Intervention: European Thinkers from Vitoria to Mill*, ed. Stefano Recchia and Jennifer Welsh (Cambridge: Cambridge University Press, 2013). For further comment, see Sankar Muthu, *Enlightenment Against Empire* (Princeton: Princeton University Press, 2003), chapters 4–5, and the concluding chapter of my *Liberal Peace* (New York: Routledge, 2011).

which is bestowed on them by other hands than their own, will have nothing *real*"("Nonintervention," 122). Authentic governance is much more like poetry than pushpin.[15]

In *Considerations on Representative Government* Mill later discusses the importance of nationality for legitimate governance and the significance of its autonomous creation:

> A portion of mankind may be said to constitute a Nationality, if they are united among themselves by common sympathies, which do not exist between them and any others which make them co-operate with each other more willingly than with other people, desire to be under the same government, and desire that it should be government by themselves or a portion of themselves, exclusively. This feeling of nationality may have been generated by various causes. Sometimes it is the effect of identity of race and descent. Community of language, and community of religion, greatly contribute to it. Geographical limits are one of its causes. But the strongest of all is identity of political antecedents; the possession of a national history, and consequent community of recollections; collective pride and humiliation, pleasure and regret, connected with the same incidents in the past.[16]

15. For an exposition of the "romantic individualist" elements and "republican moralist" in John Stuart Mill's political thought, see H. S. Jones, "John Stuart Mill as Moralist," *Journal of the History of Ideas* 53 (1992), 287–308.

16. John Stuart Mill, *Considerations on Representative Government*, in *Essays on Politics and Society*, ed. John M. Robson (Toronto: University of Toronto Press; London: Routledge and Kegan Paul, 1977), 546 (*CW* 19).

In short, there is no universal form of free government. Authentic freedom is the right and capacity to discover and make your version of self-determined governance for you and your fellow citizens. Britain and the United States both have democratic governments protective of individual liberty. But the UK head of state is hereditary, and the UK has an established church. Imagine if the Kennedys, Bushes, or Obamas suddenly declared themselves hereditary heads of state, while making the vice presidency the democratically elected head of government, or if any American president made his religion the official state religion.

John Stuart Mill provides his last and most powerful direct argument for nonintervention in focusing on likely humanitarian consequences when he explains that it would be a mistake to export freedom to a foreign people that was not in a position to win it on its own. In addition to not being "real," forcibly imported freedom would have "nothing *permanent*" to it ("Nonintervention," 122, emphasis added).

A people given freedom by a foreign intervention would not, he argues, be able to hold on to it. Connecting *permanence* to *reality*, he notes that it is only by winning and holding on to freedom through local effort that one acquires a true sense of its value. It is only by winning the "arduous struggle" for freedom that one generates the political capacities to defend it adequately against threats of foreign invasion or of domestic opposition, whether by force or subtle manipulation ("Nonintervention," 123). The struggle mobilizes citizens into what could become a national army and mobilizes as well a capacity and willingness to tax themselves for public purposes.

Mill is not romanticizing self-determination. Self-determining representation does not necessarily mean good government.

Good government for Mill is a complex amalgam of participation and competence, popular engagement and expert bureaucratic direction, which are all sustained by education. Lacking the right conditions of popular adherence to law and popular engagement in policy, democracy and the policies adopted by democratic governments can be destructive. Educated elites have vital roles to play. The best that can be said for popular self-determination is that under the right conditions it is better than autocratic rule, and especially better than an imposed foreign autocracy.[17]

Mill thus argues: If liberal government were to be introduced into a foreign society, in the knapsack of a conquering liberal army, the local liberals placed in power would find themselves immediately in a difficult situation. Not having been able to win political power on their own, they would have few domestic supporters and many nonliberal domestic enemies. They then would end up doing one of three things:

1. They would begin to rule as previous governments did, by repressing the opposition and acting to "speedily put an end to all popular institutions." Indeed, "when freedom has been achieved *for* them, they have little prospect of escaping this fate" ("Nonintervention," 122, emphasis added). The intervention would have done no good. Lacking deep domestic support, it simply would have created another oppressive government.

17. See Mill, *Considerations on Representative Government,* and Dennis Thompson, *John Stuart Mill and Representative Government* (Princeton: Princeton University Press, 1976), esp. chapters 1 and 2. But also see the discussion of the imperial exception discussed below in Chapter 2.

2. They would simply collapse in an ensuing civil war because the imposed government lacked the popular support to achieve and hold power on its own. In this scenario, intervention will have produced not freedom and progress but a civil war with all its attendant violence.

3. The interveners would have continually to send in foreign support and effectively become a permanent occupation. Rather than having established a free government, one that reflected the participation of the citizens of the state, the intervention would have created a puppet government, one that reflects the wills and interests of the intervening and only truly sovereign state. "No people ever was and remained free, but because it was determined to be so; because neither its rulers nor any other party in the nation could compel it to be otherwise." ("Nonintervention," 122)

Let us see now the extent to which modern international law and the practice of states embeds this nonintervention default position.

INTERNATIONAL LAW

Nonintervention has become firmly entrenched in international law today, but it was a weak guide to action in the nineteenth century. It was only in the twentieth century that it became influential and regulative of actual practice.

In the nineteenth century, great debates did shape public decisions on the use of force. In addition to material interests, statesmen debated ethical values that might or might not be served by intervening. From the 1820s to the 1840s, the British

Parliament debated interventions in Spain, Greece, Belgium, Texas, Egypt, Poland, and Portugal.[18] But while interests and principles were central, the legal dimension was secondary. In Mill's day, international law had little to say about when war was justified. The laws of war and peace (*jus ad bellum*) were largely discretionary. There were laws of war concerning how to fight a war justly (*jus in bello*), and there were laws of peace telling statesmen what to do to avoid a war (neutrality laws and the like). If states chose war, the laws of war would apply; if they chose to stay at peace or to be neutral, then they had to follow other rules respecting sovereignty.[19] Whether to go to war, or declare war, however, was a matter of legal discretion.

Beginning with the Kellogg-Briand Pact of 1928, and reaffirmed by the UN Charter in 1945, international law both opposed war as a matter of state discretion and was highly protective of the domestic jurisdiction of states.[20] The UN Charter—international law's supreme and authoritative source—states in Article 2(4):

> All Members shall refrain in their international relations from the threat or use of force against the territorial integrity or political independence of any state, or in any other manner inconsistent with the Purposes of the United Nations.[21]

18. Jasper Ridley, *Lord Palmerston* (London: Panther, 1972), 31; Kenneth Bourne, *The Foreign Policy of Victorian England, 1830–1902* (Oxford: Clarendon, 1970).

19. Lassa Oppenheim, *International Law: A Treatise*, 2 vols. (London: Longmans, 1920), 1: 221; and see the valuable discussion in Eliav Lieblich, *International Law and Civil Wars: Intervention and Consent* (London: Routledge, 2013).

20. For discussion, see Yoram Dinstein, *War, Aggression, and Self-Defence*, 3rd ed. (Cambridge: Cambridge University Press, 2001), chapters 3–5.

21. UN Charter, Art. 2(4). On the charter's authority, see UN Charter, Art. 103.

The UN itself is prohibited from intervening in matters "essentially within the domestic jurisdiction" of any state (except when the Security Council approves measures to prevent or stop international threats to peace or breaches of the peace or acts of aggression, discussed in the subsequent chapters). Article 2(7) states:

> Nothing contained in the present Charter shall authorize the United Nations to intervene in matters which are essentially within the domestic jurisdiction of any state or shall require the Members to submit such matters to settlement under the present Charter; but this principle shall not prejudice the application of enforcement measures under Chapter VII.[22]

The review session of the International Criminal Court (ICC), June 2010, clarified what the "threat or use of force" means.[23] The criminal uses of force were defined to include:

- planning, preparation, or execution of all forcible acts, including "invasion, armed attack . . . or occupation" by armed forces of one state on the territory of another state;
- "bombardment . . . or any weapon used . . . against the territory of another state";
- "blockade of the ports";
- "attack on the armed forces of another state";
- "use of armed forces" present by agreement in another state beyond the terms of that agreement;

22. UN Charter, Art. 2(7).

23. See Rev. Conf. of the Rome Statute, 13th plenary meeting, June 11, 2010, I.C.C. Doc. RC/Res. 6 (The Crime of Aggression) and the amendments. See id. Annex 1, Art. 8 *bis*.

- allowing territory to be used by one state for an attack on another state;
- and sending armed bands, or taking "substantial involvement therein," to attack another state.

These standards do not take effect until 2017, and even then they take effect only for parties to the Rome Statute of the ICC, which excludes some of the most powerful pillars of the international legal order, such as Russia, India, China, and the United States. Still, the ICC revisions track customary international law, as reiterated in General Assembly Resolution 3314 (1974), International Court of Justice rulings in the Nicaraguan and Bosnian cases, and the *Tadic* ruling of the International Criminal Tribunal for the former Yugoslavia.[24]

Everything short of what is included in the ICC's list—less coercive than an economic blockade, such as mandatory enforced economic sanctions, or the sending of armed bands—is considered permissible interference. The underlying assumption is that other means do not illegally impinge on territorial integrity or political independence, and are not from the legal point of view "intervention." Other forms of interference may be prohibited by treaty, such as by the World Trade Organi-

---

24. U.N.G.A. Res. 3314, Dec. 14, 1974; Case Concerning the Application of the Convention on the Prevention and Punishment of the Crime of Genocide (*Bosnia and Herzegovina v. Serbia and Montenegro*), Judgment, I.C.J. Reports 2007, p. 43; Military and Paramilitary Activities in and against Nicaragua (*Nicaragua v. United States of America*), Merits, Judgment, I.C.J. Reports 1986, p. 14; International Criminal Tribunal for the Former Yugoslavia, Appeals Chamber, Prosecutor v. Tadic, July 15, 1999 (Case no. IT-94-1-A). These are widely shared international understandings of the law. But it should be noted that in addition to opposing the latest standards affirmed at the ICC Review in 2010, some states, including the US, dissented from or rejected earlier ICJ and other court rulings.

zation for trade disruptions. But these latter interferences are akin to breaches of contract rather than crimes of intervention, subject to other states retaliating with their own trade sanctions, not force.

The International Court of Justice in its 1986 judgment in the Nicaragua case tried to clarify the definition of nonintervention: "the principle of non-intervention involves the right of every sovereign State to conduct its affairs without outside interference. . . . The Court considers that it is part and parcel of customary international law."[25] The Court further specified that "the principle forbids all States or groups of States to intervene directly or indirectly in the internal or external affairs of other States" and that "a prohibited intervention must accordingly be one bearing on matters in which each State is permitted, by the principle of State sovereignty, to decide freely. One of these is the choice of a political, economic, social and cultural system, and the formulation of foreign policy. Intervention is wrongful when it uses methods of coercion in regard to such choices, which must remain free ones. . . . The element of coercion . . . defines, and indeed forms the very essence of, prohibited intervention."[26] But in *DRC v. Uganda* (2005), the Court seemed more expansive, noting that coercion could be exerted by means other than armed force, saying that *Nicaragua* had made it clear that the principle of non-intervention prohibits a State "to intervene, directly or indirectly, with or without armed force, in support of the internal opposition within a State."[27]

The issue partly turns on what is considered domestic juris-

25. ICJ Reports 1986, para. 202.
26. Ibid., para. 205.
27. ICJ Reports 2005, para. 16.

diction. As Ian Brownlie has suggested in his influential text-
book, this appears to involve a tautology, for the international
prohibition against intervention in domestic jurisdiction itself
requires understanding what international law makes international and what it leaves as domestic.[28] The expansion of
human rights law, for example, permits states to sanction with
trade or foreign aid measures violations of internationally recognized human rights.[29]

All of this means that the current understanding of illegal intervention is coercive interference: *forceful intervention is clearly
coercive and hence—absent self-defense, consent, or Security Council authorization—is illegal.*

Force is illegal unless it is (1) in individual or collective self-
defense against an armed attack; (2) invited by the state intervened in; (3) a response to a "threat to international peace and
security" authorized by the Security Council; or (4) a response
to violations of the Genocide Convention and authorized by
the Security Council.

Force invited by the host state does not violate its "political
independence," so it, too, is legal.[30] Who can issue such invitations? Heads of state and of government can; invitations by di-

28. Ian Brownlie, *Principles of International Law,* 6th ed. (Oxford University
Press, 2003), 290–295.
29. See the discussion in the para. 703 (ff) p. 177 of the American Law Institute, *Foreign Relations Law of the United States, Restatement of the Law Third*
(St. Paul, MN: American Law Institute Publishers, 1986), Louis Henkin, Rapporteur. Lori Damrosch, "Politics Across Borders: Nonintervention and Nonforcible Influence over Domestic Affairs," *American Journal of International Law*
83 (1989), 1–50, offers a strong argument that actions supporting internationally recognized human rights do not constitute illegal intervention.
30. See Lieblich, *International Law and Civil Wars,* and Louise Doswald-
Beck, "The Legal Validity of Military Intervention by Invitation of the Government," *British Yearbook of International Law* 56 (1986), 189–252.

vided legislatures are not so clear. And what happens if there is no state or more than one group or nationality claims to be the "state"? We will return to this question in our discussion of secession in Chapter 3.

A good example of legal "intervention by invitation" is the recent sending of one hundred US combat troops to advise the regional effort in central Africa to capture Joseph Kony, the notorious head of the Lord's Resistance Army. As President Obama explained: "Subject to the approval of each respective host nation, elements of these US forces will deploy into Uganda, South Sudan, the Central African Republic and the Democratic Republic of the Congo."[31]

Difficult issues arise when rebels or secessionists claim to be states capable of inviting an intervention. Here, the law and ethics of civil wars—the rules of "insurgency" and "belligerency"—enter as exceptions to nonintervention. Under classic nineteenth-century international law, if rebels are "insurgents" they are in arms against their government (not merely criminals), but they have no international status. Other states can aid the sovereign government and must respect its sovereignty, unless they want to be at war with that government. If, on the other hand, the rebels succeed in securing territory, maintain a semblance of organization, and are themselves prepared to abide by the laws of war, then they become "belligerents." Since these

31. Matt Spetalnik and Laura Macinnis, "Obama Sends Military Advisers to Uganda," *Thomson Reuters 2011,* accessed October 14, 2011. For other examples see Karsten Nowrot and Emily Schabacker, "The Use of Force to Restore Democracy: International Legal Implications of the ECOWAS Intervention in Sierra Leone," *American University International Law Review* 14 (1998), 312–412; David Wippman, "Military Intervention, Regional Organizations, and Host-State Consent," *Duke Journal of Comparative and International Law* 7 (1996), 209–240.

rebels may also be fighting at sea, other governments have a problem. Should ships captured by the rebels be treated as pirate conquests? Should rebel ships be given port facilities? If the rebels are not given lawful status, other governments may well find themselves at war with a rebel "government." To maintain peace, neutrality is required. So other governments tend to recognize the belligerency of the rebels, granting them rights at sea as if they were sovereign powers.[32] I take up the matter of when such rights should be granted in the discussion of national liberation and justifiable secession.

The UN Charter gives the Security Council a special role to play in adjudicating the norms of nonintervention. Article 2(7) specifies that "[nothing] contained in the present Charter shall authorize the United Nations to intervene in matters which are essentially within the domestic jurisdiction of any state."[33] But this provision is subject to the exception of "enforcement measures under Chapter VII," which in turn are formally limited in Article 39 to measures the Security Council finds appropriate "in order to maintain or restore international peace and security." Domestic abuses generally do not—in black-and-white-letter Charter law—qualify as "international" threats.

All states have an obligation to prevent, stop, and punish genocide, though they should do so with the authorization of the Security Council of the UN. How the UN may be adding other harms, such as the standards in Responsibility to Protect,

32. Richard Falk, "Janus Tormented: The International Law of Internal War," in *International Aspects of Civil Strife*, ed. James Rosenau (Princeton: Princeton Press, 1964), 185–248; and the chapters by John Lawrence Hargrove and Rein Mullerson in *Law and Force and the New International Order*, ed. Lori Damrosch and David Scheffer (Boulder, CO: Westview, 1991).

33. UN Charter, Art. 2(7).

to genocide as justifiable reasons for intervention will be addressed in later chapters.

The rules on nonforceful coercive intervention are, on the other hand, ambiguous. States have the right to give or withhold foreign aid, and they typically impose conditions on it that interfere with domestic practices, but the recipient state can refuse the aid.

We still may want to ask whether, substantively, lesser interferences so restrict sovereign rights to territorial integrity and political independence that they should qualify as coercive intervention rather than licit interference. Some states in the developing world have sought to expand "intervention" and defend self-determination such that all unwanted interferences are declared illegitimate.[34] But in a complex interdependent world, such expansion is prone to rejection because states also have a right to freely engage in foreign relations. In effect, states that do not want to be criticized because such criticism would interfere with their rights to cultural autonomy also do not want to have their right to criticize other states restricted by inter-

34. See International Covenant on Civil and Political Rights, 999 U.N.T.S. 171 (1966); International Covenant on Economic, Social and Cultural Rights, 993 U.N.T.S. 3 (1966); Declaration on Principles of International Law Concerning Friendly Relations and Cooperation among States in Accordance with the Charter of the United Nations, GA Res. 2626 (XXV), UN Doc. A/8082 (October 24, 1970), principle vi. All embody the tension between self-determination as noninterference and the right to engage in friendly relations. Colonialism and forcible intervention are clearly barred, but other interferences all are contestable. Useful are the discussions in Joshua Castellano, *International Law and Self-Determination* (The Hague: Martinus Nijhoff, 2000), and especially Antonio Cassese, *Self-Determination of Peoples: A Legal Reappraisal* (Cambridge: Cambridge University Press, 1995), particularly chapters 3 and 4, and p. 56 on economic relations freely determined. In practice, the self-determination is limited to "political" choices, seeking to draw a line between them and economic and cultural interferences.

national authorities. On the other hand, the US has expanded the scope of nonintervention in ways most states will follow: it has declared that a cyberattack causing significant damage (such as to infrastructure, power grids, and so on) would be regarded as an armed attack that would justify self-defense in any legitimate manner that the US chooses (that is, not limited to a cyberresponse).[35]

A more traditional conundrum involves the potential equivalence between embargoes and blockades. A refusal to trade by a near-monopoly producer or monopsony consumer of a good can have an economic effect equivalent to a militarily enforced blockade. Nonetheless, the ease of evading unilateral embargoes makes such embargoes unlikely enough that the possibility has not revised international law.

This leaves ambiguous whether one state can promote its national culture in another (by funding language study or cultural exchanges) and whether it can support one political party by funding it and not another (fellow social democrats or Christian democrats).

International law's lack of clarity on nonforceful intervention calls out for deliberative guidance from international ethics. The philosopher John Rawls famously drew a very protective barrier against interference with self-determination.[36] "Outlaw states," those grossly violating human rights and aggressively in-

---

35. See David Sanger and Elisabeth Bumiller, "Pentagon to Consider Cyberattacks Acts of War," *New York Times*, May 31, 2011. For insightful analysis of the issue, see Matt Waxman, "Cyber Attacks and the Use of Force: Back to the Future of Article 2(4)," *Yale Journal of International Law* 36 (2011), 421–459. None of this stopped the US government from itself launching cyberwar, according to David Sanger, "Obama Ordered a Sped Up Wave of Cyberattacks Against Iran," *New York Times*, June 1, 2012.

36. John Rawls, *The Law of Peoples* (Cambridge: Harvard University Press, 1999), 37, 62–78.

clined, can be sanctioned and even invaded to rescue their oppressed population, if the forceful action is proportional and necessary. But other nations, including those he calls "decent hierarchical peoples," should be free from all interference, even including public state-to-state criticism or foreign aid designed to change their domestic order. Yet these states can be legitimate while violating equal human rights (such as equal protection of the laws, equal access to public service, periodic and genuine elections, universal and equal suffrage, and thc like).[37] These states must not violate the most basic rights of life and must respect freedom of worship and have some consultation mechanism to which persons can appeal to be heard. But they can establish one religion and systematically bar genders or minorities from public service and still claim the right to noninterference in the name of self-determination and international peaceful order.

One difficulty with this argument is that it is difficult to claim that a national "self" is self-determining if groups of persons are systematically excluded from political authority. Another difficulty is whether in fact these regimes are readily and peacefully tolerated in a liberal order ascribing to basic human rights.[38]

More thought needs to be given to these questions. But to this observer, Rawls's rules seem too restrictive. Still, allowing all but forceful intervention seems too accepting of coercive interference with self-determination. Perhaps a sensible middle ground would be, while affirming the illegality of all forceful

37. As in Article 21 of the "Universal Declaration of Human Rights," GA Res 217A, December 10, 1948.

38. I raise some of these concerns in "One World, Many Peoples: International Justice in John Rawls's *The Law of Peoples*," *Perspectives on Politics* 4 (March 2006), 111–123.

illegal intervention, to permit nonforceful interference that could be justified by internationally recognized human rights or that was not illegal in the target country. *Conversely, no interference should be permitted that violates local law and could not be justified by international human rights.*

So if the foreign funding of political parties is illegal in a country or if foreign films or other foreign cultural activities are barred, no foreign state could fund these activities unless they directly served international human rights. Even if they did serve human rights, the affected state could prosecute the foreign agents or recipients of foreign funding under domestic law, but it would have no claim that its international rights to noncoerced political independence had been violated.

EMPIRICAL RECORD

When we shift from an account of the normative legal standards for what respecting self-determination requires to an examination of the positive empirical record of the consequences of interventions, that record also reinforces Mill's presumption against intervention.

When we analyze a list of thirty "major US interventions" from 1898 (Philippines) to 2003 (Iraq) compiled by Michael McFaul, it is clear that only seven resulted in democracies ten years afterward. That is, only 23 percent were successful in benefiting the target country, at least as measured by the strenuous test of enhanced self-determination. The successful interventions by the US include the four post–World War II occupations—Italy, Germany, Austria, and Japan—and the more recent interventions in Grenada, Panama, and Kosovo. Two interventions of McFaul's list produced partial democracies (Bosnia and Afghanistan). The remaining twenty-one cases of US intervention—

the vast majority, 70 percent to be exact—resulted in autocracies.[39] McFaul's similar list of fifty-seven "covert military interventions," from Greece (1947) to Haiti (2004), yielded fifteen (26 percent) democracies ten years afterward, two partial democracies, and forty cases—another 70 percent—that were autocracies.

Other recent studies come to similar conclusions. Bruce Bueno de Mesquita and George Downs agree that democratization is an unlikely outcome of intervention, even by a democracy. But they assume that the motives of interveners and intervened against are likely to be in conflict, the first seeking material advantages over the second. While this may be true, it is not Mill's argument; he assumes that liberal interveners should want to promote liberty.[40]

Mark Peceny takes the opposite tack. He focuses on the effects of interventions explicitly motivated by an effort to promote "free and fair elections." Not surprisingly, he finds a better record. Electoral democracy improved in fourteen of the twenty cases of US interventions between 1945 and 1993, including the post–World War II occupations of Germany, Italy, Austria, South Korea, Italy, and Japan. The record, however, in addition to being limited to the US and the period of the Cold War, neglects the many interventions motivated by related liberal values, such as property and liberty.[41]

Alexander Downes and Jonathan Monten offer an empirical test much closer in spirit to Mill's own, though they limit their

39. Michael McFaul, *Advancing Democracy Abroad* (Lanham, MD: Rowman and Littlefield, 2010), 205–208.

40. Bruce Bueno de Mesquita and George Downs, "Intervention and Democracy," *International Organization* 60 (2006), 627–649. Given their assumptions, it is unclear why any democracy would want to promote democratization.

41. Mark Peceny, "Forcing Them to Be Free," *Political Science Quarterly* 52 (1999), 549–582.

study to the twentieth century and explore changes in democratization, rather than Mill's own three outcomes. They limit their data set to successful "foreign imposed regime changes" (fircs) (but they exclude military failures and interventions that result in imperial control). They find that "fircs" do improve the democracy score of target states, especially if the fircs involve institutional changes (explored as "peacebuilding" below in Chapter 5). But their conclusions confirm the small likelihood of successful liberal democratization by foreign imposition, when these target states are compared with likely outcomes without an intervention. Absent a concentrated effort, high levels of economic development, and ethnic homogeneity (all Millian concerns), interventions rarely produce democratization.[42]

Camille Strauss-Kahn and I are engaged in what we hope is a comprehensive empirical assessment of the effects of interventions. As listed in Appendix 2 and summarized in Table 2 below, we have identified 334 major, overt interventions since 1815.[43] An intervention for our purposes is an armed attack by one state in the territory of another state that is designed to intervene (come between) that second state and its population in order to change or protect its political regime, to liberate or restrain a rebellious population. Of such interventions, 135 were by liberal countries; 199 were by nonliberal countries. (Some were mixed— by liberals and nonliberals intervening together—and we code one as joint: the Maria da Fonte War in 1846, described in Chapter 2.) We assume mixed motives for all the interveners,

---

42. Alexander Downes and Jonathan Monten, "Forced to Be Free: Why Foreign-Imposed Regime Change Rarely Leads to Democratization," *International Security* 37 (Spring 2013), 90–131.

43. See the data appendix that describes the statistics. Inevitably, we do not have sufficient comparable information on covert interventions.

Table 2
The Record of Interventions: 1815–2010

	TOTAL	1815–1850	1850–1900	1900–WW1	WW1	WW1–WW2	WW2	WW2–1991	1991–2010
Number of cases	334	60	83	16	32	20	36	76	11
Number of years	195	35	50	15	4	23	5	46	19
Number of liberal regimes	49	8	13	29	29	29	29	49	49
Liberal	135	12	43	10	14	6	15	29	6
Success	107	11	34	10	11	4	13	19	5
Empire	73	6	29	9	9	2	11	5	2
Oppressive	13	2	1	0	0	2	0	7	1
War	18	3	9	0	0	0	2	4	0
None	19	3	4	1	2	1	2	5	1
Failure	28	1	9	0	3	2	2	10	1
Nonliberal	199	48	40	6	18	14	21	47	5
Success	114	28	24	3	8	9	16	22	4
Empire	73	13	15	3	8	7	16	11	0
Oppressive	55	11	7	0	4	6	11	13	3
War	36	5	7	2	3	2	7	8	2
None	7	4	2	0	0	0	0	0	1
Failure	85	20	16	3	10	5	5	25	1

but assume that the liberal interveners were more likely to include liberal motives—freedom, property, rule of law, representative government—in their interventions than the nonliberal interveners were. Only 221 were successful, in the limited sense that they militarily succeeded in invading rather than being repulsed and defeated or having no effect. In these narrow terms, only 66 percent succeeded, 34 percent failed altogether.

But what were their effects on the target state? Among the successful 221, 56 led to a new or renewed civil war within two years; 68 led to a deepened autocracy; and 146 led to empire—that is, the interveners stayed on to rule.[44] Only 26 produced a government no worse in democratic and civil liberties measures than the preceding government. That is, only 12 percent were potentially successful in advancing the cause of liberty and democracy. (Ironically, 7 of those 26 were produced by interventions by nonliberal states that collapsed an autocratic government, allowing liberals to take power, leading us to presume that producing a constitutional liberal government was not their major purpose.) In short, liberals succeeded in avoiding renewed civil war, a deepened autocracy, or imperial rule only 19 times—in 18 percent of militarily successful, liberal-led interventions.

The record seems to fully confirm Mill's warning. Eighteen percent, less than one out of five, is not great odds for democratic liberation by intervention, given the risk in lives and national treasure, unless there really is no other alternative.

Let me conclude this chapter with two points.

First, Mill's concern for violations of self-determination (ex-

---

44. The negative outcomes add up to more than 211; some cases produced more than one of these harms.

ternally imposed self-determination is inauthentic) and his concern for its humanitarian consequences (renewed autocracy, civil war, or empire) are both well founded. His skepticism is partly reflected in established international law that bans all forceful interventions unless they are by a government's invitation or justified by self-defense, motivated by a determination to stop genocide, and authorized by the Security Council in order to preserve or restore international peace and security. Even well-intentioned interventions designed to promote liberty should be approached skeptically. According to the aforementioned assessment that Camille Strauss-Kahn and I have undertaken, the empirical record of history shows few successes, at best one out of five.

These percentages do not prove that interventions are always or even usually counterproductive. We cannot be sure that the situation would not have turned out to be even worse from a humanitarian point of view if no intervention had taken place. To make that judgment scholars would need to assess the humanitarian costs of nonintervention in the cases where intervention did not take place. They would need to consider every case in which intervention might and should have been considered, but did not take place, and assess its consequences. This we have not done (nor is it clear how one would go about doing this).

Equally important, it might be the case that interventions solely motivated by humanitarian concerns have good consequences for liberty and those motivated by self-interested goals, such as territory, natural resources, strategic advantages, prestige, or profits, have bad consequences. We cannot rule this out. Even though the vast majority of interventions appear to have mixed motives, the essential motivation might determine outcomes. (But in this regard it is worth noting the curious anomaly that some successful liberations were produced by nonliberal interveners.)

More important, one cannot measure the value (or lack thereof) of intervention simply by successful democratization or continued independence and reduced autocracy (the last two, our measures). Adding, as we do, the additional dangers of imperialism and a return to civil war is a step better than simply considering changes in domestic regime. But ending slaughters is clearly as important as, if not more important than, regime changes, even liberal ones. Interventions that stop the killing can be morally justifiable, even if the regime is no more democratic or liberal than the previous regime. The problem is, of course, measuring the real concern, shortened lives, reliably across history while also incorporating an assessment of the human costs of oppressive government. Regimes are a proxy for decent self-determination, but a weak and opaque one.

The case for trying an empirical assessment is thus simple but far from perfect. Consequences should count. The overall balance of the evidence should make one skeptical of trusting that good consequences are likely to follow. The burden of proof should be placed on the intervener.

Second, we need to ask: can we create a better global regime for the use of force across borders? Given the importance Mill attaches to humanitarian protection, self-defense, self-determination, and nonintervention, it is not surprising that he envisaged elements of an ideal world in which all four would have a better prospect of being realized. Like many other nineteenth-century liberals, he thought that material and moral progress would make a difference. The spread of free governments (which to be stable would need to rest on nationality, *one* nationality), commerce, and international federalism in a "universal congress of mankind" is conducive to international harmony and peace. Less conventionally, Mill stressed moral education above institutional reform and highlighted the political enfranchisement of women.[45]

Cognizant of the fact that such an ideal world is remote in the extreme, Mill discussed the value of multilateral decision making to better regulate the likely use of force. "When a struggle," he urges, "breaks out anywhere between the despotic and the democratic principles, the powers should never intervene singly; when they interfere at all, it should be jointly, as a general European police."[46] But even that stricture, he hastens to add, is an ideal standard suitable only "if it were possible, as it will be in time, that the powers of Europe should by agreement among themselves adopt a common rule for the regulations of wars of political opinion."[47] Clearly this consensus had so far proven elusive in Europe, where for generations Russia and Austria typically intervened on opposite sides from France and the UK.

Today, of course, Europe and the wider international community have evolved standards for the nondefensive uses of force. The Responsibility to Protect doctrine enunciated at the 2005 UN General Assembly Summit outlines the principles of legitimate intervention against genocide, crimes against humanity, war crimes, and ethnic cleansing when the Security Council so approves. Whether these principles will prove ef-

45. On "universal congress," see "The Spanish Question," in *Miscellaneous Writings*, ed. John M. Robson (Toronto: University of Toronto Press; London: Routledge and Kegan Paul, 1989); on women, see *The Subjection of Women* (London: Oxford University Press, 1924), 115; and for his general international theory, see Miller, "Mill's Theory of International Relations."

46. In his 1837 essay on "The Spanish Question," Mill assessed the British and French intervention to halt a "prolonged civil war"; *CW* 31: 374.

47. Ibid., 31: 16.

fective in practice is being determined in Libya, Syria, and elsewhere.

Despite the impressive practical and ethical merits of nonintervention, Mill and many today find that intervention is sometimes both feasible and justifiable. I turn to these reasons to sometimes "override" or "disregard" nonintervention in the next two chapters.

Before drawing this discussion of the case for nonintervention to a close, let me suggest one important lesson for considering exceptions to the default rule of nonintervention. The case against intervention that has been set out in this chapter means that all interventions need to address the dangerous outcomes that accompany them. For any intervention to be justifiable, at a minimum it must anticipate its potentially dangerous outcomes and put in place measures to try to prevent those outcomes both by designing procedural checks to improve decisions and by taking peacebuilding measures (which I will describe in the chapters that follow) to address the likely negative side effects. Otherwise—as in the vast majority of cases where a foreign entity is considering intervention in the affairs of a sovereign society—it should not proceed.

2

Exceptions That Override

In the previous chapter, I noted that arguments against intervention have drawn on an appreciation of the dangers of starting a war (since wars are unpredictable); the duty to respect national self-determination (because foreign intervention is an inauthentic revolution); and the inevitable humanitarian harms attached to the use of force, which include the casualties of conflict and the likely outcomes of renewed civil war, renewed autocracy, or imposed imperial rule. Thus all three of my principles—national security, self-determination, and humanitarian protection—argue for nonintervention, the normative default principle.

But just as I showed in the previous chapter that nonintervention is a puzzle for cosmopolitan humanitarianism, so I will demonstrate in this chapter that intervention is a puzzle that can be explained in light of the powerful reasons not to intervene. This is because the world is complicated and requires exceptions to even the most compelling rules. So we see that external moral factors can *override* the nonintervention paradigm; or internal presuppositions of the nonintervention paradigm may not hold, so we can *disregard* them in a particular case.

Let us start with four types of overrides that may tip the balance against nonintervention. The first is self-defense, or national security concerns, for which I consider two examples: rescuing citizens in an emergency and ideological warfare in an international civil war. There are two humanitarian protection concerns: ending protracted civil wars and preventing (or stop-

ping) massacres. And then there is postwar reform, intervening after a just war to restore justice and prevent future wars.
(This last I save for Chapter 5.)

Again, I want to draw on and question Mill and explore
modern analogues. Mill argued that there were indeed good reasons to override what should be the usual prohibition against
intervention. In these arguments, the considerations against intervention are present, but other more important values, such
as threats to national security and humanitarian concern for
suffering, are what Mill calls "considerations paramount" ("Non-
Intervention," 123). These threats trump any considerations
militating against intervention. Although interventions usually
do more harm than good, according to Mill, there are legitimate exceptions.

Like many liberals, Mill dismisses, without much attention,
some arguments in favor of intervention to promote "territory
or revenue" in order to enhance national power, prestige, or
profits. However prevalent those motives might have been in
history, for Mill they do not justify intervention. Mill explicitly
rejects the claims of contemporary politicians who exulted in
the aggressive posturing that later came to be called jingoism
and in crudely rapacious conquests.[1] But he also implicitly rejects the arguments of those whom we now call hard realists.
Their arguments justify without noticeable exception any and

1. Mill elaborates: "Does it answer any good purpose to express ourselves as
if we did not scruple to profess that which we not merely scruple to do, but
the bare idea of doing which never crosses our minds? Why should we abnegate the character we might with truth lay claim to . . . We are the only people
among whom, by no class whatever of society, is the interest or glory of the
nation considered to be an sufficient excuse for an unjust act; the only one
which regards with jealousy and suspicion, and a proneness to hostile criticism,
precisely those acts of its Government which in other countries are sure to be
hailed with applause, those by which territory has been acquired, or political
influence extended"; "Non-Intervention," 114–115.

all gains in territory or revenue. The argument runs as follows: the interstate system is anarchic without enforceable legal or moral standards; each state consequently has nothing except its own resources to rely on for security and welfare; all territory and revenue have strategic significance, because they all can be translated in military advantage, and therefore their value is relative among states. Any relative gain is thereby justified as essential for national security: all gains are relative, and states should fight rather than forgo a material gain.[2]

The Hobbesian version of this argument stresses the roots of competitive conquest found in the uncertainties that accompany international anarchy and the competitive drives of human nature when not constrained by coercive force.[3] Contemporary game theoretic versions stress informational asymmetries (we know more about our own preferences and risk tolerances than we can know about others') as sources of conflict that overwhelm the rational disincentives to armed conflict.[4]

But many realists wisely draw limits to predation. Even Thomas Hobbes warned about the dangers of ostracism if a state breaks all its commitments. Some note that differences in technology allow states to tame rivalries by distinguishing between defensive measures and offensive ones, while others still question whether all increases in territory or revenue produce strategic gain, warning of the dangers of "imperial overstretch."[5]

2. Morton Kaplan, *System and Process in International Politics* (New York: John Wiley, 1957).

3. Michael Doyle, *Ways of War and Peace* (New York: Norton, 1997), chapter 3 on Hobbes and Realism.

4. James D. Fearon, "Rationalist Explanations for War," *International Organization* 49 (1995), 379–414.

5. Robert Jervis, "Cooperation Under the Security Dilemma," *World Politics* 30 (January 1978), 167–214; Paul Kennedy, *The Rise and Fall of the Great Powers* (New York: Vintage, 1987).

With equal disdain, Mill also rejects justifications for intervention associated with other arguments that favored intervening to promote an "idea" or ideology ("Non-Intervention," 118).
Here he condemns not just religious wars but the revolutionary democratic liberalism of the French revolutionaries and
their American "friend of the People," Thomas Paine, who proclaimed in 1791 that if "monarchical sovereignty, the enemy of
mankind and the source of misery," were abolished, and sovereignty were "restored to its natural and original place, the nation . . . throughout Europe, the cause of war would be taken
away."[6] These strictures also appear to apply to the promoters of
the "Freedom Agenda" during the George W. Bush administration, who seem to have found democratizing Iraq in 2003 to be
one of the legitimate goals that justified that costly intervention.

While rejecting those arguments for intervention, Mill finds
that some instances of national security and humanitarian protection can dominate self-determination and, in certain speci-
fiable contexts, justify intervention. Let us turn to them now.

SELF-DEFENSE OF CITIZENS

First, Mill noted, "We must except, of course, any case in which
such assistance is a measure of legitimate self-defense" ("Non-
Intervention," 123). Acknowledging the primacy of national self-
help in an anarchic international system, just war philosophers
and international lawyers typically raise the difficult cases of
intervention to enforce the rights of nationals or rescue them
from unjust imprisonment. Although Mill does not address
this problem in "Non-Intervention," he was well aware of the

6. Thomas Paine, "The Rights of Man" (1791), in *Complete Writings*, 2 vols.,
ed. Eric Foner (New York: Oxford University Press, 1995), 1: 342.

claims made to regard one aspect of national security as protection of nationals abroad.[7] Citizens overseas are usually subject to the laws of the jurisdiction in which they are residing. When a foreign state comes between those citizens and the local authorities, such rescues have frequently been classified as interventions, sometimes even as "humanitarian," as Oppenheim called it in his classic text on international law.[8] But the actual classic cases are uncomfortable, carrying more than whiffs of imperial pretension.

The British foreign secretary, Henry John Temple, 3rd Viscount Palmerston, persuaded the cabinet to send gunboats to blockade the port of Athens in 1850 in order to obtain restitution for Don Pacifico, a Jewish resident of Athens, victimized by an anti-Semitic mob. Significantly, Pacifico was a British subject, by virtue of his birth in Gibraltar. In a long and heated speech before Parliament, Palmerston justified the action:

> As the Roman, in days of old, held himself free from indignity, when he could say, Civis Romanus sum [I am a Roman citizen], so also a British subject, in whatever land he may be, shall feel confident that the watchful eye and the strong arm of England will protect him from injustice and wrong.[9]

7. Mill also skips over preemptive and preventive wars in this essay. For a lucid discussion of the problem of preventive war, see Ariel Colonomos, *The Gamble of War* (New York: Palgrave, 2013). I discuss the problems associated with preemptive or preventive interventions designed to remove a looming threat before an attack takes place in *Striking First* (Princeton: Princeton University Press, 2008); but I will overlook them here, focusing instead on realized threats, actual attacks.

8. Lassa Oppenheim, *International Law: A Treatise*, 2 vols., 9th ed., ed. Robert Jennings and Arthur Watts (1920; New York: Longmans, Green, 1992), 440–444.

9. Hansard (UK Parliament Official Report), 3rd Series, cxii, pp. 380–444.

The US equivalent involved a naval bombardment of Grey-town, Nicaragua, four years later in reprisal for an attack on the US consul. In a case that came before the US Circuit Court of Appeals in *Durand v. Hollins*, affirming the authority of the president to use force, the court declared: "Under our system of government, the citizen abroad is as much entitled to protection as the citizen at home."[10]

Since those times, the concern has been that rescue would turn into imperial conquest, as it did in numerous places in Africa and the Far East for Britain and France. Modern cases of citizen rescue by the US, in countries ranging from the Dominican Republic in 1965 to Grenada in 1983, generated widespread international condemnation. Might the international community develop guidelines for legitimate rescue?

One exception to the general condemnation was the Israeli rescue of hostages at Entebbe in Uganda in July 1976. Two militants from the Popular Front for the Liberation of Palestine and two from the Baader Meinhof Gang had hijacked a French airliner on its way from Israel to France on June 27. After landing at Entebbe Airport, they released 150 passengers and kept 100 others, those identified as Israeli or Jewish.[11] What made the case different was the manifest threat to the passengers of the hijacked airliner, the inefficacy of other potential measures, and the apparent complicity of the Ugandan government of Idi Amin in isolating the Israeli passengers as hostages. Equally important was the limited aim of the rescue—

10. See *Durand v. Hollins* (4 Blatchf. 451; 43 Hunt. Mer. Mag. 583, Sept. 13, 1860) and "The Greytown Bombardment Responsibility of Navy Officers," *New York Times*, September 15, 1860. For discussion, see Thomas Franck, *Recourse to Force* (Cambridge: Cambridge University Press, 2002), 76 ff.

11. BBC, "Israelis Rescue Entebbe Hostages," http://news.bbc.co.uk/onthis day/hi/dates/stories/july/4/newsid_2786000/2786967.stm.

freeing the hostages in a surgical strike. No attempt was made to overturn the murderous regime of Amin. (This would be left to Tanzania two years later.)

Nonetheless, many African, Asian, and other states at the UN sought to condemn the Israeli attack as aggression against the sovereignty and territorial integrity of Uganda, at the same time that the US, the UK, Sweden, and others sought to condemn the hijacking. Neither resolution was passed in the Security Council, but, perhaps remarkably, the condemnation of hijacking did slightly better.[12] This led Thomas Franck to conclude that the Entebbe raid had some legitimacy, though not legality.

There are no widely accepted standards for rescue, short of a determination by the UN Security Council that the situation constitutes a "threat to international peace and security" under Chapter VII, but the Entebbe norm seems to carry some weight:

Unilateral rescues should be allowed, when Security Council approval is unobtainable, and when they are also last resorts, necessary and genuinely "surgical" rescues without regime change—rescuing citizens and not seizing "territory or revenue."

SELF-DEFENSE IN AN INTERNATIONAL CIVIL WAR

Mill's prime example in "Non-Intervention" of the national security override focuses on a less familiar, but even more problematic set of cases: internationalized civil war. In an international system characterized by ideological conflicts that cross borders, such as the wars waged between Protestantism and Catholicism in the sixteenth century, or liberalism and despotism in Mill's own time, nonintervention can neglect vital trans-

12. Franck, *Recourse to Force*, 82–85.

national sources of national security. "If . . . this country [Great Britain], on account of its freedom, should find itself menaced with attack by a coalition of Continental despots, it ought to consider the popular party in every nation of the Continent as its natural ally: the Liberals should be to it, what the Protestants of Europe were to the Government of Queen Elizabeth" ("Non-Intervention," 123).

Simply put and in the extreme case, if everyone of each ideological faction truly aligns with its fellows overseas, irrespective of collective national interests or interstate borders, and if others are intervening in support of their faction, then not intervening in support of yours is dangerous.

As Mill implies, this kind of logic led Sir Nicholas Throckmorton, Elizabeth I's ambassador in France, to advocate intervention in support of fellow Protestants by warning: "Now when the general design is to exterminate all nations dissenting with them in religion . . . what will become of us, when the like professors [believers] with us shall be destroyed in Flanders and France."[13]

It also resonates in twentieth-century Cold War logic and neatly matches the rhetoric of the Reagan Doctrine, which pledged, "We must not break faith with those who are risking their lives . . . on every continent from Afghanistan to Nicaragua . . . to defy Soviet aggression and secure rights which have been ours since birth. Support for freedom fighters is self-defense." Reagan added this "rollback" to the original "containment" the-

13. Quoted from Lord Burghley's State Papers in Wallace MacCaffrey, "The Newhaven Expedition: 1562–1563," *Historical Journal* 40 (1997), 1–21. For an insightful and wide-ranging analysis of religious internationalism in this period, see John Owen, "When Do Ideologies Produce Alliances?" *International Studies Quarterly* 49 (2005), 73–99.

ory of the Truman Doctrine. It also fits the equally interventionist Brezhnev Doctrine of the Soviet Union.[14]

Is transnational intervention or counterintervention for the purposes of engaging in defensive civil war across international borders a just and wise policy? Let us look at Mill's first example—an interventionist expedition to "Newhaven" (now Le Havre in Normandy, France) in 1562.

In 1559, Queen Elizabeth successfully intervened to roll back the Catholic threat in Scotland. She sent troops to assist the more powerful faction of Scottish Protestant lords who were struggling against a regime sustained by intervening French forces. When her more radical advisers pressed her to do the same in France, she reluctantly agreed to intervene in support of the French Protestant nobles in Normandy only to see them defect to a better deal with their own monarch.[15]

The case does not seem to vindicate the policy. For even during the polarizing religious wars of the sixteenth and seventeenth centuries, Queen Elizabeth learned from the disastrous 1562–1563 armed expedition to Newhaven. She learned to limit intervention to vital English national security (for example, to

14. Ronald Reagan, State of the Union Address, 1985. President Truman's doctrine promising to defend free peoples from external or internal aggression was presented to a joint session of Congress in justification of the assistance he proposed for Greece and Turkey in March 1947. General Secretary Brezhnev presented his doctrine in a speech at the Fifth Congress of the Polish Worker's Party in November 1968, following the intervention against the Czechoslovak Prague Spring. Brezhnev proclaimed: "When forces that are hostile to socialism try to turn the development of some socialist country towards capitalism, it becomes not only a problem of the country concerned, but a common problem and concern of all socialist countries." For a moral argument against Cold War rollback and a defense of containment, see Ian Shapiro, *Containment: Rebuilding a Strategy Against Global Terror* (Princeton: Princeton University Press, 2008).

15. MacCaffrey, "The Newhaven Expedition," 19.

controlling Scotland and preserving the independence of the Low Countries) and to armed action only with the support of strong local allies. She also developed a policy of alternately aligning with Catholic Spain and Catholic France and success-fully played them against each other.[16] A half-century later, Cardinal Richelieu wisely aligned with the Protestant principalities that would support France against the Catholic Holy Roman Empire and Catholic Spain, which were its greatest threats.

Similar caution should be inferred from the record of the twentieth-century Cold War. In practice, early in the Cold War there were covert interventions by the US in Albania and China, as well as Soviet efforts to control local communist parties in Europe and elsewhere. Much later, Reagan and Brezhnev practiced their doctrines in Nicaragua and Czechoslovakia, respectively.[17] But the exceptions to Cold War interventionism were at least as important. The exceptions included the West's support for Tito's Yugoslavia and the East's support for Third World nationalists, not to speak of the effective combination of East-West détente with triangulation devised by the Nixon administration to exploit the Chinese split from the Soviets in

16. See R. B. Wernham, *Before the Armada* (London: Cape, 1966), and G. D. Ramsey, *The Reign of Elizabeth I*, ed. C. Haigh (London: Macmillan, 1984), who describe dual balancing against both foreign and domestic threats. According to R. B. Wernham, *The Making of Elizabethan Foreign Policy, 1558–1603* (Berkeley: University of California Press, 1980), Elizabeth may have realized that Philip of Spain was playing the same double balancing game, protecting Elizabeth in the early years of her reign from French domination by urging the pope to forbear excommunication (28 ff.) and later authorizing an armada to attack England when Protestant forces seemed in the ascendant in France (74 ff.).

17. See Tim Weiner, *Legacy of Ashes: The History of the CIA* (New York: Doubleday, 2007), 45–46, 58–61; and for a general comparison, the classic by Zbigniew Brzezinski and Samuel P. Huntington, *Political Power: USA/USSR* (New York: Viking, 1961).

the 1970s. Imagine the strategic costs to the US and its allies if attempts to achieve détente with the USSR and the Chinese split had been rejected because both were communist.

Consistent as the logic of internationalized civil war is, probing the actual examples suggests that Mill's caution to hew to the "counter" in intervention must be heeded. Moreover, we should go beyond Mill (and Throckmorton, Brezhnev, and Reagan) in order to adopt a bias toward more proximate conceptions of "legitimate self-defense" rather than reactive counterinterventions. The rampant interventionism invoked in Cold War style diplomacy is much too costly, both in treasure and lives, to qualify as national security.

The most prominent British utilitarian after Mill, Henry Sidgwick, made a similar argument in his *Elements of Politics*, more than thirty years after Mill's "Non-Intervention." Sidgwick follows Mill's thesis on nonintervention as the required international policy among civilized governments, and he similarly considers rare instances in which it may be overridden, such as to assist legitimate claims for national liberation from an oppressive state. But he unusually adds an argument justified by national security for preventive intervention that resembles Mill's exception for global civil war. This could arise when a "revolutionary party" adopts "an aggressive attitude toward foreigners, by acting avowedly on principles that they not only profess to be applicable to other states, but that they actually threaten to aid in applying elsewhere if they succeed at home."[18] Sidgwick then warns that the "aggressiveness," in addition to being acted upon at home, must be "threatened" abroad and must be "definite and unmistakable." Otherwise, he wisely

18. Henry Sidgwick, *The Elements of Politics*, 3rd ed. (1891; London: Macmillan, 1919), 261–262.

warns, "the foreign intervention will be justly open to the charge of causing the evil that it is designed to avert." Sidgwick makes no specific historical reference, but he may have had in mind aristocratic opposition to the French revolutionaries of 1789–1792, who indeed seemed to pose such a threat, but whose actual threat was probably increased by the preventive counterintervention the aristocratic parties launched against it.[19]

A similarly dangerous stretch is evident in recent efforts to justify intervention for the purpose of tilting or correcting the global balance of power. Some have justified the recent US counterinsurgency in Afghanistan as a necessary effort to preserve global deterrence against insurgent attacks on the US and its allies, to control Central Asia, and to enhance American credibility against the challenge of the rise of China.[20] After rejecting these as inadequate justifications for intervention in Afghanistan by the US, political philosopher Richard Miller raises the possibility that in other circumstances righting the balance of power in one's favor would be sufficient justification. He notes "the balance of power can have momentous consequences" and references expanding Soviet foreign bases and clients during the Cold War and China's competitive rise today.[21]

Miller sensibly rejects both of those rationales as well, but primarily because US policy is not fully a product of rational decision making. This is clearly a good reason to be skeptical of calculations of strategic advantage as a justification for in-

19. See Simon Schama, *Citizens: A Chronicle of the French Revolution* (New York: Knopf, 1989), 581–618, and Stephen Walt, *Revolution and War* (Ithaca, NY: Cornell, 1996).

20. Richard Miller, while defending the ethics of intervention for geopolitical balancing, details and rejects these specific justifications in "The Ethics of America's Afghan War," *Ethics and International Affairs* 25 (Summer 2011), 103–131, especially 119–121.

21. Ibid., p. 121.

flicting deaths through armed intervention. But there are more fundamental reasons to be skeptical of geopolitical intervention, including the availability of more ethical alternatives to interventionist "external" balancing as a means to enhance national security. They include "internal" balancing (measures such as investing more in arms production), reducing vulnerabilities (such as excessive dependence on foreign oil), and accommodating former enemies to win them over to your coalition.

Absent a proximate, imminent, and credible threat to national security, the balance of ideological or material power is simply too hypothetical, too abstract, and too uncertain to justify the certain and present infliction of death that armed intervention entails.

REDUCING HARM IN AN ONGOING CIVIL WAR

The first two examples are thus cases of the national security principle overriding the self-determination norm against intervention; they are self-regarding. The next two are other-regarding—humanitarian protection overriding self-determination. One of the most relevant today is suffering from protracted civil war. Rather than national security, humanitarian protection of noncombatants overrides self-determination.

This third exception was relevant for Mill, but also pertinent for today's debates on multilateral mediation and peacekeeping.[22] It covers, Mill said, a "protracted civil war, in which the

22. For a discussion of the circumstances favoring successful peacekeeping and peacebuilding in a civil war context, see Michael Doyle and Nicholas Sambanis, *Making War and Building Peace* (Princeton: Princeton University Press, 2006), and the large literature we cite. For discussions of the ethical issues raised in reconstruction, see the article by Stefano Recchia, "Just and Unjust Postwar Reconstruction," 165–188, and related articles in the special section in *Ethics and International Affairs* 23 (Summer 2009).

contending parties are so equally balanced that there is no probability of a speedy resolution; or if there is, the victorious side cannot hope to keep down the vanquished but by severities repugnant to humanity, and injurious to the permanent welfare of the country" ("Non-Intervention," 121). He is arguing that some civil wars become so protracted and so seemingly irresolvable by local struggle that a common sense of humanity and sympathy for the suffering of the noncombatant population calls for an outside intervention to halt the fighting in order to see whether some negotiated solution might be achieved under the aegis of foreign arms.[23]

Mill here cites the partial success of outsiders in calling a halt to and helping settle the protracted midcentury Portuguese civil war and the Greek-Turkish conflict. Outsiders can call for separation or reconciliation in these circumstances. On the one hand, two peoples contending a single territory have been forced to partition it. Greece was thus separated from Turkey in 1829.[24] Belgium seceded from Holland in 1830 following the forceful mediation of two liberal statesmen, one British, one French: Lord Palmerston and François Guizot. I will explore these sorts of interventions as "disregards" in the next

23. Here Mill appears to loosely follow an argument first developed by the eighteenth-century legal theorist Emmerich de Vattel. See the chapter by Jennifer Pitts in *Just and Unjust Military Intervention: European Thinkers from Vitoria to Mill,* ed. Jennifer Welsh and Stefano Recchia (Cambridge: Cambridge University Press, 2013).

24. Gary Bass, *Freedom's Battle* (New York: Knopf, 2008), chapters 4–12, treats this conflict under the rubric of humanitarian concern. It fits there but also as a war for secession, as noted below. Conflicts typically overlap: great powers forcibly mediated a protracted civil war with large casualties and promoted the secession of a new nation, Greece, from an established empire, Ottoman Turkey.

chapter. Relevant here, though, is a situation when two factions are struggling to control and reform a single state, each in order to fulfill its own political vision, and are forced to share it. Impartial mediation imposed this kind of power-sharing reconciliation—the "equitable terms of compromise" insisted upon by Mill—on the Portuguese factions in the 1840s.

Liberal arguments supporting humanitarian protection fall into various camps. Some liberals—strong cosmopolitans—hold that the rights of cosmopolitan freedom are valuable everywhere for all people. Any violation of them should be resisted whenever and wherever it occurs, provided that we can do so proportionally—without causing more harm than we seek to avoid.[25] But other liberals, such as notably Mill and other just war theorists, often called communitarians, limit the cases that justify intervention. They place equal weight on the collective right to self-determination and think that it should be difficult to override it.

In practical terms, the two arguments are likely to produce similar prescriptions. The human costs of interventions tend to be so high that only the most egregious of massacres can justify them proportionally as harms that outweigh the value of self-determination. But in one of the best debates in international ethics, David Luban and Michael Walzer highlighted

25. See, for example, the influential works of David Luban, "Just War and Human Rights," *Philosophy and Public Affairs* 9 (Winter 1980), 160–181; and Hadley Arkes, *First Things: An Inquiry into the First Principles of Morals and Justice* (Princeton: Princeton University Press, 1986). Both Luban and Arkes are cosmopolitans in this sense, but their conceptions of which rights are fundamental differ profoundly, the first tending toward the social democratic and the second libertarian in orientation, with correspondingly large differences in judgment on interventions.

significant differences in a discussion of whether to intervene in Nicaragua against the brutal Somoza dictatorship.[26] In the end, Luban emphasized the extra fifty thousand deaths suffered by the Nicaraguan opposition as they fought to overthrow Somoza without the help of outside intervention. Walzer focused on the much more locally legitimate regime that the opposition became as it struggled to win wider domestic support, the kind of support that would, in Millian terms, allow it to rule in a more legitimate and sustainable fashion once it won.

Mill, like Walzer much later, worried about legitimate and sustainable consequences. So it is worth examining his case for humanitarian intervention in a civil war. The intervention that Mill appears to have had in mind in "Non-Intervention" took place in 1846 in Portugal. The intervention seemed to produce two generations of peace in Portugal among the contesting factions under the rules of King Pedro (1853–1861) and King Luis (1861–1869). It looked "ill at the commencement," Mill comments, but "it could be justified by the event . . . a really healing measure" ("Non-Intervention," 121–122).[27]

One of the leading historians of Portugal, H. V. Livermore, described the political scene in the first half of the century during the reign of Queen Maria as follows: "There were now three main currents of opinion in Portugal: absolutist, moderate and radical. Each had its constitutional and institutional

---

26. David Luban, "Just War and Human Rights," and Michael Walzer, "Moral Standing of States." The essays appear consecutively in *International Ethics*, ed. Charles Beitz et al. (Princeton: Princeton University Press, 1985), 195–243.

27. This is called the "Maria da Fonte Rebellion" in various encyclopedias of war, including Michael Clodfelder's *Warfare and Armed Conflicts: A Statistical Encyclopedia of Casualty and Other Figures, 1494–2000,* 3rd ed. (Jefferson, NC: McFarland, 2008), 189.

preferences: the absolutists stood for no written constitution and the traditional *cortes*, summoned and not elected; the Chartist moderates for an *octroye* charter and a parliament of two houses; the Septembrist radicals for the constitution of 1822 and a *cortes* of a single chamber."[28] Britain intervened in 1827 with a naval force, but only, Prime Minister George Canning claimed, for the sake of "nonintervention," in order to deter a right-wing intervention supported from Spain.

Civil strife was endemic, with Dom Miguel posing the leading threat of absolutist rule with his near-constant rebellions against his niece, Queen Maria. In the 1830s, Britain supported Queen Maria and her moderate Chartist monarchist ministers against the Miguelista threat. By 1846, Miguel had been expelled and Portuguese politics had split between the last two groups, the Chartists and the Septembrists—the first "moderate" and pro-monarchical and the second "radical" and pro-constitutionalist (the constitution of 1822). When the Septembrist constitutionalists took up arms, Palmerston, then foreign secretary, was cross-pressured between his ideological preference for the Septembrist constitutionalists and Britain's established relationship with Queen Maria and her Chartist, monarchist advisers. When Miguelista-inspired peasants rose in support of the Septembrist rebels, France and Spain agitated for intervention in support of the queen.

Palmerston then sent Colonel Wylde as a special envoy to exercise what Palmerston called "a perspective of force" that involved pressuring both parties and avoiding either a Chartist-monarchist or a Septembrist-Miguelista victory. Wylde's mis-

28. H. V. Livermore, *A New History of Portugal,* 2nd ed. (Cambridge: Cambridge University Press, 1976), 274.

sion was secret, mostly it appears to shield it from Queen Victoria and Prince Albert, whose cousin was married to Queen Maria, and whose interests they unequivocally favored. Palmerston thus played a delicate balancing act. He instructed Wylde to play either a purely impartial mediatory role, urging on Queen Maria the importance of aligning herself with national opinion, not relying on foreign intervention and avoiding thereby "the fate of the Stuarts in England in the 17th century and the Bourbons in France in the 18th."[29] Or, Palmerston further directed Wylde, should both parties agree, he should take on the additional role of "umpire and mediator to prescribe to both the terms and conditions of arrangement."[30]

To avoid a unilateral Spanish intervention in support of Queen Maria, Palmerston accepted a joint Anglo-Spanish armed force that cornered the recalcitrant Septembrists in Oporto. But Palmerston then pressured both sides. He required the queen to restore the constitution and civil liberties and deal with the constitutionalist rebels indulgently, including safeguarding their property, on the view that former rebels might well shift from opponents to become someday "very useful servants of the Crown." Palmerston correspondingly instructed Wylde to tell the constitutionalist rebels that the British government would do nothing for them but secure their place in a restored, constitutional Portuguese monarchy. For that, they would be required to lay down their arms.[31]

29. Letter from Palmerston at Foreign Office to Col. Wylde, November 25, 1846; this and subsequent Palmerston letters are from Palmerston Papers, University of Southampton.

30. Letter from Palmerston to Col. Wylde, from Foreign Office, February 17, 1847.

31. See Letter from Palmerston to Col. Wylde, April 5, 1847. And see Jasper Ridley, *Lord Palmerston* (London: Constable, 1970), 317–320, and W. Smith,

Nonetheless, genuine stability took a few more years. Its decisive impetus was less the compromise of 1847 than the (unpredictable) reform led by the wise and industrious King Pedro, who replaced his mother in 1853. During his short reign (he died of cholera in 1861), Pedro helped construct a political center that served as the foundation for more extensive administrative reforms and the launching pad for an ambitious program of road and rail construction that began the economic modernization of the countryside.[32] Still, England remained a constant presence, promoting the interests of British merchants in Portugal, bullying the Portuguese overseas when Britain's trade and colonial interests required interference, and, overall, limiting the effective sovereignty of Portugal and thus undermining the self-determination that Mill had endorsed in 1859.

This suggests two lessons.

First, as a humanitarian measure, an armed intervention may be necessary to halt a civil war, but it is unlikely to be sufficient. Additional measures—reforms designed to build a self-sustaining peace—will be needed to make the intervention stick. Ideally, these would be domestic measures, but if they fail to build a peace, either the intervention will need to be repeated or the civil war will resume.

Second, unilateral interventions for these purposes, even when well motivated, have a tendency to succumb to self-dealing and imperial control. Multilateral peacebuilding is preferred, when feasible.

Both of these lessons are relevant today to UN peacekeeping operations, the precursors of modern civil war settlements, in

---

Anglo-Portuguese Relations, 1851–1861 (Lisbon: Centro de Estudios Historicos Ultramarinos, 1970), 16.

32. Livermore, *New History of Portugal,* 288–290.

El Salvador, Mozambique, Namibia, and Cambodia. While half fail, half also succeed, leading to the question of how to achieve sustainable peacebuilding, which is addressed in Chapter 5.

Interventions, even justified interventions, are never enough. Can they be better implemented? Can they be multilaterally governed to encourage less exploitation? We will return to this in Chapter 4, where we reexamine this question with the contemporary interventions in Libya and Syria.

CLASSIC HUMANITARIAN INTERVENTION

Lastly, one can intervene for humanitarian purposes. When we see what is classically called a pattern of "massacres," the development of a campaign of genocide, the institutionalization of slavery—violations that are so horrendous that in the classical phrase repeated by Walzer they "shock the conscience of mankind"—one has good ground to question whether there is any legitimate connection between the population and the state that is so brutally oppressing it.

In his "Non-Intervention" essay, in discussing protracted civil wars, Mill has already raised "severities repugnant to humanity" as closely related humanitarian reasons to forcibly mediate a civil war. And humanitarian motives sometimes arise in cases when nonintervention must be disregarded (the theme of the next chapter). But lacking the advantages of a twentieth-century perspective, Mill does not directly consider the case of an established, civilized government turning to massacre its own subjects outside the context of a civil war. He does not appear to have anticipated how barbaric the thoroughly civilized could be.[33]

---

33. It may be interesting to note, however, that writing roughly at the same time, Giuseppe Mazzini developed a more explicit argument for humanitarian

For Michael Walzer, the contemporary theorist of intervention most thoroughly inspired by Mill, humanitarian intervention is different from civil war. It also involves much suffering, for here the government is in altogether too much control. The just war tradition has claimed that outsiders can intervene for the purpose of humanitarian protection.

But the intervener should have a morally defensible motive and share the purpose of ending the slaughter and establishing a self-determining people.

Furthermore, interveners should act only as a "last resort," after exploring peaceful resolution.

They should then act only when it is clear not only that the mission is militarily feasible but also that they will save more lives than the intervention itself will almost inevitably wind up costing, and even then with minimum necessary force.[34]

It makes as little moral sense to rescue a village and start World War III as to destroy a village in order to save it.

Humanitarian motives have often been exploited, as they appear to have been in the US intervention in Cuba in 1898.[35] Even though often abused, those motives can apply in a reasonable case, such as the Indian invasion of East Pakistan in 1971, designed in part to save the people of what became Ban-

---

intervention in the case of genocidal violence against ethnic or religious minorities. See the discussion by Stefano Recchia in Welsh and Recchia, *Just and Unjust Military Intervention.*

34. See Michael Walzer, *Just and Unjust Wars* (New York: Basic, 1977), 101–108; Thomas Weiss, *Humanitarian Intervention* (Cambridge: Polity, 2007); and Alex Bellamy, *Just Wars* (Cambridge: Polity, 2006), for valuable surveys of the policy debates.

35. Walzer, *Just and Unjust Wars,* chapter 6, "Interventions," 102–104.

gladesh from the massacre that was being inflicted upon them by their own government (in West Pakistan). Despite India's mixed motives, this was a case of legitimate humanitarian intervention. It allowed the people of East Pakistan to survive and form their own state, as Walzer has persuasively argued. Vietnam rescued the Cambodians from Pol Pot's genocide of his own people in 1978, but only after more than a million died. Moreover, the rescue seemed to have been far from the primary intention. In recent times, intervention in Rwanda in 1994 could have been justified in these terms, well before 500,000 to 1 million Rwandans were slaughtered. The tragedy of these interventions was that the help arrived too late.

The policy challenge appears to be both warning and action. Samantha Power, in her influential assessment of the Rwandan genocide, concluded that "the US government knew enough about the genocide early on to save lives, but passed up countless opportunities to intervene."[36] That does not mean early warning is not difficult. As early as the spring of 1992, the Belgian ambassador warned his government of a planned "extermination" of the Tutsi. Additionally, academics, Human Rights Watch, and a UN human rights rapporteur in 1993 all warned of an impending genocide. And famously, the peacekeeping force commander in Rwanda, General Romeo Dallaire, sent the now notorious January 11, 1994, cable to the UN's Department of Peacekeeping Operations, where his request to seize an arms cache was denied.[37] Admittedly, other information did cloud

36. Samantha Power, "Bystanders to Genocide: Why the United States Let the Rwandan Tragedy Happen," *Atlantic Monthly,* September 2001, p. 86; and, more generally, Samantha Power, *A Problem from Hell: America and the Age of Genocide* (New York: Basic, 2002).

37. Linda Malvern, *A People Betrayed* (London: Zed, 2000); Gerard Prunier, *The Rwanda Crisis* (London: Hurst, 1995); Howard Adelman and Astrid Suhrke,

the picture. The US ambassador in Kigali and the head of the UN mission in Rwanda described the tensions and early killings as a continuation of a long-standing civil war that the Arusha Peace Agreement had been designed to end, an agreement that the peacekeeping operation was deployed to monitor and assist.[38]

Nonetheless, and on balance, there was adequate warning. The real question was why it was not heeded. Preventive, even responsive, action fell afoul of commitments not to act. The legacy of Somalia radically undermined a willingness to engage in robust peacekeeping that cast a deep pall over both Washington and the United Nations. This led senior officials in Washington to read the Rwanda events as "civil war"—meaning stay out—rather than "genocide"—meaning act to prevent or stop. This event produced the sad effort in April and May, as genocide spread, to refuse to name acknowledged "acts of genocide" as "genocide." The reluctance to act in Washington and London, as well as prior complicity with President Habyarimana's side in the civil war by France, stymied concerted action.

This is not to say that all could have been saved. Early preventive action would have required recognizing as early as 1992 or 1993 warning signs of the dehumanization of Tutsis and the

---

eds., *The Path to Genocide* (London: Transactions, 1997); and the valuable schema for prevention outlined by Gregory Stanton in "Could the Rwandan Genocide Have Been Prevented," *Journal of Genocide Research* 6 (June 2004), 211–228.

38. The UN peace operation was planned on the basis that all that was necessary was a monitoring and assisting mission, deployed with the full consent (and indeed active lobbying) of both parties, the government and the Rwandan Patriotic Front rebels. This was a misreading of the situation on the ground in 1993, as Dallaire later argued and the *Report of the Independent Inquiry into the Actions of the United Nations during the 1994 Genocide in Rwanda* (December 15, 1999; S/1999/1257) concluded. (Disclosure: I served as the external peacekeeping expert for the inquiry and prepared first drafts of the peacekeeping sections of the report.)

organization of death squads. This would have produced a radically more capable peacekeeping force (UNAMIR) than the lightly armed peacekeeping operation actually deployed without a protection of civilians mandate. But even at the outbreak of the killings, well-armed US, Belgian, and French troops deployed in the region and sent in to evacuate westerners could instead have supplemented a strengthened UNAMIR mandate and have been used to save large numbers of Tutsis and moderate Hutus from the Hutu Power killing machine.[39] Instead, the Security Council withdrew peacekeepers, weakening UNAMIR, and resisted action.

There is no simple solution. But the appointment of special advisers and offices whose primary task is to keep a watch out for looming genocides might make a difference in assessing conflicting reports and mobilizing attention without ulterior agendas.

Francis Deng, a respected former foreign minister from Sudan, was appointed by the UN secretary-general to play this role. But the task of mobilizing costly action for purely humanitarian purposes remains a continuing challenge.

Some kinds of violence or oppression make a mockery of authentic "arduous struggle." When faced with genocide or slavery, decent states must override nonintervention. But the same two ills that accompany humanitarian intervention in civil wars arise.

---

39. See Stanton, "Rwandan Genocide." See also Alan Kuperman's skeptical reading of whether a large-scale reduction in lives lost was possible after the genocide began, *The Limits of Humanitarian Intervention: Genocide in Rwanda* (Washington, DC: Brookings 2001), and Colonel Scott Feil's response to Kuperman, "Preventing Genocide: How the Early Use of Force Might Have Succeeded in Rwanda," *Report to the Carnegie Commission*, 1998.

How can one prevent a repeating cycle of violence? How can one avoid imperial exploitation of humanitarian crises?

These are not problems long past. They arise with each new intervention, and they arose in Libya and Syria in 2011. I will address those crises in Chapter 4. But next I turn to Mill's second set of reasons for intervention: those for "disregarding" non-intervention.

3

Exceptions That Disregard

Arguments against intervention have taken the form of claims about three principles: duties to avoid threats to national security; duties to respect national self-determination; and duties of global humanitarianism. These principles have at least two exceptions: either external moral factors can override the nonintervention paradigm or they can provide arguments to disregard it. We have explored why some external considerations call for overriding nonintervention. Mill called them "considerations paramount."

Here we explore another set of considerations that can favor intervention. Rather than being overridden, internal presuppositions of the nonintervention paradigm may not hold, so nonintervention can be disregarded in exceptional cases. The first disregarding example occurs when more than one nation struggles in one state's territory; and secession is the just outcome. The second, when other states have already intervened and unbalanced the local self-determining struggle, and counterintervention is the right response. And the third arrives when the polities in question may not have a singular self or be capable of self-determination; and then, Mill claims, benign imperial rule is the right response.

In those circumstances, the principle of national self-determination that nonintervention is designed to protect is not relevant. The local government in effect loses its claim to rule as the representative of a singular national authenticity; there is no one "self" to be determined. The reasons for nonintervention, Mill then claims, should be *disregarded*—they operate, he explains, in "an opposite way[;] . . . the reasons themselves do not exist" and intervention "does not disturb the balance of forces on which the permanent maintenance of freedom in a country depends" ("Non-Intervention," 123). Mill discusses and develops three cases in his classic essay for which an intervention serves the underlying self-determining and humanitarian protection purposes that nonintervention was designed to uphold.

SECESSION AS NATIONAL LIBERATION

The first case for disregarding is when too many nations contest one piece of territory, such as when an imperial government opposes the independence of a subordinate colonized nation, or when there are two distinct peoples, one attempting to crush the other. Under these circumstances, respecting "national" self-determination cannot be a reason to shun intervention. What is missing is the "one" nation.

Only once a people has demonstrated, through its own "arduous struggle," that it truly is another nation can foreigners intervene to help the liberation of an oppressed people. Then decolonization or secession is the right application of the self-determination principle, allowing a people to form its own destiny.

The case is not one people struggling to define itself. Instead, two or more peoples are involved, with one more powerful crushing the other. If there is a great imbalance of power between the two, no indigenous struggling can lift the "foreign" yoke. Victory in an autonomous arduous struggle, which ordinarily proves the fitness of a movement to rule a people, is not an adequate test of fitness for independence in some cases.

One example Mill might have had in mind was the American Revolution against Britain. But Mill specifically referenced the 1848–1849 failed Hungarian rebellion against Austria ("Non-Intervention," 124), and the wars of independence of Greece and Belgium. The distinguishing feature of these three examples is the role international assistance played in their outcomes.[1]

The Greeks won their independence following a bloody rebellion against the Ottoman Empire and after being crushed by an Ottoman-Egyptian force in the Peloponnese in 1825–1826. Only after the Russian-British-French naval intervention sank a large portion of the Ottoman-Egyptian fleet in the Bay of Navarino in 1827 did the tide turn. Two more years of armed conflict, with the assistance of a French expeditionary force, won back the Peloponnese, then central Greece, and eventual recognition as an independent state in 1832.[2]

BELGIAN INDEPENDENCE

The case for Belgian secession from the Netherlands in 1830 was the most welcome for Mill. Here, liberal international intervention was early, diplomatic, and, despite notable crises in the middle, effective.[3] Belgians were united by a shared Catholic religion and angered by discrimination against them in the civil service and army and inequalities in political representation

1. Mill groups the last two with the "protracted civil wars" (improbably in the Belgian case), but he distinguishes them as national movements leading to separation, not civic rebellions whose outcome, if mediated, should be conciliation, as occurred in Portugal in 1846.

2. For a thorough account emphasizing the altruism of the British intervention, see Gary Bass, *Freedom's Battle* (New York: Knopf, 2008), esp. chapters 1–3.

3. See Kenneth Bourne, *The Foreign Policy of Victorian England, 1830–1902* (Oxford: Clarendon, 1970), 30–33.

compared with the Protestant Dutch north. Belgian animosity toward the Kingdom of the Netherlands festered following the unification imposed by the post-Napoleonic Vienna settlement, which had built up a large Netherlands in an effort to create a strong power containing France on France's northern flank. Inspired perhaps by Louis Philippe's bourgeois revolution in France and establishment of a constitutional monarchy in 1830, the Belgian elite rose against King William's autocratic Dutch rule.

In retrospect it is not at all clear that secession was inevitable. Crown Prince William of the Netherlands saw the need for political reform and administrative devolution. Political equality might have appeased the Belgians; differences between French-speaking Walloons and Dutch-speaking Flemish might have been exploited. As it turned out, clumsy oppression and the nationalist spirit of the times united the Belgians.[4]

The international environment was also favorable. While the autocratic powers of Prussia, Austria, and Russia were opposed to another outbreak of liberal nationalism, the British and French, in their new liberal entente, were sympathetic to popular rule. The fortuitous rebellion in Poland stymied autocratic intervention that might have propped up Dutch rule, and the French intervened to roll back the Dutch forces that had seized Antwerp.

Nonetheless, the prospect of independence did not resolve the crisis. France encouraged the newly freed Belgians to either unify with France or accept a French prince as their new monarch (which many were inclined to do). This aggrandizement

4. Paul Schroeder, *The Transformation of European Politics, 1763–1848* (New York: Oxford University Press, 1994), 671–691, and Joel S. Fishman, *Diplomacy and Revolution: The London Conference of 1830 and the Belgian Revolt* (Amsterdam: CHEV, 1988).

of French power was completely unacceptable to Britain, and the fiery British foreign secretary, Palmerston, was prepared to threaten war to make this clear.[5] The French backed down, and a former German princeling, Leopold, became king of the independent nation.

Mill, in a later essay, noted that the Belgians met the nationality test. They had a distinct national identity warranting a claim to independence: "The Flemish and the Walloon provinces of Belgium, notwithstanding diversity of race and language, have a much greater feeling of common nationality, than the former have with Holland, or the latter with France."[6] And Mill concluded in yet another essay that international intervention was warranted in these cases, noting that

> whenever two countries, or two parts of the same country, are engaged in war, and the war either continues long undecided, or threatens to be decided in a way involving consequences repugnant to humanity or to the general interest, other countries have a right to step in; to settle among themselves what they consider reasonable terms of accommodation, and if these are not accepted, to interfere by force, and compel the recusant party to submit to the mandate. . . . This new doctrine has been acted on by a combination of the great powers of Europe . . . between Holland and Belgium at Antwerp.

5. Jasper Ridley, *Palmerston* (New York: Dutton, 1970), 123–127.

6. John Stuart Mill, *Considerations on Representative Government,* in *Essays on Politics and Society,* ed. John M. Robson (Toronto: University of Toronto Press; London: Routledge and Kegan Paul, 1977), 546 (*CW* 19).

Treating the Dutch attempt to forcibly retain Belgium as equivalent to a foreign invasion, he then concluded: "Is any motive to such interference of a more binding character—than that of preventing the liberty of a nation, which cares sufficiently for liberty to have risen in arms for its assertion, from being crushed and trampled out by tyrannical oppressors, and these not even of its own name and blood, but foreign conquerors?"[7]

The similar Hungarian revolution of 1848 was for Mill a disturbing case, a more complicated model of what was wrong with nonintervention in circumstances of genuine national liberation. For here, the local oppression was compounded by "foreign conquerors" of a sort that left no room for the kind of ambiguity raised by whether the Dutch were, or were not, "foreign" in the territory once recognized as theirs. No such ambiguity arose when the Austrians, driven from Hungary, called in the Russians to rescue their rule. Like Mill, I save this for separate treatment later in this chapter.

TWENTY-FIRST CENTURY RULES FOR SECESSION?

What rules should be followed in the ordinary case of one nation rebelling against a dominant nation in one territorial state? A war of secession differs from a civil war, in which the national struggle will decide which faction is better suited to rule by its ability to recruit followers, elicit their sacrifices in military action and taxes paid, and, in the process, define the terms of legitimate rule. A smaller nation too must struggle to define

7. John Stuart Mill, "Vindication of the French Revolution of 1848" (1849), in *Essays on French History and Historians,* ed. John M. Robson (Toronto: University of Toronto Press; London: Routledge and Kegan Paul, 1985), 346 (*CW* 20).

and determine itself, but no amount of national struggling can win adherents from the dominant nation. Nonintervention makes less sense in national secession. Once the rebels establish the local representative character of the movement for secession, internationals can assist, as France did the American states in 1778. And Mill notes such assistance might well have been legitimate to assist Hungary in its effort to break from Austria in 1848. But statespersons have long been hard-pressed to identify reliably when a people is truly a people, and to recognize consistently what steps are needed to prove its fitness for independence and justify foreign assistance.

The numerous anticolonial movements in Latin America, Africa, and Asia, and the secessions of East Timor from Indonesia and Kosovo from Serbia, also seem to fit well within this category. But they also illustrate the perplexities of "just" assistance. The record of assistance and eventual recognition is varied, ranging from recognized new states and UN members such as South Sudan and East Timor to widely accepted but contested states such as Kosovo, to states of limited recognition such as South Ossetia or Abkhazia or Somaliland.[8]

Some genuine national movements receive no assistance whatsoever and go unrecognized. Such is the Republic of Somaliland in northern Somalia, probably the only well-governed part of the country. Rebelling against the same atrocities committed by Siad Barre's regime that brought down the rest of Somalia in 1991, Somaliland won its effective autonomy on its own, without external assistance. It has a defined territory (the

---

8. For a good account of the legal standards see Joshua Castellano, *International Law and Self-Determination* (The Hague: Martinus Nijhoff, 2000), and the classic Antonio Cassese, *Self-Determination of Peoples: A Legal Reappraisal* (Cambridge: Cambridge University Press, 1995).

former colony of British Somaliland), a population (of about 3.5 million), and a functional government that also enjoys widespread local legitimacy (97 percent of the population endorsed independence in one 2001 referendum).[9] Somaliland has persevered despite its lack of natural resources, absent an external power for a patron (apart from some trade-mission interest from Ethiopia), without a single country recognizing its independence, and in the face of the strong African norm of *uti possidetis* ("as possessed at independence") in support of colonial boundaries.

At the other extreme are East Timor and South Sudan, both independent and the two newest member states of the United Nations. Both had clear markers of identity separation from their dominant countries in religion (both with significant Christian populations). Neither was fully a part of the established borders of the postcolonial successor state of Indonesia or Sudan. Both fought incorporation for decades and were forcibly ruled. Both acquired the attention of relevant regional neighbors (Australia for East Timor, the African Union for South Sudan), international patrons (Portugal for East Timor and the US Christian community for South Sudan), and multilateral organizations (the UN in both cases). Both also had significant actual and potential natural resources (oil in both cases) to attract attention.

In between are cases such as South Ossetia (closer to unrecognized and dependent) and Kosovo (closer to independent and fully recognized). South Ossetia had a long history of resistance to Georgia, moot when both were incorporated into

---

9. See Alison Eggers, "When Is a State a State? The Case for the Recognition of Somaliland," *Boston College International and Comparative Law Review* 30 (2007), 211–222, esp. 218.

the Russian Empire and the Soviet Union. But with the breakup of the USSR, the South Ossetians rebelled against the prospect of being incorporated into Georgia. Russia's initial support for Georgia curbed Ossetian independence. But as Georgia, under President Mikheil Saakashvili, leaned toward NATO and the West, Ossetia (as well as the Abkazian minority) found support in Russia. When in August 2008 President Saakashvili attempted forcible reunification of the de facto Russian-controlled areas of South Ossetia, the Russians intervened, crushing Georgian forces and driving them back, deep into Georgia proper. Russia has provided Russian passports to Ossetians and Abkazians and pledges support for those entities from "outside attack," effectively guaranteeing their independence.[10] But only Russia and a few of its close allies recognize South Ossetia's independence from Georgia. With few natural resources, it is also totally dependent on Russia for its continued existence.

Kosovo, too, had a long history of resistance (to the rule of the dominant Serbian forces) and a separate identity (in the Muslim religion). At the breakup of the former Yugoslavia, Kosovo, as an autonomous province rather than a constituent republic, lacked the full legal status that would have warranted independence. But it was close to that legal status, and its effective autonomy was forcibly repressed by Serbian nationalists just before the breakup. A long record of peaceful resistance under Ibrahim Rugova demonstrated in the 1990s the Kosovars' capacity for independent self-rule. But violent resistance to Kosovar independence from the Serbian government of Slobodan Milošević provoked the emergence of the militant Kosovo Liberation Army, which responded to atrocities in an eye-for-eye spirit. The Kosovars benefited from the attention

10. "Transcript: CNN Interview with Vladimir Putin," August 29, 2008.

of key US senators (including Robert Dole) and New York congressmen (with many Albanians in their district).[11] Milošević's campaign then triggered UN attention and European monitoring. Escalating violence and ethnic cleansing triggered NATO's intervention when neither Milošević nor the Kosovars would conciliate at the meeting mediated by NATO at the French Chateau Rambouillet. The meeting broke down in February 1999, over disputes concerning NATO's role in the implementation of "autonomy" for Kosovo; but the root of difference remained that Serbia would not permit evolution toward Kosovar independence and the Kosovar Albanians wanted nothing less.[12]

Following the NATO intervention, the UN ruled the territory under its own interim administration (UNMIK), guaranteeing both its autonomy and Serbian territorial integrity. After years of fruitless mediation, Kosovo unilaterally declared independence in February 2008. Kosovo is now de facto independent, recognized by eighty-two states, including almost all Muslim states, most members of the European Union, and the US—but remains unrecognized by Russia and Serbia. Serbs in the north of Kosovo have established their own de facto autonomous zone, supported by Serbia. The legality of the declaration of independence went before the International Court of Justice (ICJ), but its ruling was narrow, limited to the legality of a declaration of independence alone, skirting the more difficult issues of what legitimate secession is and what criteria should be applied.

11. See David Phillips's lively account in *Liberating Kosovo: Coercive Diplomacy and US Intervention* (Cambridge: MIT Press, 2012).

12. Independent International Commission on Kosovo, *The Kosovo Report, "Executive Summary: Main Findings,"* 1, http://reliefweb.int/sites/reliefweb.int/files/resources/F62789D9FCC56FB3C1256C1700303E3B-thekosovoreport.htm.

SUBSTANTIVE RULES: LAW AND ETHICS

Let us start by considering the substantive rules that should govern the question of whether to assist a secessionist movement. Controversies center around both the law and the ethics of just secessions.

International law is less than fully coherent on the question, and has traditionally been divided into two schools of thought. Proponents of the constitutive theory argue that international recognition confers the requisite international personality that creates statehood. Alternatively, under the declarative theory, recognition merely registers the factual existence of other polities when those polities meet certain criteria: *a defined territory, a population, a government that can govern independently, and the capacity to engage in foreign relations.*[13]

Not all the criteria are absolutely necessary, even for the declarativists: territory is necessary, but not a defined border. The US at its founding had no fixed western or northern boundary; neither did Israel have a fixed boundary; and of course neither does Palestine today.[14] Palestine, however, unlike the other two, is not functionally independent.

Whether a people has a right to its own state is where the issue gets more complicated. Indeed, this was the very question dodged by the ICJ on Kosovo.[15] The ICJ ruled on whether

13. Convention on the Rights and Duties of States (the "Montevideo Convention"), 165 L.N.T.S. 19, Art. 1.

14. On Israel see Statement of US Representative Philip Jessup to the UN Security Council regarding the admission of Israel to the United Nations, UN Doc. S/PV.383, at 9–11 (December 2, 1948), quoted in Lori Damrosch et al., *International Law: Cases and Materials,* 5th ed. (St. Paul, MN: Thomson/West, 2009), 306–308.

15. Accordance with International Law of the Unilateral Declaration of Independence in Respect of Kosovo, Advisory Opinion, ICJ Reports, 2010, p. 403.

states have a right to have their declaration of independence recognized, but not on whether peoples have a right to declare independent statehood. Customary law suggests that peoples have a right to self-determination, a right reaffirmed by the UN Declaration on Friendly Relations.[16] "Peoples" have that right, but we are not quite sure what a people is, though shared language and culture are often mentioned.

Thus the highly regarded Quebec case before the Supreme Court of Canada in 1998 held the right of self-determination should, in the first instance, be exercised internally through the exercise of political rights within existing states before any external claim to secession or independence is raised.[17]

The court added that *external self-determination is traditionally available only to those (1) under colonial rule or (2) under foreign occupation, or possibly (3) to those people whose internal self-determination has been forcibly repressed.*[18]

Given Quebec's civic freedoms and substantial participation in Canadian politics, the Canadian Supreme Court found that none of the three exceptional circumstances held. The court noted wryly that for forty of the fifty years before the case, the prime minister of Canada had been Quebecois.[19]

In more difficult cases, such as Kosovo, South Sudan, or South Ossetia, what constitutes "colonial rule" is itself in contention. For much of the post–World War II period, the simple

16. Declaration on Principles of International Law concerning Friendly Relations and Co-operation among States in accordance with the Charter of the United Nations, UN Doc. A/RES/25/2625 (October 24, 1970).

17. Reference re Secession of Quebec [1998], 2 SCR 217; Damrosch et al., *International Law,* 329–337.

18. Antonio Cassese, *International Law,* 2nd ed. (Oxford: Oxford University Press, 2005), 334.

19. Reference re Secession of Quebec [1998], 2 SCR 217, para. 135 (quoting *amicus curiae*).

and operative "salt water theory" applied to decolonization and independence movements. Colonies in Africa and Asia were "foreign" ruled when the ruler and the ruled were separated by salt water. With the breakup of the USSR and the former Yugoslavia in the 1990s, simple salt water rules were rendered moot. Newly independent states were established at the ends of occupations—such as the Baltic States, occupied by the USSR in 1940—and others became independent by consent in the breakup of a preexisting state, such as the USSR in 1991. The former Yugoslavia raised hard questions because the rule recognizing preexisting internal political boundaries as the legitimizing criteria of separation, which was useful in the former Soviet Union, ran afoul of "beached" Serb diasporas (minorities in both Croatia and Bosnia). It also failed to accord with the long-standing demands for autonomy from Kosovo (which lacked the boundaries of a preexisting constituent republic).

International law scholars had long recognized that traditional rules of sovereignty could bump up against "just and effective guarantees" for minorities, as did the League of Nations' Commission of Rapporteurs, who examined the issue in 1921.[20] But apart from the authority allocated to the UN Security Council to intervene to prevent breaches of the peace when minority conflicts threatened war, there was no clear recourse. Peoples "appealed to heaven"—war was often the result.

International ethics fills in and provides a foundation for the substantive legal standards. For many philosophers of international ethics, self-determination is rooted in the fundamental human right of individual self-rule: *In order to rule themselves,*

---

20. See the valuable discussion bearing on the Kosovo case in Bartram Brown's "Human Rights, Sovereignty, and the Final Status of Kosovo," *Chicago-Kent Law Review* 80 (2005), 235–272.

individuals must be able to rule one another in certain collective areas where collective goods, such as fundamental laws, require collective action.[21] *But to avoid self-determination degenerating into each individual self for himself and a universal anarchy of persons, a "collective identity" is added as a special qualifier of the unit to achieve self-determination. The contemporary difficulty is identifying when multiple identities warrant independence and political recognition.*

One approach is ethnographic and substantive. We try to discern a genuine nation by cultural, historical, or democratic standards and then endow it with a legitimate claim to independent statehood.[22] Philosophers such as Giuseppe Mazzini thus make large demands: "To each nation its own state."[23] The sovereign state provides the mechanism through compulsory education, support for public culture, and a press to protect and perpetuate a national cultural identity. Empires have sometimes tolerated diverse identities (think of the Ottomans), but the best guarantee appears to be a state of one's own.

Complementarily, states, we think, tend to benefit from, and are stabilized by, single or predominant nations as their politi-

21. Daniel Philpott insightfully makes this case for the individual root of our claims in "In Defense of Self Determination," *Ethics* 105 (1995), 352–385. For a particularly helpful analytic "brush-clearing" exercise, see Avishai Margalit and Joseph Raz, "National Self-Determination," *Journal of Philosophy* 87 (September 1990), 439–461. Margalit and Raz detail why nations are the relevant unit and explore the value of self-government, affirming the instrumental value of self-determination as a way for relevant groups to exercise self-government in the appropriate circumstances.

22. For a good example of this approach, see Allen Buchanan, *Secession* (Boulder, CO: Westview, 1991).

23. Stefano Recchia and Nadia Urbinati, Introduction to *A Cosmopolitanism of Nations: Giuseppe Mazzini's Writings on Democracy, Nation Building, and International Relations* (Princeton: Princeton University Press, 2009), 13 ff.

cal foundations. And states therefore tend to cultivate national unity by creating hegemonic national churches and fostering national languages and cultures. The French Academy thus helped ensure that *langue d'oui* crowded out its rivals, independent Ireland fostered Erse, and the Croatians are now busily creating the Croatian language out of what once was Serbo-Croatian, a language shared with Serbia and Bosnia. Mill himself once suggested that singular national identity can help stabilize states and was the necessary, consensual foundation for democratic government. And Mazzini famously averred that when each nation is satisfied with its own state, international relations would tend to be more stable too. All of this is the good national "news."

THE RHETORIC OF INDEPENDENCE

These claims are not just philosophical musings. We can see these concerns and claims play out in actual declarations of national independence by statespersons calling for popular support and international recognition. These declarations are wonderfully diverse, but most follow typical patterns. Sometimes similar phrases repeat themselves in due recognition and appeal for support, as David Armitage shows in a recent book.[24]

"All men are created equal, they are endowed by their creator with certain inalienable rights; among these are life liberty and the pursuit of happiness." Americans recognize these phrases and claim them as their own; but they are also phrases (in direct

24. David Armitage, *The Declaration of Independence: A Global History* (Cambridge: Harvard University Press, 2008), esp. chapter 3. Joshua Simon, as he explained to me in discussions following the Castle Lectures, is exploring, in his graduate dissertation at Yale, similarities among the American declarations, both north and south, as settler societies.

and conscious imitation) quoted from Ho Chi Minh's declaration of independence for Vietnam in 1945.

Most declarations that I have examined include the following:

1. An assertion of a deep and wide basis for the claim to a right of self-determination, often based on human equality, "self-evidence," and the right to self-government. The US Declaration is the prime model. Alternatively, common experience of race and the oppression of slavery are invoked, as they were by the Haitian founding fathers in 1804 in a declaration rediscovered in 2010 in the British Museum.[25] And race has been reversely invoked, as it was by Texas in 1861, when Texas's secessionists proclaimed that the "original [US] confederacy had been established exclusively for the white race," and that now the federal government was challenging that establishment of privilege. Or, more recently in a rich mixture, like that of Israel, whose 1948 declaration invoked not only the Bible but also the legacy of secular immigrants whose hard work made the desert bloom, and assorted international authorities, including the Balfour Declaration and various UN resolutions (specifically, UN General Assembly Resolution 181).

2. Then follow "grievances." Independence is contentious and requires specific justification, because governments should not be lightly overthrown or expelled. Rebels need to justify the break, arguing beyond the universal right to self-government, to explain why previous governance was illegitimate. Here rebels typically invoke a "long train of

25. Damien Cave, "Haiti's Document Found in London," *New York Times,* April 1, 2010.

abuses," as the Americans did in detailing violations of the established rights of Englishmen or the Haitians did in recalling the oppressions of slavery. The Irish 1919 declaration chronicles seven hundred years of oppression. This is matched by the Georgian declaration of comparably ancient pedigree. Less antique is the Miskito Declaration of 2009 issued by Hector E. William, the "great judge" of the Miskito people in Nicaragua. It traces more than two centuries of autonomous rule and then complains about new restrictions on turtle hunting introduced by Daniel Ortega's Nicaraguan government.

3. Almost all dutifully claim that secession is a last resort. Reflecting just war doctrine, they note that rebels have "petitioned for redress in the most humble terms." But as Thomas Jefferson went on to claim, both monarch and people of the imperial state have rejected reasonable petitions for redress.

4. Then they declare independence, claim the rights of all other nations and states, and pledge to govern together, risking as did the American rebels of 1776, "our lives, our fortunes and our Sacred honor."

These claims have moral weight. Nations should be free. But the record of national liberations has "bad news" too. One difficulty with national liberation is the problem of minorities within secessionist minorities, who want to secede from the newly seceded community. Even worse is the problem of majorities within former minorities, as in Abkhazia, where at the time of secession, only 17 percent of the population was Abkhaz. Forty-six percent of the people still thought of themselves as Georgian, 14.6 percent as Armenian, and the rest as "other Slavic" nationalities. And the Abkhaz are themselves divided between Christian and Muslim communities.[26]

But the largest single problem attached to national liberations is systemic. There are six thousand languages with identifiable populations and, today, nearly two hundred independent states. Clearly, not every identity—as measured by language—currently gets its own state. Fifty-two percent of these languages are spoken by fewer than ten thousand persons each, so perhaps we can omit them from consideration. But that still leaves us a troublesome twenty-eight hundred currently unsatisfied potential claimants on statehood. Moreover, 17 percent of the languages are spoken in more than one state, leaving us with a potential diaspora and unification ("anschluss") claims. One cannot but recall the comment by Robert Lansing, former US secretary of state to President Woodrow Wilson, who remarked on his chief's commitment to self-determination: "The phrase is simply loaded with dynamite. It will raise hopes which can never be realized. It will, I fear, cost thousands of lives."[27] Completing the nation-state system—with each nation its own state—would be a disaster.[28]

26. John Waterbury, "Avoiding the Iron Cage of Legislated Communal Identity," in *The Self-Determination of Peoples,* ed. Wolfgang Danspeckgruber (Boulder, CO: Lynne Rienner, 2002), 125.

27. Robert Lansing, diary entry for November 1918, Robert Lansing Papers, Princeton University, box 40.

28. For an alternative "complicating" of the international system through local and regional devolutions, see Michael Walzer, "The Reform of the International System," in *Studies of War and Peace,* ed. O. Osterud (New York: Oxford University Press, 1987).

Procedural Rules: From Self-Administration to Self-Determination

Substantive standards, whether in law or ethics, clearly have limitations as guidelines for a policy on when to or not to support national self-determination and secession. A second approach to self-determination is intercommunal proceduralism. Here a claim, any claim, to secede undergoes a series of procedural steps beginning with self-administration that is designed to test whether something less than full secession satisfies local demands for self-determining autonomy. Marvin Mikesell and Alexander Murphy analyzed a comprehensive framework of the range of minority group aspirations and the policy responses that have addressed those aspirations. They note the variety of aspirations, ranging from recognition through access to participation to separation to autonomy and finally to independence. In many circumstances, the lesser aspirations can be met by measures far short of independence.[29] One value of doing so is that statesmen need not weigh *ex ante* claims to legitimate differentiation. (US and UK lawyers recently debated the legality of the US Declaration of Independence; 235 years later, they still could not agree.[30]) A process decides what claims have merit and the extent of deference accorded to them.

The Liechtenstein Draft Convention on Self-Administration and Self-Determination provides a useful example of a prearranged set of steps that tests the authenticity of a demand for

29. Marvin Mikesell and Alexander Murphy, "A Framework for Comparative Study of Minority Group Aspirations," *Annals of the Association of American Geographers* 81 (1991), 588.

30. Matt Danzico and Kate Dailey, "Is the US Declaration of Independence Illegal?" BBC News, October 19, 2011.

autonomy.[31] (It was drafted by H.S.H. Hans Adam II and British barrister Sir Arthur Watts in 1995 and sponsored by the sovereign Principality of Liechtenstein.) Once a state has agreed to manage these claims in a treaty, the specified standard process outlined in the treaty pertains:

The first step occurs when a group claiming autonomy is granted local communal self-administration.

Police are recruited from the group's numbers; schools are authorized in the local language if recognition of a separate language is the group's demand. These accommodations are available to any distinct group concentrated in a territorially limited area that demonstrates a capacity and willingness to bear the costs of self-organization and that is willing to grant basic civic freedoms and provide equal protection of the law.

Once instituted and tested, if minimal self-administration fails to satisfy local demands for autonomy, legislative powers could then be devolved, changing a state from central to federal in character.

And should that not prove satisfactory, the ultimate outcome of independence is available for populations demanding it and prepared to negotiate a fair distribution of previous debts and resources.

This process, as the draft treaty proposes, works better with external monitoring of the commitments states and dissident groups make to each other.

The Liechtenstein Convention is not a panacea. It could help create a plethora of many more Liechtensteins—leading some to believe that mini-states love company. But it is only for ideal situations—velvet divorces—where constitutional governments committed to minority rights seek orderly self-administration

31. See Sir Arthur Watts, "Liechtenstein Draft on Self-Administration and Self-Determination" in Danspeckgruber, *Self-Determination of Peoples*.

and are prepared to tolerate orderly secession. It is not ideal in the hardest cases, where a consensual process is not possible, making it poorly suited as a remedy for state oppression, as took place in East Timor or Kosovo and perhaps South Ossetia (though Russia clearly fomented dissent as well).

COUNTERINTERVENTION

The second instance in which the principle against intervention should be disregarded is counterintervention in a civil war. For Mill and others, a civil war should be left to the combatants. When conflicting factions of one people are struggling to define what sort of society and government should rule, only that struggle should decide the outcomes, not foreigners.

But when an external power intervenes on behalf of one of the participants in a civil war, then another foreign power can, in Mill's words, "re-dress the balance"—counterintervene to balance the first intervention. This second intervention serves the purposes of self-determination, which the first intervention sought to undermine. Even if, Mill argues, the Hungarian rebellion was not clearly a national rebellion against "a foreign yoke," it was clearly the case that Russia should not have intervened to assist Austria in its suppression. If "Russia gave assistance to the wrong side, England would aid the right" ("Non-Intervention," 124). By doing so, Russia gave others a right to counterintervene.[32]

Mill seems unduly concerned about the authenticity of the Hungarian rebellion against Austria. Despite the long history

32. For a modern interpretation stressing Hungary's success in civil reform, while not succeeding in acquiring independence, see Domokos Kosáry, *Hungary and International Politics in 1848–1849*, trans. Tim Wilkinson (Boulder, CO: Atlantic Research and Publications, 2003).

of Austrian imperial rule, Hungary had long had an independent historical identity, and the national movement in the first half of the century asserted claims to local rule that matched claims being made in Austria for more responsible government. The toppling of Prince Metternich in Austria in March 1848 opened the door to a similar breakthrough in Hungary, with the seeming sympathy and support of Emperor Ferdinand for both reform movements. Hungarian demands were moderate: more local autonomy in a federalist structure. But disputes arose over just how federal authority was to be divided. Both revolutions radicalized, with democratic republicans taking over, including a committee of safety in Vienna and republicans in Budapest inspired by Lajos Kossuth. Alarmed by the breakup of the empire, conservative forces led by Prince Windischgratz and Baron Jellachich occupied Vienna, forced the abdication of Ferdinand, and installed his nephew, Franz Ferdinand, as the new emperor. Then, in January 1849, they invaded Hungary. But Hungarian resistance forced an Austrian withdrawal, Hungary proving itself capable of the "arduous struggle" that Mill saw as the test of an independent self-governing existence.

At this point, the Austrians called in Russian forces and decisively defeated the Hungarians, leading Mill to argue that this thoroughly foreign intervention would have justified a British counterintervention, even if the national rebellion might not have warranted armed foreign support. Mill makes a persuasive argument that the principle of self-determination would not have been violated by a (counter) intervention in this case. For him only those engaged in the local struggle should decide who should rule; not foreign interveners. But the case, as well, probably, as similar cases, is more complicated ethically in at least three ways.

First, the movement did not take place in a nationalist political vacuum. Hungary's nationalist movement occurred in a political space that included minorities within former minorities, which evokes the problem of authentic national voice discussed above. Oppressed Croats, Slovenes, and Romanians were also inspired to rise and demand their rights against perceived Hungarian oppressors. In addition to the moral conundrum this posed, it opened the door to strategic exploitation by reactionary forces, as Viennese conservatives could enlist Baron Jellachich to lead Croat military forces to suppress Hungarian and Austrian rebels.

Second, the movement also did not take place in a geopolitical vacuum. Austria was a vital part of the European balance of power, according to Foreign Secretary Palmerston. Despite considerable popular sympathy in Britain and his far from reluctant attitude toward intervention, he informed Parliament:

> Austria is a most important element in the balance of European power. Austria stands in the centre of Europe, a barrier against encroachment on the one side, and against invasion on the other. The political independence and liberties of Europe are bound up, in my opinion, with the maintenance and integrity of Austria as a great European Power; and therefore anything which tends by direct, or even remote, contingency, to weaken and to cripple Austria, but still more to reduce her from the position of a first-rate Power to that of a secondary State, must be a great calamity to Europe, and one which every Englishman ought to deprecate, and to try to prevent.[33]

33. Viscount Palmerston, Hansard (UK Parliament Official Report), House of Commons Debate, July 21, 1849, Vol. 107, paras. 786–817, available at http://

The British interest, if true, merits ethical consideration. Hungarian rebellion encouraged and then itself was further encouraged by similar revolts in Milan and Bohemia. The empire was falling apart. Is a Hungarian, or any other independence movement, worth European world war? As Michael Walzer notes in his commentary on the 1848–1849 Hungarian case, it eerily parallels concerns raised by the Hungarian rebellion of 1956 against Cold War Soviet rule: was Western intervention to secure the freedom of Budapest worth thermonuclear war with the Soviet Union?[34]

The Russian imperial government in 1849 had a separate strategic concern. They did not see the Hungarian rebellion as an Austrian matter, but rather as a Russian one, as their formal declaration announcing the armed intervention in Hungary made clear:

> The insurrection in Hungary has of late made so much progress that Russia cannot possibly remain inactive. . . . [The insurgents'] revolutionary plans have swollen in magnitude in proportion to the success of their arms. The Magyar [Hungarian] movement has been adulterated by the presence of Polish emigrants forming whole corps of the Hungarian

---

hansard.millbanksystems.com/commons/1849/jul/21/russian-invasion-of-hungary. And see for background, Charles Sproxton, *Palmerston and the Hungarian Revolution* (Cambridge: University Press, 1919). It is also worth pointing out, as Count Schwarzenberg, leader of the reactionary government in Austria, did, that Britain's own record in oppressing "unhappy Ireland" hardly suited it for the role of liberator; ibid., 109. Britain was more than prepared, the count continued, to spill "torrents of blood" to maintain its authority and, he smugly added, "It is not for us to blame her."

34. Walzer, *Just and Unjust Wars*, 94. Walzer discusses both these first two complications.

army and by the influence of certain persons as Bem and Dembinski who make plans of attack and defence and it has come to be a general insurrection especially of Poland. . . . The intrigues of these insurrectionists undermined Galicia and Cracow [in Russian-ruled Poland]. . . . They still keep the vast extent of our frontiers in a perpetual state of excitement and ferment. Such a state of things endangers our dearest interests and prudence compels us to anticipate the difficulties it prepares for us. The Austrian Government, being for the moment unable to oppose a sufficient power to the insurgents, has formally requested His Majesty the Emperor [Nicholas of Russia] to assist in the repression of a rebellion which endangers the tranquility of the two empires.[35]

It is difficult to give much moral credit to the argument on grounds of self-determination. After all, Poland also should have been free. But it is worth noting that Dembinski, originally a Polish general, not Hungarian, led the 1830 failed rebellion against Russia, and now was a general in the Hungarian army, commanding thirty thousand Polish volunteers.[36]

Both the British and the Russian positions reflect ways in which concerns extraneous to national self-determination shape policy. They lead in arbitrary ways to underintervention (Britain) or overintervention (Russia).

35. "Declaration of the Russian Government on Hungary," from *The Annual Register* 91 (1849), 333–334, St. Petersburg, April 27.

36. Charles Maurice, *The Revolutionary Movement of 1848-49 in Italy, Austria and Germany* (New York: G. P. Putnam's, 1887), 453.

The third problem has to do with the systemic coherence and sustainability of the counterintervention norm. Building on Millian arguments, Michael Walzer has explored the Vietnam interventions of the 1960s. He proposes two key principles:

First, legitimate foreign counterintervention should be . . . "on behalf of a government that has established its own internal legitimacy (unlike the South Vietnamese regime, which was radically dependent on US support)."

Second, counterintervention must be measured in a way such that it does not overwhelm the local struggle, the only legitimate determinant of who should govern.[37] *Thus no one should intervene. But if one state does, another can balance. It "holds the ring" against unbalanced international intervention, making sure the local struggle is self-determinative, not the international intervention.*

This makes fine logical moral sense. But in practice, it raises more problems than solutions. Intervening only to balance forces just helps create a protracted civil war if the first intervener does not accept the balanced, Marquess of Queensberry–style rules. Each counterintervener will be morally compelled to up the ante. In the end, it can be important for long-term stability that one party wins.[38] A recent essay by Aysegu Aydin and Patrick Regan confirms the significance of these concerns.[39] With data from 1945 on, the authors find that competitive coun-

---

37. Walzer, *Just and Unjust Wars*, 97–99.

38. See Edward Luttwak, "Give War a Chance," *Foreign Affairs* 78 (July–August 1999), 36–44, and Richard Betts, "The Delusion of Impartial Intervention," *Foreign Affairs Web* 73 (November–December, 1994), http://www.foreign affairs.com/articles/50545/richard-k-betts/the-delusion-of-impartial-intervention.

39. Aysegu Aydin and Patrick Regan, "Networks of Third Party Interveners and Civil War Duration," *EJIR*, 51 (2011), 1–25.

terinterventions lengthen civil wars. Instead, if outside powers can agree and act together on one side of a conflict, they might be able to shorten the wars.

More important, they may be able to choose the "right" side to support. In an anarchic world, counterintervention may well be the best we can do. But how much better it would be if a legitimate multilateral authority could manage competitive claims for national independence, ensuring that Croats, Poles, Romanians, and Czechs all get their claims adequately heard and adjudicated. How much better too that "Russian" overinterveners are kept out and "British" underinterveners are brought in, without risking the national security of either. Determining justifiable interventions and sharing the burdens of such interventions can help ensure that there are neither too many nor too few such interventions.

The standards of justified national separation require multilateral deliberation, and interventions require the burden-sharing of joint action.

Fortuitous balance of power and international combinations, such as the ones that supported Belgium or Greece, are too rare. I turn to these multilateral innovations in our time when I consider Libya and Syria and the Responsibility to Protect. But next, I look at Mill's most controversial disregard.

BENIGN IMPERIALISM

Mill's most controversial case today is his last disregard, the allegedly "barbarous," noncivilized world into which he dumps most of Africa and Asia—the nineteenth-century colonial empires. This is his case for paternalistic intervention and beneficent imperialism. According to Mill, his principles of nonintervention only hold among "civilized" nations.[40] His example is "Oude" in India, modern Awadh, annexed by Britain in 1858.

Mill's argument for imperial rule includes four indictments of indigenous society that justify paternalistic authority. These societies allegedly suffer four debilitating infirmities—despotism, anarchy, amoral presentism, and familism—that together make them incapable of self-determination and make their potential autonomy disregardable:

1. The people are imposed upon by a "despot . . . so oppressive and extortionate as to devastate the country."
2. Despotism long endured has produced anarchy characterized by "such a state of nerveless imbecility that everyone subject to their will, who had not the means of defending himself by his own armed followers, was the prey of anybody who had a band of ruffians in his pay."
3. The people as a result deteriorate into amoral presentism, in which present gratification overwhelms the future and no contracts can be relied upon.
4. Moral duties extend no further than the family; national or civic identity is altogether absent. They lack the scope

40. Mill, however, conceives of many circumstances in which analogous forms of paternalism or benign despotism can be justified, including over children and domestically when populations are not fit for self-government. For a discussion of various forms of despotism, see Nadia Urbinati, "The Many Heads of the Hydra: J. S. Mill on Despotism," in *J. S. Mill's Political Thought: A Bicentennial Reassessment,* ed. Nadia Urbinati and Alex Zakaras, 66–97 (Cambridge: Cambridge University Press, 2007); Mark Tulnick, "Tolerant Imperialism: John Stuart Mill's Defense of British Rule in India," *Review of Politics* 68 (2006), 586–611; and Karuna Mantena, "Mill and the Imperial Predicament," in Urbinati and Zakaras, *J. S. Mill's Political Thought,* 298–318.

for extensive, stable social relations. They do not have a civic or national self-conception, identifying only with the village or valley. ("Non-Intervention," 119–120)

No civilized government, Mill concludes, can maintain a stable relationship with these uncivilized societies: "In the first place, the rules of ordinary morality imply reciprocity. But barbarians will not reciprocate" (118). Presentism discounts the future; familism and despotism preclude public accountability. Together, they undermine reliable reciprocity. And, in the next place, these "nations have not got beyond the period during which it is likely to be for their benefit that they should be conquered and held in subjection by foreigners" (118).

In these circumstances, Mill claims, the best that can happen for the population is a benign colonialism, such as he recommended during the annexation of Oude in 1857. Normal interstate relations cannot be maintained in such an anarchic and lawless environment. The most a well-intentioned foreigner owes these peoples is paternal care and education. For, like children or lunatics, they presumably can benefit from nothing else.

Given this grim judgment, it is important to note that Mill advocates neither exploitation nor racialist domination. Indeed, as Mark Tulnick has persuasively argued, the imperialism Mill recommends is, in many respects, "tolerant"—neither totalitarian nor racist.[41] Instead, it is grounded in the principles of human dignity that also form his view of just relations among "civilized" states. Significantly, Mill applies the same reasoning to once-primitive northern Europeans who "benefited" from the

---

41. Tulnick, "Tolerant Imperialism," and see Stephen Holmes, "Making Sense of Liberal Imperialism," in Urbinati and Zakaras, *J. S. Mill's Political Thought,* 319–346, for related arguments.

imperial rule imposed by civilized Romans. Unlike the much stronger paternalism of his father, James Mill, and other imperial liberals, Mill's imperial education does not require conversion to Christianity, nor does it call for the adoption of English culture—only for the cultivation of the ethos of the rule of law and the material sciences that are needed for economic progress. The duties of paternal care, moreover, are real, precluding oppression and exploitation and requiring care and education designed to one day fit the colonized people for independent national existence.

What should we make of this? Let us note that Mill never demonstrates "presentism." On its face, the judgment is incredible, when one observes the generations of labor invested in great monuments in Asia, Africa, and India—twelfth-century Angkor Wat in Cambodia, the seventeenth-century Taj Mahal, or the elaborate religious ritual and art of Benin bronzes in Africa. Ancient cultures embodying deep senses of social obligation made nonsense of presentism and familism.

Jennifer Pitts points out that J. S. Mill, like James Mill, stressed the moral and intellectual failings of the "barbarous" peoples and lumped all the varieties of social structures they exhibited, from nomadic tribes to feudal and bureaucratic empires, into one "barbarism." In doing so, both Mills, father and son, broke with earlier liberal traditions that posited a common rationality and varying societal and political regimes, as did Jeremy Bentham and philosophers such as Adam Smith and Immanuel Kant.[42]

But anarchy, corruption, and despotic oppression did afflict

42. See Jennifer Pitts, *A Turn to Empire: The Rise of Imperial Liberalism in Britain and France* (Princeton: Princeton University Press, 2003), chapter 5, passim. On Smith, see also Michael Doyle, *Ways of War and Peace* (New York: Norton, 1997), chapter 7.

many of the peoples in these regions. Two current experts, Rudrangshu Mukherjee and Thomas Metcalf, agree with Mill's indictment of the nawabs (rulers) of Oude who "abandoned the attempt to govern . . . and amused themselves with wine, women and poetry."[43] Sources contemporary to Mill, including a treaty of 1837, negotiated but never ratified, between Oude and Britain, warned that if "gross and systematic oppression, anarchy and misrule" continued, the nawabs' land would be seized. But in this regard, we would want to ask how this corruption differed, if at all, from the corruption of European despotisms, all of which according to Mill should "enjoy" their own self-determining "arduous struggle."

More significantly, while Mill's treatment does convey Britain's responsibility for some of the misrule and consequent responsibility (in Mill's judgment) to redress it ("Non-Intervention," 120), Mill does not seem able to parcel out the responsibilities of the shared causation he does acknowledge, including the responsibility not to contribute to the weakening that later justifies imperial rule. Oude's condition was very much a product of the irresponsible dependent condition to which the nawabs had been reduced by the Treaty of 1801. That treaty established the British protectorate, for which Oude paid a heavy subsidy to the East India Company, and guaranteed unfettered access for British merchants to Oude's markets. The nawabs soon found themselves without local authority (usurped by the British res-

43. Rudrangshu Mukherjee, *Awadh in Revolt, 1857–1858* (Delhi: Oxford University Press, 1984), quoting Thomas Metcalf, *Land, Landlords, and the British Raj: Northern India in the Nineteenth Century* (Berkeley: University of California Press, 1979), 33. And for context and historiography see Biswannoy Pati, ed., *The 1857 Rebellion* (Delhi: Oxford University Press, 2007), and E. T. Sullivan, "Liberalism and Imperialism: J. S. Mill's Defense of the British Empire," *Journal of the History of Ideas* 44 (1983), 599–617.

ident), incapable of fostering native industry, and responsible for seventy-six lacs of rupees ($3.8 million in 1856 dollars) in annual tribute to Britain. Mill notes that if Oude's misrule was partly occasioned by British rule, Britain may have had the obligation to correct it. But it also had an obligation not to contribute to causing it in the first place and use the misrule as a justification for annexation.[44]

Mill thus admits that the anarchy of Oude was partly "morally accountable" to British rule and known to be the case "by men who knew it well" (120). But what he does not mention is that *he* was the responsible official under the Court of Directors of the East India Company charged with the oversight of the company's relations with Oude. Indeed, Oude was his first (beginning in 1828) and continuing assignment in the London headquarters of the East India Company.[45]

Problematic as it is, and shorn of its cultural "Orientalism," Mill's argument for trusteeship begins to address one serious gap in strategies of humanitarian assistance: the devastations that cannot be readily redressed by a quick in-and-out intervention designed to liberate an oppressed people from the clutches of foreign oppression or a domestic genocide. But unilateral interveners have a special obligation to discuss how one can prevent benign trusteeship from becoming malign imperialism, particularly when one recalls the flowery words and humanitarian intentions that accompanied the conquerors of Asia and Africa. This is a problem posed by Michael Walzer: what to do

44. See Karl Marx's article in the *New York Daily Tribune*, May 28, 1858, "The Annexation of Oude."

45. For background on Mill's career in this connection, see Lynn Zastoupil, *John Stuart Mill and India* (Stanford: Stanford University Press, 1994), 87.

with the anarchy of Somalia or (for a while) Liberia and Sierra Leone and the Democratic Republic of the Congo, "failed states" in modern parlance. They are not suited to a quick intervention of the sort that split Belgium from Holland in 1830 or reconciled the Portuguese in 1846.

But for Kosovo, Bosnia, Somalia, and now Afghanistan and Congo, and for the unjustified interventions that one nonetheless would want to leave justly, like Iraq, with a stable and decent government, what stabilizing and sustaining is available to them? How does the country later become self-governing? How does one empower the locals to be self-governing? If interveners cannot or will not commit to solve this, should one intervene? And if outsiders do intervene, who will prevent imperial exploitation? And when can the interveners justly leave?

The modern answer is multilateral peacebuilding in the wake of a civil war or humanitarian crisis. It claims to be different from occupation or colonialism. It either rests upon consent of the key domestic parties or it is a multilateral rescue of a country that has experienced a humanitarian crisis, as did, for example, Somalia, Bosnia, or East Timor. It is an occupation that is designed to promote human rights and local self-determination, devoid of the controlling national interest of any particular occupier. I take it up in Chapter 5 on postwar peacebuilding.

4

Libya, the "Responsibility to Protect," and the New Moral Minimum

On March 17, 2011, the United Nations Security Council authorized "all necessary means"—the UN code words for armed intervention—against Muammar al-Qaddafi's Libya. Was it legal? Was it ethical? The casualties experienced were nowhere near the level of past humanitarian crises that warranted intervention, such as Bangladesh in 1971 (200,000–300,000 deaths; 8 million refugees) or Rwanda in 1994 (800,000 deaths). Michael Walzer thus argued that Libya did not qualify as a humanitarian intervention because it was not a genocidal massacre like Rwanda; and surely he was right. He then reasonably concluded that it was instead just an ordinary rebellion against a typical tyrant, but one incapable of succeeding on its own.[1] Intervention, he suggested, was not justifiable.

Mill probably would have agreed—and we can agree—that it was not justifiable as a classical humanitarian intervention against a massacre of the kind that any well-meaning state would have the right, and perhaps duty, to stop by overriding the nonintervention norm. It was more preventive than reactive. It was also more proactive and dependent on multilateral, procedural legitimacy than Mill would have envisaged. It was, instead, something new, an application of the Responsibility to

1. Michael Walzer, "The Case Against Our Attack on Libya," *New Republic,* March 20, 2011, http://www.newrepublic.com/article/world/85509/the-case-against-our-attack-libya, accessed July 6, 2011.

Protect (R2P or RtoP)—a new norm for humanitarian military intervention and a newly legitimate moral minimum of global order.[2] This UN-authorized protection replaces, under special circumstances, the massacre standard underlying traditional humanitarian intervention.

Where did this new norm come from? In this chapter I will trace the roots of RtoP in international law and international ethics. RtoP is in tension with established UN Charter law on the use of force, but it may be beginning to change the law. It is, on the other hand, deeply familiar to international ethics, a widening of the circumstances that allow for overriding nonintervention. It evolved out of the failures to protect the populations of Rwanda (1994) and Bosnia (1992–1995) and NATO's decision to intervene in Kosovo (1999). I will show in this chapter how RtoP has been invoked, explicitly and implicitly, successfully and unsuccessfully, in cases ranging from Myanmar and Kenya in 2008, to Guinea in 2009, and then recently, and controversially, for Libya in 2011. And the last has had severe negative consequences for international protection for Syrians since 2011.

I will argue that RtoP is both a *license for* and a *leash against* forcible intervention. As such, it has contributed to the increasing pluralism, contested and contestable, of the normative architecture of world politics. But this confusion may reduce as RtoP norms become better institutionalized in the UN, reshape the discourse of international ethics, and are accumulated in customary law. In any case, where the alternative to pluralism is a clarity that either abandons vulnerable populations or im-

2. R2P is the acronym of the International Commission on Intervention and State Sovereignty, and RtoP is the acronym adopted by the UN ("2" as "to" does not register across languages); both are discussed below.

poses unrealistic expectations of enforced human rights, contestation is a step forward. RtoP can now be a resource for responsible policy and it is the best we are likely to get if we continue to care about both vulnerable populations and national sovereignty.

Significantly, Responsibility to Protect now constitutes a floor limit to global pluralism. States should respect and attempt to further the full range of human rights as expressed in the two covenants of civil and political rights, and economic, social, and cultural rights. But what they now must do, or be liable to enforcement action, is to protect their populations from genocide, crimes against humanity, war crimes, and ethnic cleansing.[3] The meaning of sovereignty has changed. States are still sovereign, independent in their domestic affairs, but they are no longer free to commit one of those four crimes without risk of legitimate international constraint.

In 2001, a global commission chaired by Gareth Evans, the former foreign minister of Australia, and Mohammed Sahnoun, a prominent former Algerian diplomat, proposed that the international community widen the legitimate grounds for international protection to include protecting populations from serious and irreparable harm. In 2005, the UN General Assembly narrowed those protections to genocide, war crimes, crimes against humanity, and ethnic cleansing, but restricted the enforcement

---

3. These crimes are defined in detail in the Rome Statute of the International Criminal Court. Genocide is the killing or other severe harms intended to destroy a national, ethnical, racial, or religious group in whole or in part (Article 6). Crimes against humanity are widespread murder, enslavement, torture, rape, etc., against a civilian population (Article 7). War crimes are either grave breaches of the Geneva Convention against, e.g., noncombatants, or mistreatments of prisoners of war, etc. (Article 8). Ethnic cleansing is deportation or forcible transfer of an ethnic population (specified in Article 7d).

of these principles to authorization by the UN Security Council in order to preclude unilateral interventions. In other words, the General Assembly created a new global governance norm, a norm that was both a substantive license to protect more and a procedural leash to avoid intervening too much.

Responsibility to Protect was articulated as part of the *World Summit Outcome Document,* which expressed the consensus of all 191 members of the UN at its 2005 Summit.[4] Responsibility to Protect's core commitments are expressed in two key paragraphs, which are worth quoting:

> 138. Each individual State has the responsibility to protect its populations from genocide, war crimes, ethnic cleansing and crimes against humanity. This responsibility entails the prevention of such crimes, including their incitement, through appropriate and necessary means. We accept that responsibility and will act in accordance with it. . . .
>
> 139. The international community, through the United Nations, also has the responsibility to use appropriate diplomatic, humanitarian and other peaceful means, in accordance with Chapters VI and VIII of the Charter, to help to protect populations from genocide, war crimes, ethnic cleansing and crimes against humanity. In this context, we are prepared to take collective action, in a timely and decisive manner, through the Security Council, in accordance with the Charter, including Chapter VII, on a case-by-case basis and in cooperation with relevant regional organizations as appropriate, should

4. GA Res. 60/1, UN Doc. A/RES/60/1 (October 24, 2005).

peaceful means be inadequate and [if] national authorities are manifestly failing to protect their populations from genocide, war crimes, ethnic cleansing and crimes against humanity.

The paragraphs identify what have been called three "pillars."[5] The first is the responsibility of each state to protect its
own population. The second is the responsibility of the international community to assist states. The third, the most striking, is the residual responsibility of the Security Council to
take timely and decisive action if a state fails to protect its own
population from war crimes, crimes against humanity, ethnic
cleansing, or genocide.

These paragraphs appear revolutionary. They have created
much controversy. Indeed, the Pillar Three responsibility of the
doctrine of RtoP overturns established international law that
was designed to maintain national jurisdiction free from external intervention.

INTERNATIONAL LAW AND RTOP

Pillars One and Two are legally uncontroversial. The International Covenants on Human Rights, the Genocide Convention
(1948), and common Article 3 of the Geneva Conventions
make it clear that states are prohibited from inflicting those
crimes on their populations. Other states and international organizations have the right to assist countries at the request of
the countries assisted in any internationally legal activity.

But Pillar Three, enforcement by the Security Council, is

---

5. UN Secretary-General, *Implementing the Responsibility to Protect,* UN
Doc. A/63/677 (January 12, 2009). RtoP Special Adviser Edward Luck, who
did much during his mandate to refine the RtoP doctrine, wrote this report.

legally ambiguous. The Charter remains highly protective of the domestic jurisdiction of states. As discussed in Chapter 1, UN Charter Article 2(7) specifies that "nothing contained in the present Charter shall authorize the United Nations to intervene in matters which are essentially within the domestic jurisdiction of any state." The exception is "enforcement measures under Chapter VII," which in turn are formally limited in Article 39 to measures the Security Council finds appropriate "in order to maintain or restore international peace and security." Domestic abuses generally do not—in black-letter Charter law—qualify as "international" threats. The *Outcome Document* articulating RtoP is a General Assembly resolution and as such it is a recommendation, not a binding international obligation on the Security Council.[6] And while the Security Council established tribunals for the Former Yugoslavia and Rwanda in order to punish genocide and war crimes authorized by reference to international peace and security, the Security Council is neither a global legislature nor a global court. It does not set general legal precedents. Instead, it addresses specific cases according to its discretion.

It is thus not surprising that UN General Assembly President Miguel d'Escoto-Brockmann began his *Concept Note on Responsibility to Protect*, written to introduce the General Assembly reconsideration of RtoP in the summer of 2009, with the observation that "none of the documents [including the *Outcome Document* and Security Council Resolution 1674, recognizing RtoP] can be considered as a binding source of international law in terms of Article 38 of the Statute of the Inter-

---

6. Charter of the United Nations (San Francisco, 1945), 1 U.N.T.S. XVI, Art. 10.

national Court of Justice which lists the classic sources of international law."[7]

RtoP is not a treaty, Article 38's primary source of law. Yet it might be argued that RtoP is an emerging customary international law, another source of law in Article 38. Unlike treaty law, customary law is established by a pattern of general state practice when practice is motivated by a sense of its legal obligation (*opinio juris*). But a General Assembly resolution does not per se qualify as *opinio juris* (voting can be purely political), and state or Security Council practice, though significant, is not yet extensive. (But, as I will discuss later, RtoP could indeed evolve into customary law, if Security Council practice confirms and states express a continuing "responsibility" to act).[8]

But the picture was not as straightforward as the General Assembly president suggested. The Genocide Convention outlaws genocide, even if inflicted solely domestically, and is a treaty so widely endorsed that it is regarded as customary international law and, as a *jus cogens* norm, binding on parties and nonparties alike. It requires states to "prevent and punish" genocide (Article 1). It leaves interpretation of genocide to the International Court of Justice (Article 9) and invites states to

7. Article 38 cites treaties, custom, and as lesser sources general principles of law, previous court decisions, and the opinions of scholars as the sources of international law. Miguel D'Escoto-Brockmann, *Concept Note on Responsibility to Protect Populations from Genocide, War Crimes, Ethnic Cleansing, and Crimes Against Humanity* (New York: Office of the President of the UN General Assembly, 2009).

8. Lori Damrosch et al., *International Law: Cases and Materials* (St. Paul, MN: West Group, 2001), 451–466. For R2P's grounding in human rights discourse, see Dorota Gierycz, *Responsibility to Protect: A Legal and Human Rights Based Perspective* (Oslo: NUPI, 2008).

enforce protection through the United Nations (Article 8).[9] Thus, for genocide, RtoP was well-established internationally enforceable law, even if the specific role proposed for the Security Council seemed to go beyond Article 39 of the Charter. Equally powerful obligations against intervention and in favor of stopping genocide thus clashed.

Most important, the Security Council has claimed a very wide discretion in practice. It is a legal body, authorized by the UN Charter to make binding resolutions (Articles 25 and 48) on matters of "international peace and security" (Chapter VII). But it also is a political body, authorized to decide based on its own judgment of what constitutes "threats to the peace, breaches of the peace and acts of aggression" (Article 39). The Security Council has a long record of wide discretion, acting on the basis of Chapter VII against perceived "threats to the peace" that did not constitute international attacks. For instance, the Council imposed obligatory sanctions on Rhodesia (1966) and South Africa (1977), citing with regard to the obligatory arms embargo imposed on South Africa—in effect an arms blockade—that country's "massive violence" against its own population, its "military build-up," and its past record of "persistent acts of aggression" against its neighboring states.[10] Drawing up a list just three years into the expansion of Council activity that characterized the post–Cold War period, Lori Damrosch has identified a wide range of other triggers for successful Chapter VII determinations of threats against the peace, including genocide, ethnic cleansing, and war crimes (Former Republic of Yugoslavia, Iraq, and Liberia); interference with the delivery of humanitarian supplies (Former Republic of Yu-

---

9. UN GA Resolution 260 (III) A, December 9, 1948.
10. SC Resolution 418, UN Doc. S/RES/418 (November 4, 1977).

goslavia, Iraq, and Somalia); violations of cease-fires (Former Republic of Yugoslavia, Liberia, and Cambodia); collapse of civil order (Liberia and Somalia); and coups against democratic governments (Haiti).[11]

The Council's judgment thus has had wide scope, constrained arguably only by the law of the Charter and *jus cogens* norms, such as those against genocide. Many states, especially in the South, as I will discuss below, have come to view the Security Council as acting far beyond the parameters of "international peace and security" as specified in Article 39 of the UN Charter. But most legal scholars would share Yoram Dinstein's interpretation of the International Court of Justice's ruling in the Lockerbie case: the Security Council has wide discretion, but this jurisdiction may not be infinite.[12] It could not legally and manifestly violate the Charter or authorize genocide. Whether the Security Council should act to prevent or stop domestic atrocity crimes, like those prohibited by RtoP, and thus operate beyond a narrow reading of the Charter's authorization in Article 39 to maintain "international" peace was the disputed question raised by Nicaraguan diplomat and UN General Assembly President d'Escoto-Brockmann and a few states allied with him at the 2009 special session of the General Assembly. (This is an issue to which I return at the end of the chapter).

Other tensions in international law revolve around the role of the Security Council as enforcer, the International Criminal Court (ICC), and regional law. Domestic war crimes (now including ethnic cleansing) and crimes against humanity in non-

11. Lori Fisler Damrosch, ed., *Enforcing Restraint: Collective Intervention in Internal Conflicts* (New York: Council on Foreign Relations Press, 1993), 10–14.

12. Yoram Dinstein, *War, Aggression, and Self-Defence*, 4th ed. (Cambridge: Cambridge University Press, 2005), 324.

international armed conflicts are parts of international law outlawed by custom and treaties, including the Rome Statute
defining the jurisdiction of the ICC.[13] But they are not clearly
within the jurisdiction of the Security Council for its own coercive enforcement, which is limited in Article 39 to "international peace and security." The ICC has residual jurisdiction for
certain types of grave crimes committed by individuals when
states party to the court do not prosecute those crimes domestically. But major powers, including the US, China, India, and
Russia, are not parties to the ICC.

Regional law and international law are converging but clash-
ing. For example, the African Union Constitutive Act in Article 4(j), prefiguring RtoP norms and legalizing them by treaty,
recognizes the "right" of the African Union to "intervene in
a Member State pursuant to a decision by the Assembly, in
grave circumstances, namely war crimes, genocide and crimes
against humanity." But the UN Security Council is not mentioned as the requisite authorizing source of such interventions,
despite its Charter monopoly on nondefensive uses of force.[14]
In practice, the AU and subregional organizations in Africa
have often intervened without prior Security Council authorization, seeking approval only after the fact.

Thus international law is contested. The strict legality of

13. Damrosch et al., *International Law*, 990–1004.
14. The Lomé Protocol of ECOWAS makes similar commitments. See
Jean Allain, "The True Challenge to the United Nations System of the Use
of Force: The Failures of Kosovo and Iraq and the Emergence of the African
Union," *Max Planck Yearbook of United Nations Law* 8 (2004), 237, 265–266,
284, 289; and Eliav Lieblich, *International Law and Civil Wars: Intervention
and Consent* (London: Routledge Press, 2013). UN Charter Article 52 permits
regional arrangements, and Article 51 allows collective self-defense, but regional arrangements are not authorized to engage in "enforcement operations"
without the authorization of the Security Council (Article 53).

RtoP as a new basis for Security Council action supplementing global "international" peace and security thus has not yet been established formally. The Security Council may have the legal authority and states can exercise their obligation to prevent and punish genocide through the UN.[15] But the Security Council so far has neither the authority nor the legal obligation to prevent or stop the four RtoP crimes unless it determines that international peace and security are threatened. Given the supremacy of the Charter over all treaties (Article 103), a Charter revision would be needed to formally incorporate RtoP as cause for international enforcement. Short of that, RtoP will remain legally contested.

THE ORIGINS AND EVOLUTION OF THE RTOP DOCTRINE

Humanitarian intervention is also contested in international ethics: it pits the protection of global humanitarian rights against national self-determination and sovereignty. Its recent evolution as the international legitimacy norm of RtoP both reflects those tensions and helps to reconcile them. RtoP builds on, but narrows, humanitarian doctrine in ways that expand international legitimacy and address many, but not all, skeptics of humanitarian intervention.

The Kosovo crisis was a watershed event in the reformulation of the doctrine of intervention. When the UN did not protect the Kosovars, NATO did. US President Bill Clinton, echoing earlier promises by British Prime Minister Tony Blair, announced

15. Common Article 1 of the Geneva Convention imposes obligations, but they are less distinct. It requires that all states "undertake to respect and ensure respect for the present Convention"; Laurence de Chazournes and Luigi Condarelli, "Common Article 1 of the Geneva Conventions," *International Review of the Red Cross* 857 (2000), 67–87.

a "Clinton Doctrine" to the assembled NATO peacekeeping (KFOR) troops on June 22, 1999, following their successful, though belated, occupation of Kosovo:

> Never forget if we can do this here, and if we can then say to the people of the world, whether you live in Africa, or Central Europe, or any other place, if somebody comes after innocent civilians and tries to kill them en masse because of their race, their ethnic background, or their religion, and it's within our power to stop it, we will stop it.[16]

UN Secretary-General Kofi Annan three months later also endorsed the principle of humanitarian intervention, but highlighted a problem: the requirements of international law—consent by a state, individual or collective self-defense, or Security Council authorization—were missing in the Kosovo campaign. The imperative of "halting gross and systematic violations of human rights" had clashed with "dangerous precedents for future interventions without a clear criterion to decide who might invoke these precedents, and in what circumstances."[17] Both the Blair-Clinton doctrine and the Annan statement alarmed developing states of the "South," which feared that humanitarian concern might be used as a pretext for imperial intervention.[18] The G77 (132 states of the South)

16. William J. Clinton, "Remarks by the President to the KFOR Troops," Skopje (Washington, DC: Office of the White House Press Secretary, 1999).

17. Kofi Annan, "Reflections on Intervention," Ditchley Park, UK, June 26, 1998, in Kofi Annan, *The Question of Intervention: Statements by the Secretary-General* (New York: United Nations Department of Public Information, 1999), 4.

18. For Kosovo and the concept of RtoP generally see Gareth Evans, *The Responsibility to Protect* (Washington, DC: Brookings, 2008), and Alex Bellamy, "Kosovo and the Advent of Sovereignty as Responsibility," *Journal of Intervention and Statebuilding* 3 (2009), 163–184. For a valuable survey of the

condemned "the so-called right of humanitarian intervention" in Paragraph 69 of their Ministerial Declaration of September 24, 1999, three months after the NATO intervention.[19] The Non-Aligned Movement (114 countries of the South) was deeply divided, with Islamic countries overwhelmingly supportive of the NATO intervention, and non-Islamic ones (led by Cuba, Belarus, and India) opposed.[20]

The Kosovo Commission was then asked to write an objective, international, and nongovernmental report to assess the intervention. It famously concluded that the intervention was "illegal but legitimate." It was not an act of self-defense and it lacked the needed Security Council approval under Article 39, but it was a legitimate humanitarian rescue in the eyes of the commission of notables. In making the judgment the committee defined what it saw as relevant "threshold principles" for a genuine "humanitarian intervention":

> The first is severe violations of international human rights or humanitarian law on a sustained basis. The second is the subjection of a civilian society to great suffering and risk due to the "failure" of their state, which entails the breakdown of governance at the level of the territorial sovereign state.[21]

---

roots of the concept of limited sovereignty, see Anne Orford, *International Authority and the Responsibility to Protect* (London: Cambridge University Press, 2011).

19. See discussion in Ian Brownlie, *Principles of Public International Law*, 6th ed. (Oxford: Oxford University Press, 2003), 712.

20. Thalif Deen, "Third World Nations Split over Kosovo," Third World Network, http://www.twnside.org.sg/title/kosovo-cn.htm.

21. Independent International Commission on Kosovo, *The Kosovo Report: Conflict, International Response, Lessons Learned* (New York: Oxford University Press, 2000).

The principles still were noticeably wide ("international human rights or humanitarian law"), and they allowed for action if the Security Council would not act, albeit as a last resort. The Commission did not assuage the concerns of the South.

In an effort to include more viewpoints from the global South (and more representation from former government officials), Canada supported a new and more ambitious commission, one cochaired by Mohammed Sahnoun and Gareth Evans. The International Commission on Intervention and State Sovereignty (ICISS) reframed the debate as "Responsibility to Protect" rather than a "right" to intervene and, by dint of numerous meetings at the regional level around the world, built a multilateral coalition. Building on former Sudanese Foreign Minister Francis Deng's articulation of a "responsibility to protect" for internally displaced persons, ICISS identified a dual responsibility: that of governments to protect their own inhabitants and then, should governments fail to do so, a residual international responsibility.[22] International responsibility had three parts: to prevent, to react, and to rebuild.

Compared with the Kosovo Report, the ICISS report narrowed the triggers for action to the threat of or presence of "large scale loss of life" whether by action or inaction of states and "large scale ethnic cleansing." Building on classic just war doctrine underlying humanitarian intervention, the Commission specified "right intention," "just cause," "proportionality," and "right authority" as further qualifiers on when international force could be used if states failed to meet their responsibility to protect their own populations. "Right authority," furthermore, was specified ideally as the UN Security Council. "No

22. Francis M. Deng et al., *Sovereignty as Responsibility* (Washington, DC: Brookings, 1996).

better or more appropriate" authority could be found, but, at the same time, it was not the last word. In "shocking situations . . . concerned states . . . may not rule out other measures" if the Security Council does not act. And "the Security Council should take note." The ICISS had narrowed the triggers and the authority, but in 2001 much of the global South was still alarmed. Secretary-General Annan personally welcomed the report, but no UN venue would host its formal New York presentation in 2001.[23] (The Commission unveiled its report in a hotel across the street from the UN.)

This record reveals the significance of the 2005 *Summit Outcome Document* paragraphs (quoted in the introduction to this chapter) that won the unanimous assent of the 192 member states. Paragraphs 138–139 reflected four additional years of assiduous lobbying and doctrinal adjustment, overcoming the significant distrust of the international community to any intervention following the 2003 invasion of Iraq.

RtoP is both a license and leash. The two paragraphs broadened the norm of legitimate intervention beyond the limited authority outlined in customary international law and the UN Charter's authorization to avert "threats to international peace and security." They greatly narrowed the norms emerging in UN Security Council practice of the 1990s. They also narrowed the triggers for RtoP from "international human rights" or "large scale killings" (the triggers specified by the Kosovo and ICISS commissions) to four specific elements: "genocide, war crimes, ethnic cleansing and crimes against humanity." To emphasize the point, these four specific elements are repeated

23. At Secretary-General Kofi Annan's request, I approached the president of the General Assembly to see whether a room could be found. His then-chief of staff, Ban Ki-moon, after checking with the group heads, determined that a UN venue could not be allocated for something so controversial.

five times in the original two paragraphs. In addition, the assembled states removed the ambiguity in authorization found in the earlier reports and clearly restricted "right authority" to use coercive means to the Security Council when it contemplates "collective action, in a timely and decisive manner, through the Security Council, in accordance with the Charter, including Chapter VII, on a case-by-case basis" (Paragraph 139). The UN reaffirms the importance of state responsibility and the triad of prevention, reaction, and rebuilding, and that RtoP is a "responsibility"—though only undertaken on a "case by case," hence discretionary, basis.

The Practice of RtoP

The practice of RtoP has been crucial in assuring the skeptics who fear neoimperialism and in winning support for working through the UN system from those who seek stronger protections for human rights. In all these cases, although coercion was in the background, preventing armed intervention has been the key to RtoP success.

The first test for the UN was, ironically, passed by inaction, when it did not intervene in Myanmar to rescue the population from the effects of Cyclone Nargis in May 2008. After the hurricane struck and when news of the government's inability or unwillingness to deal with the disaster circulated, French Foreign Minister Bernard Kouchner and former Australian Foreign Minister Gareth Evans called for action. Evans commented: "When a government default is as grave as the course on which the Burmese generals now seem to be set, there is at least a prima facie case to answer for their intransigence being a crime against humanity—of a kind which would attract the responsibility to protect principle."[24] Evans himself soon changed his mind, and cooler heads in the UN Security Council and the Secretariat prevailed. Widespread loss of life and government incapacity to rescue—both of which were manifest and which were triggers for ICISS R2P—were not the triggers for United Nations RtoP. And to treat them as such would have undermined the thin support RtoP had achieved at the 2005 Summit. "Crimes against humanity," the closest potential trigger, includes murder, extermination, enslavement, and other crimes evidencing "widespread or systematic attacks on the civilian population . . . part of government policy . . . a consistent plan."[25] The loss of life appeared to be widespread, but there was no evidence of an intentional "policy" designed to deprive parts of the population of the means of life. Eventually regional diplomacy secured access—too late for many victims, but "late enough" to permit slow-moving regional diplomacy to work, and thus to preserve the thin political coalition behind RtoP.

Kenya in 2008 and Guinea in 2009 were crises shaped by RtoP—but implicitly, not explicitly. This indeed might be the doctrine's strongest claim: it provides an option whose mere existence encourages consensual resolutions of crises.

In Kenya, Kofi Annan, former UN secretary-general; Benjamin Mkapa, former Tanzanian president; and Graça Machel, a Mozambican liberationist and wife of former South African president Nelson Mandela, served as a mediation team. Their task was to halt ethnic killing sparked by the widely contested

24. Gareth Evans, "Facing Up to Our Responsibilities," *Guardian*, May 12, 2008, http://www.theguardian.com/commentisfree/2008/may/12/facinguptoour responsbilities.

25. Rome Statute of the International Criminal Court, July 17, 1998, 2187 U.N.T.S. 90, Art. 7.

reelection of President Mwai Kibaki, in which opposition leader Raila Odinga claimed to have been robbed of victory. Approximately 800 people were killed and some 260,000 others were displaced across the country, in a wave of deadly rioting and ethnic killings. Kouchner again invoked the specific language of RtoP.[26] Annan, however, while later acknowledging that he "saw the crisis in the RtoP prism with the Kenyan government unable to contain the situation or protect the people," did not use that language directly with the Kenyan government.[27] He did not need to. Governments in Africa, Europe, and the US were sending the same message of concern, backed with cuts, or threatened cuts, in government foreign aid (humanitarian aid continued). Moreover, the leadership in Kenya knew that RtoP was now part of the Security Council arsenal, available if their intransigence provoked sufficient international will to invoke it.[28]

26. Bernard Kouchner, Statement by Bernard Kouchner on the Situation in Kenya, January 31, 2008, http://www.ambafrance-ke.org/Statement-by-Bernard -Kouchner-on.

27. For his later reflections, see Roger Cohen, "How Kofi Annan Rescued Kenya," *New York Review of Books*, August 13, 2008. For his reluctance to use the term with the government, I rely on my interview with Kofi Annan, April 14, 2010, in New York, in which he said there was "no direct reference to RtoP." But Annan did warn the government that the entire region was concerned and that a continuation of the crisis would disrupt the entire region.

28. Elizabeth Lindenmayer and Josie L. Kaye, *A Choice for Peace? The Story of the Forty-One Days of Mediation in Kenya* (New York: International Peace Institute, 2009); Thomas Weiss, "Halting Atrocities in Kenya," in *Great Decisions* (New York: Foreign Policy Association, 2010). The EU and the US both announced that their aid to Kenya was "under review." See European Parliament resolution of January 17, 2008, on Kenya, http://www.europarl.europa.eu/ sides/getDoc.do?type=TA&reference=P6-TA-2008-0018&format=XML &language=EN; and "Kenya Violence Prompts US to Review Its Aid," *Telegraph*, January 31, 2008, http://www.telegraph.co.uk/news/worldnews/1577171/ Kenya-violence-prompts-US-to-review-its-aid.html.

The September 2009 crisis in Guinea involved coup leader Captain Dadis Camara's troops rioting against a peaceful demonstration. The international community mobilized again. Secretary-General Ban Ki-moon condemned the violence and set up a UN Commission of Inquiry. The commission report raised the possibility that "crimes against humanity" had been committed by Camara's troops. The US and the EU suspended economic assistance. Camara was attacked by one of his own officers (whom Camara may have planned to be the scapegoat for the earlier violence) and fled the country for medical assistance. An interim government initiated steps toward a democratic election with international support.[29]

LIBYA

The March 2011 UN-authorized and NATO-led intervention in Libya was the doctrine's first and most important test case. In classic United Nations Security Council language authorizing force, Resolution 1973 of March 17, 2011, authorized UN member states to "take all necessary measures . . . to protect civilians and civilian populated areas" in Libya, including by establishing a no-fly zone and enforcing an arms embargo against Colonel Muammar al-Qaddafi's regime.[30]

29. Jon L. Anderson, "Downfall: The End of a West African Dictatorship," *New Yorker,* April 12, 2010.

30. SC Res. 1973, UN Doc. S/Res/1973 (March 17, 2011) and SC Res. 1970, UN Doc. S/Res/1970 (February 26, 2011). In late March, I addressed the Libya issue in Michael W. Doyle, "The Folly of Protection: Is Intervention Against Qaddafi's Regime Legal and Legitimate?" *Foreign Affairs,* March 20, 2011, www .foreignaffairs.com/articles/67666/michael-w-doyle/the-folly-of-protection, accessed January 24, 2013. For a thorough analysis of the background to UN RtoP doctrine, see Catherine Powell, "Libya: A Multilateral Constitutional Moment?" *American Journal of International Law* 106 (2012), 298–316.

The resolution thus gave teeth to the much-heralded RtoP, as only the third time since the Security Council had invoked the doctrine, to enforce the protection of civilians. The first case was to authorize an arms embargo over the Sudan in 2005. The second case had occurred only weeks earlier, when Resolution 1970, the Security Council's first resolution, targeted Qaddafi's crackdown against Libya's rebellion by calling for financial sanctions, an arms embargo, and a referral to the ICC for criminal prosecution. Significantly, Resolution 1970 passed unanimously (that is, with the support of Russia, China, Brazil, and South Africa—all later skeptics about forcible intervention in Libya). Resolution 1973 marks the first Security Council approval of force in the name of RtoP (notably with abstentions from Russia, China, Germany, India, and South Africa). And this became controversial, putting RtoP itself in peril.

Even a few years later, it is still far too early for an accurate assessment (we still lack the archives and insiders' full accounts), but humanitarian rescue against war crimes and crimes against humanity seems to offer the best justification for the Libyan intervention. Qaddafi's regime had alienated a wide swath of Libyan society, provoking in the UN's later assessment "an almost intolerable amount of uncertainty, oppression, and serious abuse into the daily lives of citizens." This reflected years of "nontransparent allocation of resources . . . a sense of relative deprivation among Libyans," provoked by the looting of Libya's oil wealth in ways that sustained the army, the regime, and Qaddafi's personal and familial coterie while abandoning the rest of the population.[31]

31. UN, Consolidated Report of the Integrated Pre-Assessment Process for Libya Post-Conflict Planning, August 5 2011, leaked and available at http://

As the conflict escalated, the prosecutor of the International Criminal Court (to whom the case had been referred by the Security Council) found what he regarded as reasonable evidence of serious crimes. Qaddafi and his confederates were alleged to have committed deportations, rapes, forcible attacks on noncombatants, and the destruction of religious and other civilian buildings. Noting the efforts by Qaddafi's forces to cover up the crimes by hiding and destroying bodies, the prosecutor acknowledged the difficulty of accurate body counts, but suggested that the best evidence was that 500 to 700 had died in February 2011; the regime claimed "only 150 or 200 died . . . and half of them security forces."[32] In the month that followed, Qaddafi and his sons were reported to have made threats of merciless expulsion, "house to house" searches, and extermination against the rebels, their supporters, and perhaps the entire city of Benghazi.[33]

President Nicolas Sarkozy of France and Prime Minister David Cameron of the UK took the lead. Both were alarmed by the humanitarian crisis emerging as Libyans stood up against Qaddafi. Sarkozy may have been motivated in part by a wish to escape the scandal of his government's dealings with the corrupt Tunisian regime; Cameron, by a desire to be seen to be acting independently of the US in order to escape

---

www.innercitypress.com/unılibyaıvandewalle.pdf. This report and plan has been attributed to Ian Martin, a distinguished UN peacekeeper with extensive field experience in East Timor and Nepal.

32. Office of the Prosecutor, International Criminal Court, First Report of the Prosecutor of the International Criminal Court to the UN Security Council in Pursuant of UNSCR 1970 (2011), paras. 17–21.

33. For a valuable account, see Emily O'Brien and Andrew Sinclair, *The Libyan War: A Diplomatic History* (New York: Center on International Cooperation, 2011).

the shadow of Prime Minister Blair's dependence on President Bush.[34]

Other countries, including Russia and China, were deeply influenced by the demands for action from the developing world, and even more by the defection of Libya's ministers of the interior and of justice and especially of Libya's two leading diplomats at the UN, who denounced the regime's killing of innocent demonstrators and called for intervention. Especially influential at the Security Council itself was Libya's permanent representative. Like most diplomats, the members of the Council were skeptical of casualty reports and they knew of the rivalries between Qaddafi and members of the Arab League that lurked in the background of the League's denunciations of Qaddafi. But the Qaddafi family's own reported phrases—such as calls to deal with the "cockroaches" (astoundingly reminiscent of the genocide rhetoric from Rwanda in 1994)—and the pleas of the Libyan Deputy Ambassador Ibrahim Dabbashi and Ambassador Abdel Rahman Shalgam were decisive. The ambassador, well known in the UN and a Qaddafi appointee, made an unforgettable case against the growing depredations of the regime and the urgent necessity of stopping them.[35]

The US initially cautioned against action, as Secretary of Defense Robert Gates expressed the lack of US interest in Libya. France and the Arab League proposed a no-fly zone on March 15. But soon thereafter, Washington reversed itself and insisted on a full air campaign to protect Libyans threatened by Qaddafi's regime. On March 28, reacting to mounting casual-

34. Laïdi Zaki, *Limited Achievements: Obama's Foreign Policy* (New York: Palgrave Macmillan, 2012).

35. Interview with a permanent representative and SC member, October 31, 2013; interview with Ambassador Peter Wittig, Germany's permanent representative, November 11, 2013.

ties, President Obama summarized the case for armed action, in increasing order of importance:

1. The threat to regional stability in Egypt and Tunisia and the need to stand with the popular forces in the region.
2. Qaddafi's record of "extreme violence," launching jets and helicopters against civilians, cutting off water for tens of thousands in various towns including Misrata, shelling cities and towns, unleashing gunships on the people, and raiding homes and hospitals. (When his record of arbitrary arrests, torture and ordering of rapes was added in, all these led to the ICC arrest warrants.)
3. Most important was the threat of worse to come: the looming slaughter in Benghazi that could "not wait one more day."[36]

Following just war traditions, the intervention seemingly enjoyed just intentions, necessity (last resort, at least for Benghazi), and reasonable prospects of success. Qaddafi's air defenses were weak and the US and NATO could utilize Italy and sea-based naval airpower to interdict the Libyan air forces and dominate relevant airspace conveniently concentrated along Libya's coast.

Proportionality is more complex. The intervention in Libya joined legality (Security Council approval) to legitimacy (the cause of protecting civilians). But, as described above, it still strained against the letter-of-the-law role that the Charter as-

36. President Obama warned that Qaddafi bore down on the "700,000" people of Benghazi—helpfully noted to be the "size of Charlotte." The administration also reported that Qaddafi's subordinates had threatened "no mercy" and vowed to hunt the rebels down, apartment by apartment, like "rats"; US White House, *United States Activities in Libya*, 2011, pp. 2–5.

signs the Security Council and risked going beyond (as it did) the protection of civilians that RtoP envisages. It also remained ethically problematic unless it succeeded in resolving the crisis without further large loss of life and left behind a viable, legitimate, and rights-respecting Libyan polity.

All these issues provoked concerns and revealed a series of tensions and problems that will shape the Libyan intervention's legacies. The first problem is a lack of clarity about when to invoke Pillar Three of RtoP.

When does the gravity of the crimes rise to a level warranting intervention? How reliable is our information?[37]

The key to the indictment of Libya under RtoP in this case had to be threats, because much violence was averted. Postwar surveys by the Red Cross and other humanitarian agencies found a total of fewer than thirty-five hundred accountable deaths—in the "hundreds" in major cities, not thousands. Yet the National Transitional Council, the recognized interim governing body for Libya during and immediately after the conflict, claimed thirty thousand to fifty thousand.[38] Still, the Libyan conflict is closer in casualty level to Kosovo than to Bosnia or Croatia, not to speak of Rwanda. It was the *threat*

37. On these two points, making the positive case, with suggestions for reform of RtoP, see the valuable essays by Robert Pape, "When Duty Calls: A Pragmatic Standard for Humanitarian Intervention," *International Security* 37 (2012), 41–80, and Roland Paris, "The Responsibility to Protect and Libya," draft, 2012. For the negative view of the Libyan case, see Alan Kuperman, "A Model Humanitarian Intervention," *International Security* 38 (2013), 105–136, and Aidan Hehir, "The Permanence of Inconsistency," *International Security* 38 (2013), 137–159.

38. See Rod Nordland, "Libya Counts More Martyrs than Bodies," *New York Times*, September 16, 2011. Additional bodies may be found when searches deepen. This is not unusual in civil conflicts; combatants have more to do than count bodies.

of expulsions and massacres that seems to have justified the action, not the numbers already killed.[39] The case for action became persuasive when the Arab League, the Organization of Islamic Cooperation, and other regional organizations spoke out in favor of intervention, including directly to the Security Council, and individual Libyan diplomats and officials resigned in protest.

The second problem was equally grave: a lack of strategic doctrine on how to design protection, distinguishing strategic scenarios and fitting remedies to harm. The strategic scenario in March was a likely stalemate. Qaddafi probably would have been able to conquer the rebel capital Benghazi with his air force, artillery, and armor in the lead, but the commencement of allied intervention destroyed the air force and protected the civilian population from large-scale attacks. On the other hand, it was not clear that the rebels could conquer the country even if Qaddafi's air force was neutralized, unless international arms or forces on the ground aided them—aid not explicitly authorized by Resolution 1973, which only permitted the protection of civilians. President Obama hoped, as the UN Security Council strategy envisaged, that economic sanctions would undermine Qaddafi's regime, but Qaddafi had too much loose cash and gold for the sanctions to gain traction anytime soon.

This led to unpalatable alternatives: If Qaddafi stopped victimizing civilians and retained power while the rebels maintained their own territory, would partition have provided a workable solution? If Qaddafi and the rebels could not achieve political agreement, could the international community see it-

---

39. In the former Yugoslavia, 130,000–140,000 were killed before 1995, when protection was finally provided. The 10,000 margin of error fifteen years after the end of the conflict is not unusual.

self as legitimately, ethically holding the ring, watching the casualties mount, while the two sides battled it out with small arms? Or should the interveners have brushed aside the restrictions of the Security Council resolution and aided the rebels and toppled Qaddafi?

Obviously, the third option was chosen. Qatar provided funds, possibly arms; the UK and perhaps France added "trainers" on the ground for the rebels; and others, including possibly some Americans, served as bombing spotters and air coordinators. The air campaign went after targets—headquarters, communications, troop and arms depots—remote from staging areas for the direct infliction of harm on civilians.

This was all arguably necessary to end the crisis. And some of it was authorized. Resolution 1973 authorized "all necessary means" to protect not just civilians but "civilian populated areas" —including against "threats." It also, in the much-disputed Paragraph 4, authorized states to arm the rebels "not withstanding Paragraph 9 [of Resolution 1970]," which had imposed an arms embargo.[40] Ambassador Susan Rice is said to have warned the other members of the Security Council that wide, not narrow, interdiction of Libyan military assets would be taken.[41]

But the tactical use of NATO airpower to support the rebel offensive against Tripoli, the bombing of Libyan TV, and the attempted assassination by drone of Qaddafi himself arguably strained against the protecting civilian logic of RtoP.[42] It also

40. Paul Williams and Colleen Popken, "Security Council Resolution 1973 on Libya: A Moment of Legal and Moral Clarity," *Case Western Reserve Journal of International Law* 44 (2011), 225–251.

41. A senior adviser at USUN, interview.

42. Fran Townsend, "NATO Official: Gadhafi a Legitimate Target," CNN, June 9, 2011; "Libyan Rebels Take Fight to Tripoli," Associated Press, August

undermined the "Immaculate Intervention" contemplated by Russia, China, and other supporters of RtoP and the negotiated transition envisaged by Resolution 1970 and still hoped for by those who chose not to veto Resolution 1973. To the critics of the intervention, the way force was used for regime change discredited the legal authorization of RtoP, which was limited to protecting civilians.

The distinction between protection of citizens and "regime change," however, confuses at least five different strategic scenarios.

1. An oppressive but strong regime that is violating RtoP and a weak and or divided opposition. This calls for pressure and persuasion in the direction of reform, for example, by economic sanctions. This was the anticipated scenario shaping Resolution 1970 in February 2011.

2. An oppressive, strong, and violent regime that is victimizing its populations but that is also vulnerable to external military pressure for the purpose of protecting civilians, such as Libya was judged to be in March 2011, with Resolution 1973, by Russia, China, Germany, and South Africa.

3. A country that has split into a civil war among powerful belligerents, each of which enjoys popular support and each of which is violating RtoP. This scenario calls for sanctions or force and diplomacy in order to mediate a comprehensive peace settlement, followed perhaps by UN peacebuilding. Something like this occurred in El Salvador in the 1980s and 1990s, and in Cambodia and Mozambique in the 1990s.

20, 2011; "NATO Strikes Libyan Satellite TV Facility," NATO LiveNews, July 30, 2011.

4. A discredited regime violating RtoP that has lost the overwhelming proportion of bureaucratic and popular support, and faces a nearly unified opposition. In these circumstances, the opposition should be recognized and assisted in its efforts to overthrow the preexisting regime. This was the US, British, and French view of Libya in March 2011.

5. A regime that has lost all support and is committing RtoP violations, but the opposition to which is also divided and cannot govern. Then what is needed is a multilateral enforcement operation followed by a temporary UN peacebuilding trusteeship, as occurred in Kosovo in 1999.

Libya was scenario number 4. But members of the Security Council could agree only to plan for scenario 1 and then 2, and were not prepared to change when events on the ground changed, whence the subsequent strife and recrimination.

A third problem was how to manage the intervention. How can one preserve multilateral principles of impartial administration when enforcement must be delegated to the militarily competent—usually to NATO?

Security Council members complained of a "blank check" to NATO. NATO members wondered whether the intervention could be seen as a low-cost model for future protection. But it was not quite so promising. The US, while officially, in President Obama's widely noted phrase, "leading from behind," had to take the early lead in destroying Qaddafi's air force and air defenses, then continue to carry the load in refueling, logistics, air rescue, and drone attacks. France, the UK, Denmark, and Norway carried the bulk of the air combat burden. (The absence of Germany and Turkey was keenly felt.) In the process,

NATO ran out of ammunition and exhausted its contingency budgets. For NATO, it became a "success" that could not be readily repeated.[43] For the UN, procedures need to be established that allow the Security Council to remain in political control while delegating military implementation to those who can implement—not an easy balance. Brazil is exploring the development of new standards of "responsibility *while* protecting," but little progress is evident.[44]

The fourth problem was how to assist former victims to become an effective and humane government, and thereby avoid another cycle of repression and war. This was the endgame in Libya itself.

Could the transitional authorities establish a legitimate and rights-respecting regime?

It would be a sad outcome if the new regime simply replicated Qaddafi's style of oppression. Ian Martin, the newly appointed special representative for Libya, accurately diagnosed the disintegration of the Libyan state and society and the barely coordinated chaos that characterized cooperation among rebel militias.[45] Drawing on lessons from UN peacebuilding elsewhere, he proposed an extensive peacebuilding program to help reconstruct the government. He sensibly included the need for monitoring (200 unarmed military observers and 190 police

43. See Helene Cooper and Steven L. Myers, "U.S. Tactics in Libya May Be a Model for Other Efforts," *New York Times,* August 28, 2011; and Steven Erlanger, "What Libya's Lessons Mean for NATO," *New York Times,* September 3, 2011.

44. "Responsibility While Protecting: Elements for a Development and Promotion of a Concept," A/66/551 S/2011/701, November 11, 2011.

45. UN, *Consolidated Report of the Integrated Pre-Assessment Process for Libya Post-Conflict Planning,* August 5, 2011. Leaked and available at http://www.innercitypress.com/un1libya1vandewalle.pdf, 23–28.

advisers), a major role in assisting elections, and an unspecified continuing role for NATO. When the plan was leaked in 2011, the National Transitional Council rejected it as much too intrusive. This was by past standards a light "footprint," but even it was too much for the loose coalition that constituted the National Transitional Council (NTC). Deferential, as it so often is, the Security Council backed down and the NTC dictated the terms of initial assistance.[46]

By late 2012, the record was mixed. Local authorities were victimizing African and Berber minorities in the far south and west of Libya, and the militias in control of Benghazi were reluctant to cede power. Tripoli appeared to function best, but it too was subject to militias holding neighborhoods hostage. All awaited with hope the emergence of an alternative to militia rule. The National Transitional Council rejected the heavy UN footprint (on the East Timor model) that Martin planned, and now Libya's future is nearly completely in its own hands.[47]

An assessment of the Libyan intervention highlights wider implications. On the one hand, RtoP and the Libya precedent have "solved" the genocide problem. This does not mean that future genocides have been prevented, but that new standards

46. Martin provided upbeat reports to the Security Council in late 2011 and 2012 that may have delayed a realization of how anarchic Libya had in fact become. In any case, the Security Council seemed to chase events there, rather than help shape them.

47. Nicolas Pelham, "Is Libya Cracking Up?" *New York Review of Books,* June 21, 2012, pp. 66–69. Brian McQuinn, in "Assessing (In)security After the Arab Spring: The Case of Libya," *PS: Political Science and Politics* 46 (2013), 709–715, notes the absence of state authority, the lack of a monopoly of legitimate violence. Militias ruled, but violence was muted, unlike both the postwar aftermaths in Iraq and Afghanistan. The revolution was widely seen as legitimate, and the country was not riven by deep political fractures among large ethnic groups or religions. The very plurality of local control seemed to reduce the scale, if not the frequency, of violence.

preclude the trap of a genocide threshold for protection. The Darfuri suffered while the International Commission of Inquiry on Darfur to the UN researched. Months of interviewing produced an accurate conclusion that Darfur did not then constitute "genocide." Darfur slaughters lacked the intention to kill on the basis of race or ethnicity or religion—the standards required by the Genocide Convention—and then nothing happened, despite a documented record of crimes against humanity and war crimes.

With RtoP, we now have a new more credible standard for international protection. It is more restrictive than Security Council practice of intervention in the 1990s, when anything that could muster the right votes passed, and more restrictive than the "human rights" abuses set by the Kosovo Commission or the indefinite "large scale deaths" of the ICISS. But it is less restrictive than Chapter VII of the Charter ("international" threats) or the genocide standard of the Genocide Convention. RtoP includes genocide, ethnic cleansing, crimes against humanity, and war crimes. But procedurally—and unlike the doctrines enunciated by the Kosovo Commission and ICISS—RtoP avoids unilateral exploitation by the requirement of Security Council multilateral authorization. This is a reasonable combination of substantive license and procedural leash.

On the other hand, Libya has wounded RtoP. To gain approval for the intervention in Libya, Western nations secured a resolution that passed with ten votes in favor, and no vetoes. But the legitimacy, in the sense of wide support, was not fulsome. There were abstentions from the not insignificant countries of Brazil, China, Germany, India, and Russia. Brazil, Germany, and India are seeking permanent membership on the Security Council, as is South Africa and, though it voted for Resolution 1973 while on the Council, it opposed what it saw as regime change in the intervention. The Arab League supported the intervention, but only the United Arab Emirates and Qatar provided any assistance. The African Union condemned Qaddafi's violence, but it also condemned the air strikes.

Despite their support for action against Qaddafi (and Assad in Syria today, for that matter) defenders of national sovereignty in the Arab world were particularly alarmed. They rightly note that none of the veto-wielding permanent five—US, UK, France, China, and Russia—or their close allies will ever be subject to RtoP sanctions. So whatever happens in Palestine, that conflict, unlike other conflicts in the Middle East, Africa, or Asia, is shielded from RtoP sanctions. And the fact that crises in Tibet and Chechnya are similarly immune from protection assuages none of these critics. The only response is to acknowledge that the world remains unequal, and RtoP cannot itself correct that. It does restrict unilateral imperialism, because all Security Council interventions must have the support of diverse permanent members and at least four votes from the nonpermanent members. The real question is whether one wants to have a norm that helps protect some (as in Benghazi) even if it cannot protect all.

Despite the successes of the Libyan intervention, strategic confusion prevailed. The dissenters on the Security Council felt that they had been hoodwinked and sold a protection intervention that turned into a regime change intervention. The costs of this may now be visible in Syria, where, burned once, neither Russia nor China is prepared to abstain on resolutions presented by the US and the Europeans to sanction the Assad regime.[48]

48. RtoP at IPI June 28, 2011. Ambassador Puri (India): "Libya will give RtoP a bad name; resistance to sanctions in Syria is a product of Libya experience, in which NATO has run away with RtoP and is imposing regime change."

Both, in fact, vetoed resolutions on Syria, carefully negotiated in advance to limit their impacts.[49]

We need to find remedies for the confusions soon. Failing to learn these lessons makes innocent Syrians today and others in the future bear the costs of the learning exercise that the international community should have already begun in order to make RtoP genuinely responsive and responsible.

IMPLICATIONS FOR LAW AND ETHICS

The UN Charter is a "living constitution" and the UN members are nothing if not fluid in their commitments. So RtoP continues to evolve. The Security Council reaffirmed RtoP in Resolution 1674 and operationally made the protection of civilians in ongoing peace operations an important commitment.[50] In 2009, the secretary-general presented a valuable report out-

49. The Arab League imposed sanctions on Syria, as did the Europeans and the US. But the Annan mediation authorized by the Security Council lacked in 2012 a threat of more severe UN authorized measures should Assad fail to comply. Lakhdar Brahimi, who succeeded Annan in 2012, similarly was left with no UN-authorized "sticks." Syria is a much more problematic intervention in any case. But it is unfortunate that the multilateral authority and legitimacy of RtoP no longer seem available. See Neil MacFarquhar, "With Rare Double UN Veto on Syria, Russia and China Try to Shield Friend," *New York Times,* October 5, 2011, http://www.nytimes.com/2011/10/06/world/middle east/with-united-nations-veto-russia-and-china-help-syria.html?pagewanted =all&_r=0. Following the use of chemical weapons by Assad's regime in August 2013, the US and Russia agreed on a framework for monitoring the chemical disarmament of Syria in September 2013. But as of May 2014, no measures had been authorized for the protection of Syrian civilians, whose death toll exceeded 100,000.

50. S.C. Res. 1674, UN Doc. S/Res/1674 (April 28, 2006). Protecting civilians during an established and authorized peacekeeping operation is not, however, the same as legislating intervention whenever a government harms or threatens to harm its own nationals.

lining what the UN could and should do to help prevent and rebuild with the consent of the affected state.[51] It identified three pillars. The first reaffirms national responsibility; the second specifies measures of assistance the international community could and should offer to assist states in meeting their national responsibilities; and the third covers international responsibility, including the variety of measures the UN could and should take to ensure protection. By emphasizing prevention and rebuilding, the report further distanced RtoP from a focus on coercive intervention.

In the summer of 2009, as noted above, the General Assembly considered the secretary-general's report and RtoP more generally at a special meeting organized by General Assembly president and strong RtoP critic Miguel d'Escoto-Brockmann, a former Sandinista commandante and Nicaraguan foreign minister. Highlighted by an invitation to Professor Noam Chomsky to address the General Assembly, the session was designed by d'Escoto-Brockmann to roast the doctrine.

Instead, a considerable majority of states—both developing and developed—reaffirmed their commitment. But many also warned of abuses that might follow from it. On behalf of the 118 member states of the Non-Aligned Movement, Ambassador Maged Abdelaziz of Egypt, while condemning the four crimes covered by RtoP, expressed concern that the doctrine could be abused by opening up the possibility of unilateral intervention or extending its triggers beyond the four elements, attempting thus to legitimize "intervention in the internal affairs of states."[52]

51. UN Secretary-General, *Implementing the Responsibility to Protect*, UN Doc. A/63/677 (January 12, 2009).

52. A. Maged Abdelaziz, Statement by the Permanent Representative of Egypt on Behalf of the Non-Aligned Movement (New York: Permanent Mission of the Arab Republic of Egypt, 2009).

Only a handful of states, including Venezuela, Cuba, North Korea, and a few others, acknowledged sufficient "buyer's remorse" and pushed to reject outright the commitment made in 2005. Most southern states shared the concerns the Non-Aligned Movement expressed, and with China, for example, averred: "The concept of 'RtoP' applies only to the four international crimes of 'genocide, war crimes, ethnic cleansing, and crimes against humanity.' No state should expand on the concept or make arbitrary interpretations."[53] Not authorizing an intervention in Myanmar implicitly excluded health, climate, and natural disasters as appropriate triggers for RtoP.[54] Thus, when it came to a consensus endorsement of the secretary-general's report, the best that could be achieved was a tepid "takes note" rather than the more full-throated "approves" or "endorses" that traditionally signal approval in UN jargon.[55]

From the standpoint of international law, the commitment to RtoP was not legislative—not equivalent to either a Charter amendment of Chapter VII or an international treaty. But it was part of a twofold process bending the meaning of "international threats to the peace" as defined by the Council under Chapter VII.

First, while far from settled, RtoP is beginning to build the record of general practice supplementing the sense of obligation

53. Z. Liu, Statement of Ambassador Liu Zhenmin at the Plenary Session of GA Debate on Responsibility to Protect (New York: Permanent Mission of China, 2009).

54. Kyaw Zwar Minn U, Statement of the Deputy Permanent Representative of the Union of Myanmar to the United Nations on Agenda Item 44 and 107 (New York: Permanent Mission of Myanmar, 2009).

55. Dept. of Public Information, "Delegates Weigh Legal Merits of RtoP Concept," GA/10850, July 28, 2009, un.org/News/Press/docs/2009/ga10850 .doc.htm.

that builds customary international law. The RtoP norm does not quite qualify as *opinio juris vel necessitatis*—acting on the basis of legal obligation—that is required for the formation of customary international law, but the repeated use of "responsibility" is approaching the normative commitment that evidences obligation.[56] And the continued use of RtoP language in Security Council and Human Rights Council resolutions and presidential statements, even after Libya, suggests that the norm is surviving.[57]

Second, it is important to recognize that the vast majority of states in 2009 were explicitly and implicitly endorsing the RtoP elements of genocide, war crimes, crimes against humanity, and ethnic cleansing as legitimate causes for the Security Council (when necessary) to authorize coercive force.

They were attempting to transcend the national, unilateral standards explored by Mill and other moral philosophers. The United Nations has set standards by both broadening the principles and narrowing practice. Since General Assembly resolutions are not binding measures that could amend the UN Charter, states in effect were trying to redefine and broaden the standard that does authorize force, Chapter VII's "international peace and security." At the same time, these states were also denying the Security Council the discretion it had exercised so often in the 1990s to autointerpret "international peace and security," seemingly without restraint or credible attention to "international." Will this new assertion of an au-

---

56. The standards from the North Sea continental shelf cases (*Germany v. Denmark* and *Germany v. Netherlands*), Judgment, 1969 I.C.J. 3, 45, para. 77.

57. Maggie Powers, "Responsibility to Protect: Dead, Dying or Thriving?" (Columbia University, MA Thesis in Human Rights, 2014), 4.

thoritative interpretive role by the General Assembly create a lasting precedent?[58]

RtoP could not claim clear legality, but it could claim "legitimacy" after the 2005 summit outcome. In this light it is worth recalling that Security Council action during the Rwandan genocide was in part stymied by claims from Rwanda (then on the Council) and its few supporters on the Council that the crisis was a domestic issue, not one subject to international authority.[59] Ironically, the increasing power of the norm is reflected in the way in which the US invoked humanitarian concerns generally and the way in which Russia invoked RtoP explicitly to try to justify their interventions in Iraq (2003) and Georgia (2008), respectively. But the experience of Libya and now Syria will prove decisive in strengthening or weakening the doctrine.[60]

58. The Charter has been informally amended before, as when states chose to define Security Council abstentions not to have the effect of permanent member vetoes despite Article 27's provision that substantive decisions of the Security Council have the "affirming" and "concurring votes" of the five permanent members. This process of deliberation and interpretation is well covered in Ian Johnstone's *The Power of Deliberation* (Oxford: Oxford University Press, 2011).

59. See the important personal account by the former Czech permanent representative to the UN, and then–Security Council member, Karel Kovanda, "The Czech Republic on the UN Security Council," *Journal of Genocide Studies and Prevention* 5 (2010), 192–218.

60. For a well-argued brief in favor of US support for RtoP, see Matthew C. Waxman, *Intervention to Stop Genocide and Mass Atrocities,* Council Special Report no. 49 (New York: Council on Foreign Relations, 2009). For the latest presidential commitment, see Sophie Quinton, "Obama Highlights Efforts to Prevent Genocide," *National Journal,* April 23, 2012; Global Centre for the Responsibility to Protect, Policy Brief, January 2010; and Security Council, Update Report no. 3, January 11, 2010.

This has implications for international ethics. On its face, it defines and limits acceptable communitarian standards from an international point of view. *The principle of sovereignty can protect states from a wide range of international interferences, but no longer from proportional, Security Council–endorsed actions to prevent or stop the four harms outlined in the RtoP doctrine.*

It also clarifies the question of just authority. *The Security Council has that legal authority to act against international threats. It also now has the legitimacy to address domestic crimes against humanity, war crimes, ethnic cleansing, and genocide.* We should not assume that it will resolve the most important issue of political will: getting states to take these principles seriously, abide by them, and be willing, where justified, to enforce them.[61] Nor does RtoP resolve debates in moral philosophy. Much of the value of ethical thinking is that it constantly questions received standards in the name of security, solidarity, and human welfare, and RtoP should not be immune from this critique.

61. At a special, unofficial meeting, a "retreat of the Security Council" at Pocantico in May 2001, all the permanent representatives of the fifteen members were prepared to acknowledge that R2P was a legitimate cause of action for Security Council enforcement, but none was prepared to publicly issue a statement that it constituted a general responsibility to act. The case-by-case language of paras. 138–139 reaffirmed in 2005 this reluctance.

5

Postbellum Peacebuilding

According to Mill, a just victor does not need to halt at the restored border. Following a successful defensive war against an aggressor, it can cross the border, intervening in order to remove a "perpetual menace" to peace and its security.

> So, again, when a nation, in her own defense, has gone to war with a despot, and has had the rare good fortune not only to succeed in her resistance, but to hold the conditions of peace in her own hands, she is entitled to say that she will make no treaty, unless with some other ruler than the one whose existence as such may be a perpetual menace to her safety and freedom. ("Non-Intervention," 123)

Mill's implicit reference was the exile of Napoleon to Elba, off the Italian coast, in 1814 and then subsequently far in the south Atlantic to St. Helena in 1815, after his "perpetually menacing" threat had indeed been proved by his return to France and the costly campaign that led to his second defeat at the Battle of Waterloo.

This justification for postwar intervention is one more override based on national security, but it also raises the more general concern of the rights and duties of victors after war. This is the problem of *jus post bellum* (justice after war) and "peacebuilding" (assisting a political transformation that helps make peace last). The point is again that consequences count: even

well-intentioned interventions can produce more harm than
good if the intervention is incapable of transitioning to a self-
determining, rights-respecting, welfare-enhancing, stable government. We have seen in Chapter 1 that most interventions,
whether well intentioned or not, lead to one of three harmful
consequences: subsequent civil war, an oppressive regime, or a
dependent colony. Mill's eloquent warnings notwithstanding,
not all interventions have these consequences. Just intervention postbellum is possible, but difficult.

Mill clearly worried about the consequences of postbellum
intervention whether in interstate or civil wars. In his remarks
on post–Civil War Reconstruction in the US South, Mill explicitly noted the need not just to remove Jefferson Davis from
office but to "break altogether the power of the slaveholding
caste" so that its members did not "remain masters of the State
legislatures [where] they w[ould] be able effectually to nullify a
great part of the result which ha[d] been so dearly bought by
the blood of the Free States."[1]

The history of harmful interventions suggests that interveners, even in just interventions, should have an obligation to take
care that a justifiable postbellum transition is achieved. This in
turn raises three questions: First, what are the applicable rules
under international law for lawful occupations, and are they
adequate? Second, what postbellum transformations are morally permissible, or even required? And, third, are permissible
transformations effective in achieving a just and stable peace?

This chapter leads to two conclusions. First, existing occupation law is inadequate, and should be reformed to permit trans-

1. See Eric Foner, *Reconstruction: America's Unfinished Revolution* (New York:
Harper, 2002) for background and Mill's letter to Parke Goodwin quoted in
Michael St. John Packe, *The Life of John Stuart Mill* (New York: Macmillan,
1954), 427.

formational peacebuilding. Second, legitimate peacebuilding strategies will succeed only if they win the self-determining consent of the temporarily occupied.

INTERNATIONAL LAW

In traditional, pre–twentieth century international law, the use of armed force was not unlawful. States were permitted to, at their will, conquer territories, annex them, and assume sovereign rights over their populations.[2] The Peace of Westphalia of 1648 imposed limits against forcible religious conversion, but there were few other limits on the use of force.[3] In the nineteenth century, at the same time that the rules for the conduct of war evolved, a set of norms emerged to civilize the outcomes of war by constraining the rights of belligerent occupation. These norms emphasized an occupation's temporary character, one preliminary to the disposition of a peace treaty. An occupation could not legalize annexation, which was permitted only through a surrender agreement of an established sovereign.[4] In the meantime, the laws of occupation established rights for

2. Lassa Oppenheim, *International Law: A Treatise*, 2 vols., 9th ed., ed. Robert Jennings and Arthur Watts (1920; Oxford: Oxford University Press, 2008), 699.

3. Leo Gross, "The Peace of Westphalia," *American Journal of International Law* 42 (1948), 20.

4. Needless to say that does not imply that the surrender agreement was voluntary in any larger sense or that these same norms applied outside the developed world of Europe, North America, and Japan. For influential treatments of the law of occupation, see Eyal Benvenisti, *The International Law of Occupation* (Princeton: Princeton University Press, 1993); and Morris Greenspan, *The Modern Law of Land Warfare* (Berkeley: University of California Press, 1959). For a classic and now shocking example of the nonapplication of humanitarian law outside Europe and North America, see Elbridge Colby, "How to Fight Savage Tribes," *American Journal of International Law* 21 (1927), 279–288.

occupiers and rights for the occupied. When the Kellogg-Briand Pact of 1928 and the UN Charter of 1945 outlawed wars of aggression and established the principle of national self-determination, territory acquired by force was generally deemed illegitimate.

There thus emerged a tension between, on the one hand, the record of surrenders—which seemed to allow for complete discretion, even (as after World War II, "unconditional surrender") transferring complete sovereignty to the occupier—and, on the other hand, the law of occupation, which became the only operative, general law governing postbellum responsibilities.

Today the United Nations Charter governs both sets of rules. Article 2(4) prohibits the use or threat of force among states other than in individual or collective self-defense, and Article 2(7) prohibits the UN's interference in domestic affairs, other than as required to preserve international peace and security when so determined by the Security Council. Nothing but a defensive war—and no other use of force—can be fully legal without Security Council authorization.

The Hague Regulations of 1907 and the Geneva Convention (IV) of 1949 still define the accepted laws of occupation. Their essence is conservation: occupiers have a duty to protect the occupied, maintain law and order, protect private property, and ensure the delivery of social services, such as public health care (Article 56). In turn, the occupied population has duties not to resist the occupiers (if they wish to enjoy protected civilian status), to follow lawful regulations, and even to pay taxes to cover the expenses of the occupation. Conservation thus supplanted transformation—occupiers are not permitted to reform the laws, promote human rights not already recognized in local law, change the constitution, democratize, or promote social equity. They must instead preserve the status quo ante bellum. The 1907 Hague Convention summarizes the requirements as follows:

> *Article 43. The authority of the legitimate power having in fact passed into the hands of the occupant, the latter shall take all the measures in his power to restore, and ensure, as far as possible, public order and safety, while respecting, unless absolutely prevented, the laws in force in the country.*[5]

The Geneva Convention shifts the focus of responsibilities directly to the rights of "protected persons" in the occupied territory and substantially enhances those rights. But while more flexible, the Convention also stresses conservation of laws and the constitution, unless changes are necessary to respect the rights of the protected set forth in the Convention, as in Articles 47 and 64.

> *Article 47. Protected persons who are in occupied territory shall not be deprived, in any case or in any manner whatsoever, of the benefits of the present Convention by any change introduced, as the result of the occupation of a territory, into the institutions or government of the said territory, nor by any agreement concluded between the authorities of the occupied territories and the Occupying Power, nor by any annexation by the latter of the whole or part of the occupied territory.*[6]

5. Hague Convention no. IV, Respecting the Laws and Customs of War on Land, Annex, Art. 43, October 18, 1907, 36 stat. 2277; T.S. no. 539, Art. 43 [hereinafter Hague Convention].

6. Geneva Convention relative to the Protection of Civilian Persons in Time of War, Art. 47, August 12, 1949, 75 U.N.T.S. 287, 6 U.S.T. 3516 [hereinafter Geneva Convention].

> *Article 64. The penal laws of the occupied territory shall remain in force, with the exception that they may be repealed or suspended by the Occupying Power in cases where they constitute a threat to its security or an obstacle to the application of the present Convention. Subject to the latter consideration and to the necessity for ensuring the effective administration of justice, the tribunals of the occupied territory shall continue to function in respect of all offences covered by the said laws. The Occupying Power may, however, subject the population of the occupied territory to provisions which are essential to enable the Occupying Power to fulfill its obligations under the present Convention, to maintain the orderly government of the territory, and to ensure the security of the Occupying Power, of the members and property of the occupying forces or administration, and likewise of the establishments and lines of communication used by them.[7]*

Article 43 of the Hague Convention, concluded seven years before the outbreak of World War I, is understandable as a

---

7. Ibid., Art. 64. On the limitations of occupation law, see David J. Scheffer, "Beyond Occupation Law," *American Journal of International Law* 97 (2003), 842–849; and Kristen E. Boon, "Obligations of the New Occupier: The Contours of a Jus Post Bellum," *Loyola of Los Angeles International and Comparative Law Review* 31 (2009), 57. For a thorough discussion of the Convention and critique of US and UK occupation policy in Iraq, see Adam Roberts, "Transformative Military Occupation: Applying the Laws of War and Human Rights," *American Journal of International Law* 100 (2006), 580. And for discussion of the lack of connection between occupation law and peacebuilding, see Gregory Fox, *Humanitarian Occupation* (New York: Cambridge University Press, 2008); and Ralph Wilde, *International Territorial Administration* (New York: Oxford University Press, 2008).

rule to limit constitutional changes among European states sharing a common sense of civilized comity. Barring a "standing menace" or the collapse of civil order, occupations of other legitimate sovereigns should be temporary and conservative. But the Geneva Conventions of 1949 are harder to explain. In the aftermath of World War II and the Holocaust, and in the middle of radical attempts to de-Nazify Germany and create new legal orders across western and eastern Europe, the Conventions may reflect attempts by each bloc, capitalist and communist, to limit the transformations imposed by the other. But they do not reflect what each did in its own sphere based on the unconditional surrender agreements they imposed. Nor do they reflect what one might want to, or should, do in the aftermath of anything but a limited war among states recognizing each other's legitimacy.

Jus Post Bellum

Turning to the ethics of just war, what should occupiers be allowed to do and what should they be held responsible for doing? Complementing traditional *jus ad bellum* and *jus in bello*, scholars are arguing that we must also assess *jus post bellum*, or justice after war. This raises the question of whether, like the traditional justices, justice after war should be judged semi-independently. Can interventions be in accordance with the requirements of *jus ad bellum* and *jus in bello* but fail the principles of *jus post bellum*, and vice versa? Whatever one thinks of the justice of going to war with Iraq, can the US leave without helping Iraqis build a legitimate state? Former US Secretary of State Colin Powell has called this (when he thought about occupying Iraq in 1991) the "Pottery Barn Doctrine: You break it, you own it." But is it possible?

In our time, the classic reference is "de-Nazification" in Germany following World War II and the breaking up of the imperial principle, the militarist faction, and the *zaibatsu,* or industrial and financial business conglomerates, in Japan. The Allies clearly had a right to end German and Japanese aggression and drive their armies back to their borders. But were they entitled to also reform Germany and Japan? If so, what cost, Michael Walzer asks, should the victors and vanquished pay to guarantee reliable security?[8] Alternatively, when instead should the victors relinquish the goals of unconditional surrender and peacebuilding in order to spare the lives that a campaign for total conquest will cost?

Walzer poses, and also sharpens, this modern moral conundrum, but without fully resolving it. Should a negotiated arrangement have been struck with Nazi Germany, had it been willing to surrender to the Western Allies? The special nature of the evil of Nazism makes it apparent that this was not a deal many, including Walzer, would have wanted to be made, even to save the lives of many Allied soldiers and noncombatant Germans. But Walzer does not address Mill's argument for postwar pacific reconstruction. He, like many liberals, would have preferred a German revolution that toppled Nazism and with which the Allies could then have made peace. But he also argues that Nazi leaders should have been punished and, lacking a German revolution, that occupying Germany was necessary. But the trial would have been an act of "collective

8. Michael Walzer, *Just and Unjust Wars* (New York: Basic, 1977), 111–124. In a recent essay, Walzer revises his arguments, noting the importance of reforming regimes subject to humanitarian interventions rather than leaving genocidaires in power. See Michael Walzer, "The Triumph of Just War Theory," in *Arguing About War* (New Haven: Yale University Press, 2004), 3–22.

abhorrence" for their crimes, rather than an act to prevent future aggression.[9]

Walzer further argues that Japan's government should have been accommodated. Thus the atomic bombs dropped on Hiroshima and Nagasaki, along with the firebombing of Tokyo and other Japanese cities, were unjustified as violating *jus in bello* restrictions on killing noncombatants.[10] Indeed, the US dropped the two atomic bombs on military targets, but with radically disproportionate effects on noncombatants. The evident purpose behind the destruction of those cities was to coerce the Japanese war cabinet into surrender. Unfortunately, the two bombs were barely adequate for the purpose of persuading the war cabinet to surrender on terms likely to make the peace last. The victors conceded the continuation of an imperial figurehead but demanded the authority to reconstruct Japan. It is not at all clear that the war cabinet would have accepted this demand without the shock of the two bombs or the entry of the

9. Walzer, *Just and Unjust Wars*, 117. See also Gary Bass, "Jus Post Bellum: Postwar Justice and Reconstruction," *Philosophy and Public Affairs* 32 (2004), 384, for an exploration of the justice of these kinds of settlements; Bass limits his arguments to the demonstrably necessary case of postgenocide. For valuable overviews, see Stefano Recchia, "Just and Unjust Postwar Reconstruction," *Ethics and International Affairs* 23 (2009), 165–188; and Brian Orend, *The Morality of War* (Toronto: Broadview, 2006), especially chapter 7.

10. They were unjustified in that Japan did not pose a "supreme emergency" that might have justified overriding the rules on noncombatant immunity if following them would have resulted in the victory of a genocidal regime. As important, the overridings needed to be necessary and effective; Walzer, *Just and Unjust Wars*, 263–268. Walzer argues that Japanese militarism was not a genocidal regime in the way in which Nazi Germany was. But if Japanese militarism was dangerous to its neighbors, as it surely was, and needed to be reconstructed domestically, as it probably did, to reduce that danger, then measures beyond external constraint or negotiated accommodation were required.

USSR into the war against Japan. Both together seemed to have tipped the decision toward surrender.[11]

Leaving Japan in the hands of those who launched the conquest of Asia would have been unwise. For cynics, talking about noncombatant protection in the era of the bombings of Shanghai, Nanjing, Coventry, London, Hamburg, and Dresden is akin to handing out speeding tickets at the Indianapolis 500. But it is reasonable to ask whether there were other, more just means of coercing the Japanese war cabinet into a sufficiently complete surrender that would have permitted political reconstruction. For example, would a detonation of a demonstration bomb have worked? What about a protracted naval blockade that prohibited Japan's access to any goods other than food and medicine necessary for survival? Neither of these seemed promising at the time. The looming competition with the Soviet Union also colored US estimations of how to end the war.[12] But in retrospect, humane alternatives may have been worth further exploration.

11. Ian Buruma surveys the debate on the issue in "The War over the Bomb," *New York Review of Books,* September 21, 1995, pp. 26–34. Tsuyoshi Hasegawa, in *Racing the Enemy: Stalin, Truman, and the Surrender of Japan* (Cambridge: Harvard University Press, 2005), discusses the difficulty of persuading the Japanese cabinet to limit negotiations to the preservation of the emperor, after the atomic bombs on Hiroshima and Nagasaki had been dropped; see 205–251.

12. For insights on the debate within the US, see Leon Sigal, *Fighting to a Finish: The Politics of War Termination in the United States and Japan, 1945* (Ithaca, NY: Cornell University Press, 1988); and McGeorge Bundy, *Danger and Survival: Choices About the Bomb in the First 50 Years* (New York: Vintage, 1988). For a balanced assessment of Truman's leadership, see Joseph Nye's *Presidential Leadership and the Creation of the American Era* (Princeton: Princeton University Press, 2013), especially 81–83.

ETHICAL PEACEBUILDING

In a seminal article on the ethics of postwar peacebuilding, Gary Bass addresses the ethics of political reconstruction. He sensibly suggests that justice after war should be tailored to addressing the causes that brought about the war.[13] If, on the one hand, genocide provoked a humanitarian response, then the criminal regime that committed genocide should be reconstructed, the perpetrators prosecuted, and the victims compensated. The obvious model here is de-Nazification following World War II, along with the Nuremberg Tribunals and Germany's financial compensation for Holocaust victims. If, on the other hand, a traditional aggression takes place, such as an attempt to seize a province or valuable oil field, other rules should apply. Under these circumstances the right response is a return to the status quo while perhaps imposing additional external measures to ensure that the aggressor is unlikely to repeat the aggression.

EXTERNAL MEASURES

The just defender thus has a right to improve the prospects that aggression will not be repeated. Historically, beyond the return of conquered territory, defenders have demanded the cession of strategic provinces or outposts to reduce the capacity for renewed aggression. Following World War I, Germany lost its overseas colonies and substantial contiguous territories,

13. See Bass, "Jus Post Bellum." For a wide-ranging analytic survey of the elements of transitional justice, see Jon Elster's *Closing the Books: Transitional Justice in Historical Perspective* (New York: Cambridge University Press, 2004); the discussion of "restoration" France in 1814 and 1815 is especially apposite.

including most of Alsace-Lorraine to France and West Prussia to a reconstituted Poland. So, too, the US demanded the cession of strategic islands from Japan following World War II. Some of these territories were held in residual sovereignty for Japan, as Okinawa was until 1972, while others were held as UN Trust Territories under a special strategic mandate of the Security Council.[14] Their purpose was to put the US in a dominant position in the western Pacific, in part to deter a remilitarization of Japan. But each ran up against the competing demand of self-determination, and, in the end, ceded to it by restoring the territory to its national sovereign or recognizing independent statehood.

Reflecting the challenges of holding strategic territory permanently, reparations and other restrictions on future capacities have been levied on past aggressors. The most famous (or infamous) of these were the reparations required of Germany following World War I, mandated by the "war guilt" clause (Article 231) of the Treaty of Versailles. Reparations were set at 132 billion marks (about $442 billion in 2012 US dollars).[15] This imposition raises questions of who should pay: were all parties equivalently responsible? And whether the effects are counterproductive: would they produce resentment or impoverish the world economy? Restrictions have also been placed on armaments. After World War I, the German army was limited to 100,000 troops (and no tanks) and to 15,000 sailors and six battleships. This may well be a better strategy for peace, but,

14. Palau, independent in 1994, was the last of these.

15. See Margaret MacMillan, *Peacemakers* (London: Murray, 2001). Unusually and adding to the penalty of the reparations (and thus eroding the prospects for long-term peace), the Treaty of Versailles required Germany to acknowledge "war guilt" and try the kaiser and other senior officials (the last requirement observed only in the breach).

again, one needs to consider whether it produces incentives to evade, how it will be enforced, and whether the limitations are credible.

External measures might well indeed be sufficient to reduce the capacity for future aggression. The most prominent modern example of capacity limiting postbellum is the peace imposed on Iraq following Saddam Hussein's aggression against Kuwait in 1990. The United Nations Security Council imposed the peace on Iraq through Resolution 687, the so-called "Mother of All Resolutions" (named in mockery of Hussein's empty threat of inflicting the "Mother of All Battles" in defense of his occupation of Kuwait). The cease-fire resolution dictated the demarcation of Iraqi-Kuwaiti contested borders and imposed compensation obligations on Iraq for damage done in Kuwait and to Iraq's foreign financial creditors. It also mandated a disarmament regime enforced by international economic sanctions.[16]

Such external measures have the virtue of preserving the internal self-determination of even aggressor states, but they can easily fall short of what seems necessary both as a matter of national security and humanitarian sympathy. As Bass notes, wars sometimes leave defeated aggressors on "the verge of anarchy," with broken governments incapable of providing secu-

16. For a thorough analysis, see Ian Johnstone, *Aftermath of the Gulf War: An Assessment of UN Action*, IPA Occasional Paper (Boulder, CO: Lynne Rienner, 1994). The disarmament regime and its sanctions were later lightened by Oil for Food, which was designed to protect vulnerable civilians and their nutritional and medical needs from the effects of the sanctions imposed to coerce Iraqi compliance. The effects were nonetheless devastating for Iraqi civilians, and the regime engendered massive corruption, some of which spilled over onto UN officials; see the account in Kofi Annan, *Interventions* (New York: Penguin, 2012), 319–334.

rity or minimal social protections.[17] An occupation thus becomes morally necessary. It then produces legal obligations of occupation, but also a conundrum of how to leave justly. To whom is sovereignty to be restored if the state is itself collapsed or "failed"?

Sometimes, the root causes of aggression are deep within a regime's structure. This militarism, the perpetual menace Mill identified in Napoleon's rule of France, is an ideology and set of institutions fostered by the rulers. It is itself the problem and must be changed.

And lastly, interventions, unlike ordinary wars of self-defense, presuppose a focus on the domestic regime of the state intervened against. Justifiable interventions are necessarily grounded in overriding or disregarding a state's sovereignty in order to rescue a population from its government or free an oppressed nation seeking to secede. External measures do not address these problems.[18]

INTERNAL MEASURES

The principles of UN trusteeship that applied to colonial trust territories after World War II provide one guide to just peacebuilding for foreigners exercising authority over another people. Article 76 of the UN Charter requires state trust holders "to promote the political, economic, social and educational advancement of the inhabitants of the trust territories and their predevelopment towards self-government or independence." This

17. Bass, "Jus Post Bellum," 403.
18. See the article by Brian Orend, "Justice After War," *Ethics and International Affairs* 16, no. 1 (2002), 43–57, on the democratic norms for reconstructing domestic regimes.

applied only to designated trust territories and specifically not to UN member states (according to Article 78). Legally, states are either independent, or, if conquered, protected by the laws of occupation of the Geneva Conventions that prohibit transformation. Transformation thus can be guided only by broad ethical principles, specific surrender agreements and Security Council authorizations.

Assuming that sovereignty is temporarily in the hands of another state or international organization, what is permissible and what is required in the way of transformation? In these circumstances, the occupying state is something like a "trustee," or "conservator," for the interests of the people.[19] Three guiding principles seem appropriate.

First are the terms of the surrender (pre-Charter), the enabling Security Council resolution, or the peace treaty among competing factions in a civil war that the foreign force is mediating or implementing.

These are decisive legal and ethical constraints on postbellum reconstruction, the legally binding standards for authoritative action. I discuss their authorizing and limiting role below in regard to the peace process in Cambodia.

This first principle is essential but is not a sufficient guide because there may be no formal surrender (as in Iraq in 2003). Moreover, the Security Council will itself need guidance in the design of the mandate it authorizes. Many Security Council mandates and peace treaties are themselves open-ended and require substantive interpretation to fix their policy content.[20]

19. Gerald Helman and Steven Ratner, "Saving Failed States," *Foreign Policy* 89 (1992–1993), 3–20.

20. See Ian Johnstone, *Rights and Reconciliation: UN Strategies in El Salvador* (Boulder, CO: Lynne Rienner, 1995).

And when the peace post–civil war is less than voluntary, the issue becomes what terms the foreign mediator should pressure the parties to accept. This will require standards.

Thus second are the basic norms of human rights, such as those embodied in the Universal Declaration of Human Rights (1948), claimable by all persons.

These basic norms of individual, civil, political, and economic rights should limit what the peacebuilder or occupier can do and indicate what it should strive to foster. They cannot, however, be a fixed rule, or recipe for action. No state today fully meets these exacting standards of human rights or those of the subsequent human rights treaties inspired by them. But peacebuilders in temporary sovereign authority should regard human rights standards as normative: to be fostered where feasible and not to be violated without cause.

And third, the principle of self-determination should guide.

Peace treaties are ambiguous and human rights are abstract and open-ended, and inevitably need to be balanced and given local specificity by culture and methods of actual consent.[21] The challenge of legitimate and effective peacebuilding is balancing these three, sometimes contradictory, principles and adjusting to the particular circumstances of each case.

21. My views on this question owe much to conversations with legal advisers and peacekeepers in Cambodia (1993), El Salvador (1994), Vukovar (1998 and 1999), and Brcko (1999 and 2000). For an eminently pragmatic rendering of these issues and how to make them effective, see Ambassador R. William Farrand's *Reconstruction and Peace Building in the Balkans: The Brcko Experience* (Boulder, CO: Rowman and Littlefield, 2011). This book is remarkable among other reasons for being one of the very few studies of peacebuilding written by someone intimately informed about (not to speak of responsible for) the complexities of transitional governance as they emerge at the leadership level.

Transforming Iraq, 2003

The UN Security Council faced these questions as it considered what mandate to give the coalition that invaded Iraq. Importantly, it asserted in Resolution 1483 that the occupation was an "occupation" and that therefore the Geneva Conventions applied.[22] This entailed responsibilities for maintaining public order, such as preventing looting, and for protecting the inhabitants from abuses, including torture or other inhumane treatment.[23] It then went on to specify that the "Oil for Food" program (the provision of humanitarian assistance funded through Iraqi oil sales monitored by the Security Council) should be concluded, but that the remaining financial balances of the program and ongoing oil sales should be handled according to best international market practices, with the proceeds to be used for the benefit of the Iraqi population.[24]

The most striking provision of Resolution 1483, given the limitations of occupation law, was the requirement that the "Authorities" (later termed the CPA, Coalition Provisional Authority) facilitate the "establishment of an internationally recognized, representative government of Iraq."[25] This purpose was further

22. Paragraph 5 of the resolution specifically cites The Hague and Geneva Conventions. See SC Res. 1483, UN Doc. S/RES/1483 (May 22, 2003). For discussion, see Frederic Kirgis, "Security Council Resolution 1483 on the Rebuilding of Iraq," ASIL Insights, http://www.asil.org/insigh107.cfm, 12/5/2012.

23. The looting of the National Museum and National Library had already occurred when 1483 passed. Paragraph 6 requires the authorities to assist in the return of stolen goods. The abuses at Abu Ghraib prison were revealed subsequently. The US and the UK, apparently key drafters of SCR 1483, were under pressure to recognize their "occupation."

24. The agreement also specified that 5 percent be used for the Kuwait compensation fund established following the first Iraq War.

25. See SC Res. 1483, para. 22.

elaborated in the preambular paragraphs as "[encouraging] the efforts of the people of Iraq to form a representative government based on the rule of law that affords equal rights and justice to all Iraqi citizens without regard to ethnicity, religion, or gender." Resolution 1483 probably reflected long-standing norms in favor of democratic governance as integral parts of peacebuilding and UN standards more generally.[26] It may also have reflected concerns that some members of the US Defense Department had been contemplating handing over sovereignty to an unrepresentative (and shady) group of former exiles led by Ahmed Chalabi, though the US sought to assure the international community that this was not the case.[27]

In any case, Resolution 1483 filled the gaps in occupation law. Authorized under Chapter VII, 1483 was legally binding on all states as part of the UN's authority to address breaches of international peace and security. It could not rewrite occupation law (only a treaty can), but it provided definitive authority for this particular case for transforming Iraq.

Self-determination, human rights, and occupation authority are often in tension. In a thoughtful study of what should have been the occupation policy in Iraq, Noah Feldman set out principles drawing on the idea of trusteeship as a duty to facilitate self-determination.[28] He described four steps that occupiers should

26. See Thomas Franck's influential survey of the issue, "The Emerging Right to Democratic Governance," *American Journal of International Law* 86 (1992), 46.

27. See David Phillips, *Losing Iraq: Inside the Postwar Reconstruction Fiasco* (New York: Basic, 2005); and Thomas Ricks, *Fiasco: The American Adventure in Iraq* (New York: Penguin, 2006), 56–57.

28. Noah Feldman, *What We Owe Iraq: War and the Ethics of Nation Building* (Princeton: Princeton University Press, 2004), 59–62. The related importance of building a wide coalition including all prepared to live within a constitutional regime of viable tolerance is stressed by Andrew Arato, "Constitution-Making in Iraq," *Dissent,* Spring 2004.

take. The first is establishing order, providing the security that the population has a right to expect when a government has been overturned and that is necessary for the population to begin to express itself. Second is guaranteeing freedom of speech and assembly, allowing the population to define itself and its goals. Third is serving as an impartial mediator among factions, giving each a chance to present its case to the people. Finally, fourth is holding democratic elections for a constituent assembly that will itself shape a constitution and government. These elections should be neither too early—before a viable state has been restored (police and courts), parties have formed, and a responsible press can inform the public—nor too late, when the occupation appears colonial and the population is rebelling against its paternalism. Then, when all the above criteria have been met, the occupier must leave, having returned self-determination and effective self-government to the people and their own government.

"Liberal Peacebuilding" as Multilateral Imperialism?

There has arisen in the literature on peacebuilding a concern that both state reconstruction and holding elections as exit strategies are new forms of imperialism, imposed by the UN or regional organizations such as NATO on vulnerable postconflict societies.[29] This view gains some persuasive force when one

29. For a good recent survey, see Philip Cunliffe, "Still the Spectre at the Feast: Comparison Between Peacekeeping and Imperialism in Peacekeeping Studies," *International Peacekeeping* 19 (2012), 426–442. For the seminal but still relevant critique, see Roland Paris, "Peacebuilding and the Limits of Liberal Internationalism," *International Security* 22, no. 2 (1997), 54–89; and his updated reassessment "Saving Liberal Peacebuilding," *Review of International Studies* 36 (2010), 337–365.

adds that neither liberal states nor electoral democracies are absolute requirements of justice. Both state reconstruction and elections respond to a need for secure protection and human rights, but as John Rawls has observed in *The Law of Peoples,* neither peace nor basic rights logically requires either a liberal order or an electoral democracy.[30]

Rawls argues that a concern for the basic human rights—including subsistence and the absence of extreme abuses, such as torture, and guarantees of freedom of speech and religion—that are essential for human dignity and for international security are compatible with what he calls "decent hierarchical societies." These do not meet the egalitarian standards of "justice as fairness" that would be chosen by free and independent individuals (including the standards of equality of opportunity and democracy of his *Theory of Justice* for example). They are, instead, hierarchical societies without elected governments. But they do not abuse basic rights and, having pledged nonaggression, can be assumed by liberal democratic peoples to be sufficiently safe that they warrant respect for their sovereignty and a mutual regime of nonintervention and peace. These societies do not guarantee equal protection of the laws. They tolerate, for example, systematic discrimination against racial or other minorities, women, or other religions, and they limit voting rights or legislative and bureaucratic posts to males or members of the established religion. But they do have consultation mechanisms, such that even those without equal rights have their interests listened to and taken into account by the established hierarchy.

30. John Rawls, *The Law of Peoples* (Princeton: Princeton University Press, 1999). For "Kazanistans" see 75–78. And for a related argument that the human right to democratic government should not be enforced across borders, see Charles Beitz, *The Idea of Human Rights* (Oxford: Oxford University Press, 2009), 174–180.

Together, Rawls argues, these guarantees are sufficient for liberal peoples to extend the democratic peace they institute among themselves to decent hierarchical societies, which he significantly calls "Kazanistans," implying that certain traditional Muslim hierarchical societies might qualify.

Some liberal philosophers disagree with Rawls, holding that, even in ideal theory, Rawls's rights are insufficiently egalitarian to guarantee mutual respect for human dignity. Political scientists have speculated that the regime Rawls described is such an abstract construct that few actual states will meet its criteria for rights and peace without also being electoral democracies.[31] But Rawls's argument is hypothetical, arguing for the possibility of complete toleration of nondemocratic, nonliberal societies by liberal societies. He makes a powerful case for a duty of toleration, including nonintervention with regard to the decent hierarchical societies.[32] And these arguments build on a long tradition of liberal thought, exemplified by Mill and others, in favor of indigenously determined self-determination.

But these arguments for nonintervention, though legitimate, are not equally relevant for peacebuilding.[33] Peacebuilding in-

31. For the first point, see Charles Beitz, "Rawls's Law of Peoples," *Ethics* 110 (2000), 669–696. For the second point, see, for example, Michael Doyle, "One World, Many Peoples: International Justice in John Rawls's *The Law of Peoples*," *Perspectives on Politics* 4 (2006), 111–123.

32. He parallels, with differing grounds, the arguments made for nonintervention by Kant for all societies but the aggressive and by J. S. Mill for all but the exceptions noted in previous chapters.

33. Peacekeeping in the sense employed here takes the form of UN or regional organization-mandated military forces and civilian officials who are charged with implementing a peace treaty through monitoring a cease-fire or facilitating assistance or (under extreme circumstances) authoritative administration. Peacebuilding, or postconflict reconstruction, involves reconstructive activities designed to establish or reform a state and economy. This latter can occur with consent on a bilateral basis or with UN or regional organization

volves what foreigners should and should not do when they are in a position of legal or legitimate authority—not what locals can do and what foreigners, as part of an established international order of sovereign independence, should tolerate.

In a post–civil war conflict situation, the peace treaty will govern the norms of foreign interference. But in the age of human rights, where UN peacebuilders have discretion, it would be hard to understand how foreigners on their own authority could deny equal participation in constitution making to women or minority claimants. Partly, of course, this is a product of UN norms in favor of equal human rights. In addition to free speech and assembly, the Universal Declaration of Human Rights (1948) specifies in Article 21:

1. Everyone has the right to take part in the government of his country, directly or through freely chosen representatives.
2. Everyone has the right of equal access to public service in his country.
3. The will of the people shall be the basis of the authority of government; this will shall be expressed in periodic and genuine elections which shall be by universal and equal suffrage and shall be held by secret vote or by equivalent free voting procedures.[34]

But the preference for democratic decisions is also a product of the fact that in the postconflict situation it is not clear *ex ante* who should have leading authority to determine the con-

---

authorization and can include, under rare circumstances, enforcement powers. See Michael Doyle and Nicholas Sambanis, *Making War and Building Peace* (Princeton: Princeton University Press, 2007), 10–11, for definitions and discussion.

34. Universal Declaration of Human Rights (UDHR), GA Res. 217A, UN Doc. A/810 (1948).

tent of self-determination, again unless that has been settled by a peace treaty. If temporary peacebuilding authority has been delegated to the UN, peacekeepers cannot say to one minority or religion, class, race, gender, or ethnicity that it does not have legitimate standing in an effort to write a constitution specifically delegated to the supervision of international authorities. It is not sufficient that such groups merely be consulted. The question of what constitutes equitable participation may indeed have been the root of the preceding armed conflict.

The deputy head of the UN's peacekeeping department, Edmond Mulet, recently recounted how the electoral logic works. When he was special representative overseeing the peacebuilding process in Haiti, he consulted influential local political figures about what should be done about upcoming elections, looming in the wake of the devastating earthquake the country had just experienced. All agreed that the country was not ready to go through an electoral contest. The governing party offered to simply retain political power—backed up with international support. Opposition leaders were equally happy to carve up the ministries among themselves and began suggesting friends and relatives for the various posts. But neither agreed that the other had a legitimate right to govern. In these circumstances, with the opposition and governing parties each nominating itself to take power illegitimately, an election seemed the least corrupt and most legitimate alternative.[35]

Moreover, peacebuilding authority arises only in distinct circumstances. States that possess effective sovereignty—a monopoly on domestic violence—are not candidates for peacebuilding,

35. See Mulet's remarks at the International Day of Democracy, September 16, 2013, hosted by the International Peace Institute and available on the IPI website at http://www.ipinst.org/news/general announcement/397-video -democratization-at-the-sharp-end.html.

no matter what their domestic regime. As long as they do not engage in aggressive war or genocide and suffer defeat, these states are members in good standing of the international legal order. The current world order tolerates military and civilian oligarchies (China, for example, is a permanent member of the Security Council) and numerous monarchies and personalist dictatorships (like those of Saudi Arabia or North Korea or Venezuela or, until recently, Libya and Syria), with and without elections. As long as they do not require bilateral foreign aid from the US to survive (which limits some foreign aid programs to rule of law–abiding democratic regimes), they are free enough from constraint to sustain whatever regime power-holders choose.[36]

Nor are most civil wars settled by international peacebuilding. When a civil war is resolved by conquest, the winner imposes its constitutional regime. When it is resolved by a negotiated elite pact, the reconstituted oligarchy rules. It is only when there is no victor and the elites, warlords, or others are incapable of arriving at their own peace agreement that international mediators and UN authorized peacebuilders become relevant.

36. Other countries have their own similar criteria for the continued awarding of aid. The US government Millennium Challenge Corporation "partners" only with selected countries. "For a country to be selected as eligible for an MCC assistance program, it must demonstrate a commitment to just and democratic governance, investments in its people, and economic freedom as measured by different policy indicators," which include indicators for the ease of private sector business formation, civil liberties, democratic governance, etc. And "According to MCC's statute, a country may have its eligibility or assistance suspended or terminated if the country has: engaged in activities contrary to the national security interests of the United States; engaged in a pattern of actions inconsistent with MCA eligibility criteria; or failed to adhere to its responsibilities under a MCC program agreement."

CAMBODIA, 1991–1993, A "SYSTEM OF LIBERAL DEMOCRACY,
ON THE BASIS OF PLURALISM"

This was the story of the Cambodian peace process.[37] Following the toppling of Prince Sihanouk's regime by a US-inspired
coup led by Lon Nol in 1970 and the devastation inflicted by
the Khmer Rouge genocide of the late 1970s, Vietnam invaded
Cambodia in December 1978. But Hun Sen, the Vietnamese-
installed strongman, could not root out the Khmer Rouge and
its Sihanoukist allies in the 1980s. And Hun Sen's forces could
not come to a power-sharing agreement with the Khmer Rouge
and the Sihanoukist faction in negotiations between 1987 and
1990 mediated by Indonesia and Australia.[38] It was only then
that Security Council mediators stepped in.

In the Paris Peace Agreement of 1991, substantial compromises with justice were incorporated that governed the activities
of international peacebuilders. The genocide inflicted by the
Khmer Rouge was brushed aside (at least temporarily) as the
"unfortunate practices of the recent past." But an essential element of the bargain struck was that the factions agreed to desig-
nate the UN as an interim administrator, which would conduct
a "free and fair" election to determine the future sovereignty
of Cambodia. One could not count on the commitment of any

37. The quoted phrase in the subheading is from the Paris Peace Agreement, 1991.

38. See Steven Ratner, "The Cambodian Settlement Agreements," *Ameri-
can Journal of International Law* 97 (1993), 1; Richard Solomon, *Exiting Indo-
china* (Washington, DC: U.S. Institute of Peace Press, 2000); the chapters by
Jin Song and Nishkala Suntharalingam in Michael Doyle, Ian Johnstone, and
Robert Orr, eds., *Keeping the Peace: Multidimensional Operations in Cambodia
and El Salvador* (New York: Cambridge University Press, 1997); and Michael
Doyle and Nicholas Sambanis, *Making War and Building Peace* (Princeton:
Princeton University Press, 2007), chapter 5.

one of the four factions—ex-Leninist, ex-Maoist, ex-republican, or ex-royalist—to the "liberal democratic pluralism" the peace accords envisaged. But democracy was the only constitution on which they could agree after autocracy and oligarchy had failed. One value of elections as a coordinating solution was their very uncertainty *ex ante*—each faction thought it could win.[39] A second value was important but much more difficult to achieve in practice. This was a commitment that the next set of elections would also be free and fair. Tolerating a loss in one election was a precondition of being able to compete again and perhaps win.

The usual norm in peacebuilding is that forming a government should be left to the process itself, in which all relevant groups have *prima facie* equal standing. This produces a bias in favor of democratic procedures that allow, but make unlikely, the handing over of authority by the wide range of participants to one ruler, a narrow oligarchy, a military junta, or, in pluralist societies, one ethnicity or one religion. In short, it does not preclude tyranny, but it structurally limits tyrannies to tyrannies of the majority. And it biases procedures for drafting new constitutions in favor of power-sharing pacts and constitutional limitations that protect minorities in order to represent the widest possible consent.

Thus the UN secretary-general's report of 2001, *No Exit Without Strategy* (NEWS), explores criteria of success and failure in peacekeeping operations and outlines when to close an operation, either because it has succeeded or failed. It offers a menu of peacebuilding activities that include building state institu-

39. Michael Doyle, *UN Peacekeeping in Cambodia: UNTACS Civil Mandate* (Boulder, CO: Lynne Rienner, 1995). Disclosure: I served as an international monitor during the Cambodian elections that were organized and certified by the United Nations, April–June 1993.

tions such as a bureaucracy, army, and police force; economic development; and democratic elections. These are ideals toward which most operations should strive.[40] Elections are seen as part of a typical exit strategy because they permit a transfer of state authority, temporarily in the hands of international peacekeepers, to a government chosen by the majority of the voters.

As do many strategy documents, NEWS sets forth ideals. It indicates, but does not develop, all the actual hard and incompatible choices that vary from conflict to conflict. In an ideal world, special representatives heading peacebuilding operations can choose security first; or establish the rule of law; or implement a rational budgetary and fiscal process, in which the government relies on nationally derived revenues; or foster local self-governance; or launch self-sustaining economic development.[41] All of these would serve as better, even ideal, exit strategies compared with democratic elections or the mere expiration of a mandate. If elections are held before there is stable order, or reliable information from a free press, or responsible political parties, they can simply ratify hatreds and extremism.[42] Calendar-

40. Report of the Secretary-General, *No Exit Without Strategy: Security Council Decision-Making and the Closure or Transition of United Nations Peacekeeping Operations* (S/2001/394), April 20, 2001. Disclosure: in March 2001, I chaired the UN Secretariat working group drafting the report and presented it to the Security Council in April for its approval.

41. Numerous studies in the field are recommending priorities along these various lines, including Kimberly Marten's *Enforcing the Peace* (New York: Columbia University Press, 2004); Severine Autesserre's *The Trouble with the Congo* (New York: Cambridge University Press, 2010); Ashraf Ghani and Clare Lockhart's *Fixing Failed States* (New York: Oxford University Press, 2008); and Nicholas Sambanis and my own list (including our "seven step plan," with security first) in *Making War and Building Peace* (Princeton: Princeton University Press, 2007), 337–342.

42. Edward Mansfield and Jack Snyder, "Democratic Transitions, Institutional Strength and War," *International Organization* 56 (2002), 297–337.

driven exit dates neglect rational assessments of whether the purposes of the intervention or peacebuilding actually have been fulfilled.[43]

Unfortunately, special representatives do not operate in those ideal worlds. Instead, they need to take into account what the factions will tolerate and measure that against what sustainable peace seems to require. Ideally, again, this balance will be incorporated in the peace treaty that the parties will have negotiated. But this will be far from a perfect consensus. Factions will be tempted to defect (become "spoilers" in Stephen Stedman's phrasing) and resort to force unless they can be assuaged, sidelined, or overawed.[44] For example, in Cambodia, the Khmer Rouge defected quickly, and Yasushi Akashi, the special representative in charge of the UN peacekeeping operation, had to rely on, and balance, the rivalry between Hun Sen's "State of Cambodia," which had military and bureaucratic capacity, and Prince Ranarridh's FUNCINPEC Party, which enjoyed the traditional legitimacy of his father, Prince Sihanouk.

If that is not enough compromise, they will also have to take into account what the troop contributors will bear in terms of cost, time, and casualties, and what their own missions will accept as achievable mandates. Elections became the Cambodian exit strategy in 1993 not only because the factions could not agree on who would rule, but also because the troop contributors insisted on leaving in the summer of 1993 rather than bearing the additional costs of staying until order, the rule of law, and fiscal sustainability were in place.[45]

43. Fen Hampson and Tod Lindberg, "'No Exit' Strategy," *Policy Review*, December 1, 2012.

44. Stephen Stedman, "Spoiler Problems in Peace Processes," *International Security* 22, no. 2 (1997), 5–53.

45. In spring 1993, both the Japanese battalion and the Australian battalion had announced their decisions to leave. The Japanese had been driven out by

An ideal peacebuilding effort will be both national and local. A successful national election that establishes a legitimate government in the capital may do nothing to promote local reconciliation of disputes over land, public policy, and municipal authority among contesting ethnic, religious, and class factions at the local level. The local disputes, unless resolved, can quickly erode the national-level reconciliation. The problem is that foreign peacebuilders are in a poor position to lead local reconciliation, which varies with each locality. Colonial administrations rarely achieved this degree of control. Multilateral peacebuilders typically lack the mandate, the capacity, and the relevant legitimate standing to be effective at the village level. Instead, at its best, national reconciliation empowers a newly legitimate state to manage its own disputes at the local level. Sadly, this translation from national to local legitimacy has proved elusive.[46]

The alternative to a national electoral exit strategy in the vast majority of cases is thus not an organic, ground-up, or locally derived communal consensus. Nor is it a stable, economically viable state experiencing the rule of law. The alternative in most cases, as it was in Cambodia, is a return to civil war. In these circumstances, democratic election as an exit strategy is what is tried when everything else has been tried and failed. It is the last, not the first, choice. And elections are—unfortunately, but frequently—conducted before state institutions are secure,

the traumatic loss of a Japanese national murdered by disgruntled electoral division employees (not by the Khmer Rouge, as originally thought). The Australian Parliament resolved on the rapid exit as security deteriorated throughout Cambodia in March and April 1993.

46. But for an experimental analysis of what international assistance can do to promote local-level village cooperation, after a central government has been established, see James Fearon, Macartan Humphreys, and Jeremy Weinstein, "Can Development Aid Contribute to Social Cohesion After Civil War? Evidence from a Field Experiment in Post Conflict Liberia," *American Economic Review: Papers and Proceedings* 99 (2009), 287–291.

before a reliable rule of law is in place, before a responsible press and well-organized political parties have been established, and before the electorate is well informed. Elections, as they were conducted in Cambodia in 1993, were held in the midst of escalating civil violence inflicted by the Khmer Rouge insurgency and by Hun Sen's violent provocations—conditions far short of the ideal circumstances favoring "free and fair" polls of the popular will. But they were held *then* because the peacekeepers were unwilling to take additional casualties and ordinary Cambodians were fed up with the inflation that the spending by the UN operation had helped engender. The alternative to election was a return to full-scale civil war. The election created a government that could be internationally recognized, and thus legally assisted to combat the Khmer Rouge insurgency, and a constituent assembly authorized to write a constitution.[47]

THE POLITICAL LOGISTICS OF PEACEBUILDING

Can international peacebuilding actually work? There have been many failures to impose a legitimate and stable domestic regime through foreign occupation, as Mill so presciently warned. We need only think of the US intervention in Cuba in 1898 and again in 1907; in the Philippines from 1898; in Nicaragua in 1912 and Haiti in 1915. Rule of law, private property, democracy

---

47. The constitutional assembly was required to operate on the basis of a two-thirds supermajority for ratification, ensuring that the agreement of the two major factions—FUNCINPEC (the princely party of Sihanouk's son) and SOC (Hun Sen's State of Cambodia)—was required for ratification. This had the fortunate and not accidental effect that a coalition government was the likely outcome. No other government would have been functional and legitimate, since FUNCINPEC had the most votes, and the SOC controlled the military and civil capacities of the state.

promotion, and strategic dominance were joint aims in those cases. In all those cases there was a failure to establish a democratic government. From 1920 to 1932, the UK failed in Iraq and Palestine—and from 1882 to 1954 in Egypt—to leave behind friendly, rule of law–abiding semi-democratic governments. In the postwar period, the Soviet Union failed in Eastern Europe to leave behind stable, self-sustainable communist governments.

On the other hand, the postwar occupations by the US, UK, and France in Germany and western Austria, as well as the US occupation in Japan, were all instances of successful democratic transplant. How was this done and how can these successes be repeated?

First, there was in each case a complete defeat. In no case was there just a liberation of one group that was then freed to rule in its own interests. A complete defeat offered a fresh slate for transformation. Second, the occupiers were able to draw upon indigenous traditions of liberal capitalism and representative rule, including the liberal constitutional regimes that governed both Germany and Japan in the 1920s. Each occupation thus had a restorative aspect to it. Third, the occupation could identify a common foreign enemy against which the new regime could mobilize alongside occupiers. Soviet communism served this purpose for the Allies in postwar Germany. In other cases, a domestic "enemy" was exploited through a strategy that often included offering new opportunities for hitherto subordinated classes now newly advantaged by expropriating former landlord or ruling classes. In Korea and Japan, land reform and labor rights operated in this fashion. Fourth, there was an assured departure. That is, the occupiers drew a public distinction between occupation and imperial rule. The occupiers were known to be temporary.

And fifth, the occupiers were well prepared. As David Edelstein has noted, as early as 1943, the US set up schools at the University of Virginia and at Yale to train future administrators of Germany and Japan. In 1943, it was not clear that the Allies were going to win the war. Nonetheless, the US began that early to develop adequate language and other civil administration skills, and undertook long-term planning.[48] Compare this with the US occupation of Iraq in 2003. A story in the *New York Times* quotes a senior US staff officer of the Third Infantry Division saying that, after successfully taking Baghdad, his division had *"no further orders whatsoever."*[49] That is, expecting that the war would be an easy victory (it was) and that peace would almost automatically follow (it rarely does), their superiors provided no instructions on how to occupy or govern, or on what was to happen next. This was a striking and, as we now know, a consequential difference. This lack of preparedness, in conjunction with the weakness of democratic traditions in Iraq, the incomplete defeat of the insurgents (to put it mildly), and the very slow pace of reconstruction made the challenges of a successful occupation in Iraq become clear.

Much can be learned from these unilateral measures, but they need to be supplemented by the lessons of multilateral peacebuilding. Multilateralism introduces severe coordination costs, but it also mobilizes new capacities, curbs the more ex-

48. For a thorough analysis of establishing strategically friendly regimes, see David Edelstein, "Occupational Hazards," *International Security* 29, no. 1 (2004), 49–91. Edelstein is defining success differently, not in terms of democracy or self-determination but in terms of US security interests. For a discussion of democracy promotion, see Carnegie Council on Ethics and International Affairs, *Multilateral Strategies to Promote Democracy* (New York: Carnegie Council, 2004).

49. Michael Gordon, "Catastrophic Success: The Strategy to Secure Iraq Did Not Foresee a Second War," *New York Times*, October 19, 2004, and Ricks, *Fiasco.*

treme forms of national self-dealing, and adds impartial implementation through multilateral management, which can elicit widespread cooperation.[50] The question, of course, is how to do this.

There have been many successes in establishing self-sustaining self-government. They include Namibia, El Salvador, Cambodia, Mozambique, and East Timor. By "success," I mean an end to large-scale civil war (fewer than one thousand battle deaths) and something very modest on the scale of democratic rule—that is, some degree of participation, a national election, but not necessarily a resolution of all the other problems that we know are associated with early democracy. There have also been equally striking failures to establish a democratic rule of law, including Rwanda in 1994, Bosnia throughout the 1990s, Liberia and Angola, also in the 1990s, and Somalia from the 1990s up until the present.

Though slow learners, the international community is beginning to grasp the key factors to success. Nicholas Sambanis and I have identified two key factors: consent and international capacity.

First, success requires consent through a comprehensive and negotiated peace settlement. In short, a good exit depends on a good entrance. This requires a genuine, comprehensive, negotiated agreement (not a mere truce) that brings all the relevant players together to negotiate a future preliminary constitution under which they are all prepared to compete peacefully. This

50. Nicholas Sambanis and I address the costs and value of multilateral peacebuilding at some length in *Making War and Building Peace* (Princeton: Princeton University Press, 2006). Page Fortna, in *Does Peacekeeping Work?* (Princeton: Princeton University Press, 2008), offers a cogent argument for its successes; Charles Call, in *Why Peace Fails* (Washington, DC: Georgetown University Press, 2012), addresses the record of many failures.

kind of agreement seems to make a difference. When the UN enters under Chapter VII enforcement authority, without consent, as in Bosnia or Somalia, or with heavily coerced consent, as NATO did in Bosnia after Dayton, achieving a successful participatory peace is much more difficult.[51] It is not impossible. The peace in East Timor and between East Timor and Indonesia is still holding, but it is important that the peace enforcement operation transform itself into a consent-based operation. It can do this by organizing a national convention to outline a peacebuilding strategy, as Lakhdar Brahimi attempted to do for Afghanistan in the Bonn meetings in 2002. There he helped identify plans to call a Loya Jirga (traditional, popular assembly) to ratify a peacebuilding strategy.

Second, a major international investment of peacebuilding resources helps transform agreements into self-determining successes. Multidimensional peacebuilding on the cheap is a prescription for failure. One needs to have as much "international capacity" as is needed to counterbalance both "local incapacity" and "local hostility." The more local hostility (measured by deaths, refugee displacements, and the stronger, more numerous and hostile factions) and the less local capacity (measured by the incapacity of the government and poverty of the economy) there are, the larger the "international capacity" needs to

51. As Stefano Recchia commented on a draft of this argument, this unfortunately means that peacebuilding is most likely to succeed in the easier cases, when comprehensive peace agreements can be achieved. Since the UN often tackles the harder cases, when the parties cannot settle the conflicts on their own, the challenges of successful peacebuilding become evident. For a good discussion of some of the tensions between peacebuilders and local elites, see Michael Barnett and Cristoph Zurcher, "The Peacebuilder's Contract," in *The Dilemmas of Statebuilding,* ed. Roland Paris and Timothy Sisk (London: Routledge, 2008), 23–52.

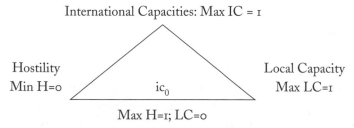

International Capacities: Max IC = 1

Hostility
Min H=0

ic_0

Local Capacity
Max LC=1

Max H=1; LC=0

Figure 1. The peacebuilding triangle. Hostility is measured by refugees and casualties and increases toward the center. Local capacity is measured by gross domestic product per capita and institutional capacity; it increases from the center to the right. International capacity, measured by troops and budget of the peacekeeping operation, increases from base to peak. The overall relative area of the triangle measures the prospects for successful peacebuilding. The proxies are discussed in the source, Michael Doyle and Nicholas Sambanis, *Making War and Building Peace* (Princeton: Princeton University Press, 2006), 64.

be (measured by troops, money, and authority).[52] International capacity offsets local incapacity and can launch a process of peacebuilding that restores order, builds new institutions, and launches economic development. The three can be seen as constituting three dimensions of a triangle, whose "area" is the peacebuilding probability and the prospect for peace, and whose shape differs for each country (Figure 1).

If the international community engages in a conflict area,

---

52. The sources, both for insurgents and the government, of local capacity and the hostility their conflict generates vary from case to case. For penetrating case studies of insurgent capacity see Elisabeth Wood, *Insurgent Collective Action and Civil War in El Salvador* (Cambridge: Cambridge University Press, 2003), and for insurgent violence see Jeremy Weinstein, *Inside Rebellion* (Cambridge: Cambridge University Press, 2007). The current classic reviewing the sources and effects of civil war is Christopher Blattman and Edward Miguel, "Civil War," in the *Journal of Economic Literature* 48 (2010), 3–57.

such as Rwanda in 1993–1994, with a cheap operation designed merely to monitor and facilitate, when the extremists are determined and all factions are hostile and distrustful, disaster is probably inevitable. But peacebuilding can be done effectively, and successes in Namibia, El Salvador, Cambodia, Mozambique, and East Timor are the result of significant international efforts to help transfer democratic institutions to societies that are otherwise extremely problematic prospects for democratic rule. The keys were matching the right degree of international authority (from monitoring to quasi-sovereign trusteeship); military and civilian governance assistance; and economic redevelopment to fit the nature of the dispute in question. Without grassroots economic reconstruction, the postconflict state becomes an unsustainable ward of the international community.[53] When the international capacity compensated for the amount of destruction sustained and deaths and displacements suffered, these transformations were well positioned for success.

The key to an effective strategy is a combined portfolio. Good peacemaking, composed of mediation and negotiation, generates consent and authorizes the legitimate capacities that allow peacekeeping civilians and battalions to manage a peace process. Similarly, effective peacekeeping organizes the reconstructive peacebuilding that creates new institutions and new actors through which genuine transformation toward peace can take place. Discrete force and bribes are the inducements that stop the gaps in peacemaking, peacekeeping, and peacebuilding and prevent a peace operation from becoming hostage to total

---

53. See the evidence and argument provided by Graciana del Castillo, *Rebuilding War-Torn States: The Challenge of Post-Conflict Economic Reconstruction* (New York: Oxford University Press, 2008).

spoilers who are determined to prevent peace under any terms. The force works in these circumstances because it rests on a process that incorporates the consent of the vast majority of the relevant actors and draws upon resources that the peace-building process has mobilized.[54] The four work together, each reinforcing the other in a successful combination. The absence of any is an invitation to failure.

A recent study by the Department of Peacekeeping Operations of the UN has identified key features in the operational success of these missions. They include:

- Genuine commitment to a political process by the parties to work toward peace;
- Clear, credible, and achievable mandates, with matching resources;
- Unity of purpose in the Security Council, with active diplomacy in support;
- Supportive engagement by neighboring countries and regional actors;
- Host country commitment to unhindered operations and freedom of movement;
- Integrated UN approach, effective coordination with other actors, and good communication with host country authorities and population;

54. For example, containing the Khmer Rouge from disrupting the election after their defection from the peace process was tolerated by their former ally (Prince Ranariddh's FUNCINPEC), supported by Hun Sen's military forces and conducted with the support of the UN operation. Attacks on the Khmer Rouge by Hun Sen prior to the peacebuilding process met the political opposition of FUNCINPEC, China, and Thailand. I have explored the combined portfolio strategy in "Building Peace: The John W. Holmes Lecture," *Global Governance* 13, no. 1 (2007), 1–15.

- Demonstration of credibility, strengthening of legitimacy, and promotion of national and local ownership.[55]

All these factors can clearly make a positive difference, but no one should argue that the ethical problems of *jus post bellum* have been solved by multilateral authorization and new strategies of multilaterally managed peacebuilding.[56] Manifestly, they have not been. On too many occasions the international community, as represented in the Security Council, has chosen to authorize less than adequate missions, perhaps most notably in Rwanda and Srebrenica. Under pressure from a Security Council unwilling to expend resources and assign troops, General Roméo Dallaire, the force commander of the UN operation in Rwanda, was told to "situate the estimate": to design the mission to fit available resources rather than to fit the challenges on the ground.[57] Elsewhere, the Security Council has refused to act, or has taken measures clearly inadequate toward ending humanitarian emergencies with which it has been confronted, such as in Bosnia before 1995, Darfur from 2003, and Syria today.

55. United Nations, Department of Peacekeeping Operations and Department of Field Services, *A New Partnership Agenda: Charting the New Horizon for UN Peacekeeping* (New York: United Nations, 2009).

56. For thoughtful criticisms, see Chandra Sriram, *Confronting Past Human Rights Violations: Justice vs. Peace in Times of Transition* (London: Frank Cass, 2004). For the challenges of restoring the rule of law, see Agnes Hurwitz, ed., *Civil War and the Rule of Law* (Boulder, CO: Lynne Rienner for the International Peace Institute, 2008); and Jane Stromseth, David Wippman, and Rosa Brooks, *Can Might Make Right?* (New York: Cambridge University Press, 2008). Saira Mohamed notes the value of an overall authorizing and monitoring function that might be achieved by a revised Trusteeship Council in "Note, From Keeping Peace to Building Peace: A Proposal for a Revitalized United Nations Trusteeship Council," *Columbia Law Review* 105 (2005), 809–812.

57. Roméo Dallaire, *Shake Hands with the Devil: The Failure of Humanity in Rwanda* (Toronto: Random House Canada, 2003), 56.

Nonetheless, with the revival of the Security Council after the Cold War, multilateral authorization constrained many of the dangers of unilateral exploitation. With the slow buildup of lessons—what worked and what did not—multilateral intervention has acquired the tools to avoid both political collapse and dependency. It learned, moreover, how to help build self-sustaining, self-determining peace. We should not, therefore, be judging these new forms of interventionism by the same tropes we have used to judge unilateral interventions. They can be different and, sometimes, justifiable.

Conclusion

The age of intervention is far from over. In the past twenty-five years, and despite the end of the Cold War, interventions have proliferated. Following the attack on the World Trade Center on September 11, 2001, the US intervened in Afghanistan to halt the Taliban's support of Al-Qaeda. Two years later, in 2003, the US invaded Iraq, allegedly to protect US national security, though we now think the decision was based on biased and false information. In 2014, Russia mobilized the Russian-speaking population in Crimea and seized the Crimea from Ukraine, while destabilizing the rest of eastern Ukraine.

And the record of interventions is far from consistent, even when authorized by an impartial multilateral body such as the UN. The UN authorized an overwhelming intervention in Somalia in 1992 to stop a famine and it failed. It authorized underwhelming interventions to stop genocide and crimes against humanity in Bosnia in 1993 and in Rwanda in 1994; neither provided adequate protection. NATO liberated the Kosovars by intervening in 1999 and assisted the people of South Sudan, but failed to protect the people of Darfur. In 2011, the UN authorized a rescue of the Libyans after they suffered a few thousand casualties. Starting in 2011 and continuing well into 2014, the Syrians suffered more than 160,000 deaths, with millions of internal and external refugees, but no intervention took place.

The question of intervention is thus complicated. But the principles identified by J. S. Mill 150 years ago still have moral and legal purchase. Because the globe is still far short of a global community, national security remains decisive. At the same time, we want to respect the human dignity of persons and the self-determination of communities, so that people and nations have a right to be free and safe. These principles, at times conflicting, produce standards both for and against intervention, for sometimes overriding or disregarding nonintervention and for sometimes adhering to the nonintervention norm. They specify the content of abstract moral principles of respecting rights and assessing costs—telling us whose rights are relevant and what considerations count when balancing potential consequences with moral intentions. They also give direction to the just war standards of necessity and proportionality by telling us the purposes (necessity for "what") and bases (proportionally to "what") for the use of force.

This "debate" with J. S. Mill has shown that nonintervention and intervention are two sides of the same coin. Some of the very strongest reasons to abide by a strict form of the nonintervention doctrine that protects national sovereignty are provided by a commitment to *humanitarian protection*. It is only with secure national borders that peoples can exercise the right to protect themselves as free citizens. On the other hand, this very principle of humanitarian protection, when applied in different contexts, provides justifications for overriding the principle of nonintervention and intervening to limit sovereignty. So, too, *self-determination* requires nonintervention; but rescuing an oppressed national minority can justify disregarding nonintervention. And vital *national security*, self-defense, can justify intervention and, in other circumstances, nonintervention.

But the principles are not completely symmetrical. There are good reasons not to intervene that do not, when reversed, justify intervention. Economic factors, such as financial costs, can justify nonintervention by a state, but profit certainly does not justify intervention. Similarly, security or strategic interests can justify nonintervention, but merely enhancing security or the balance of power does not justify intervention (despite its long tradition as excuse for intervention). Because the international community is inherently decentralized, global goods and bads are produced by national action. We lack a world government that could make rights and duties truly symmetrical.

No one better captured this dual logic than Mill in his famous argument against and for intervention, presented in his short essay "A Few Words on Non-Intervention," published in *Fraser's Magazine* in 1859. In the century and a half since, it has become the touchstone in debates over the vices and virtues of intervention.

By expanding on Mill, we include all races, religions, and cultures that respect the rights of others. In today's world, unlike Mill's, we actually see each other as fellow human beings, and we have institutions that stretch across national borders. But before turning to this modern impact, let us review Mill's contribution and its limitations.

MILLIAN INTERVENTION

Mill has sketched out a powerful moral geography of when to and when not to intervene, including numerous circumstances that would favor overriding or disregarding nonintervention. No international moralist who subscribes to principles of humanitarian protection, self-determination, and national security can neglect his arguments for ethical intervention.

He makes a number of major contributions. First, his method of practical reason warns policy makers that formulae cannot be abstractly applied—each conclusion is case specific. General patterns can be inferred, but their ethical significance comes from their specific application to a specific case.

Mill's truly outstanding contribution to international ethics is thus not his systematic ideal theory, of which there is little and even less that he does not contradict. Instead, it is his practical judgments that repeatedly qualify general precepts in the name of general utility and individual dignity, neither of which can be rightly understood absent a particular case. Mill favors democracy and representation, but only for peoples who are capable of exercising those freedoms well. He favors national self-determination, but only for peoples who have truly become one nation. Even then he can recommend that some nations, such as the Basques or the Bretons, should stay part of their larger political communities for "protection" or "dignity and power." Rather than "to sulk on his rocks, the half-savage relic of past times," these nationals should sublimate their nationalism in a larger unit.[1] Every general proposition is contingent, sometimes balancing competing values of human welfare, self-determination, and national security, always shaped by what is possible and beneficial in the particular circumstances. For these reasons, despite the merits of nonintervention, Mill finds that intervention is sometimes both right and feasible.

Equally important, Mill's practical reason outlines an array of varying ethics of intervention that override or disregard nonintervention. Modern discourse tends to measure all interventions as if they were humanitarian interventions. Some then meet the casualty threshold, and others do not. Concern for casualties is always relevant—theirs and ours. But an exclusive

---

1. John Stuart Mill, *Considerations on Representative Government,* in *Essays on Politics and Society,* ed. John M. Robson (Toronto: University of Toronto Press; London: Routledge and Kegan Paul, 1977), 363–364 (*CW* 19).

concern for casualties flattens and impoverishes the variety of moral discourse that Mill outlined.

For example, the debate over Kosovo was distorted from a case of disregard to one of overriding. A claim to self-determining independence was transferred into a plea for arresting genocide or halting crimes against humanity. Typically, proponents of intervention highlighted Milošević's violent repression in Kosovo, his record of crimes against humanity in Bosnia and Croatia, and the strong likelihood that he would inflict similar devastation in Kosovo. The critics then reasonably replied that the Kosovo Liberation Army had also committed atrocities and that the "West" had done nothing to stop atrocities equally bad, if not worse, elsewhere, such as in Cambodia in the 1970s.[2] What is missing from the debate is that Kosovars, who made up 78 percent of the pre-expulsion population, demanded to rule themselves as an independent nation. Missing the national self-determination claim misses the essence of the case.

There is at least one good reason for this distortion. Contemporary international law does not allow armed rescue to liberate a nation. It does legitimize forcible international action, with Security Council authorization, to stop crimes specified by RtoP. But that does not mean that self-determination should not be addressed—preferably peaceably, through mediation before resistance provokes genocide, ethnic cleansing, crimes against humanity, or war crimes.

In short, those who craft interventionist and noninterventionist arguments should and can draw on Mill, but they will

2. Among the best of these two literatures are, respectively, Samantha Power, *A Problem from Hell: America and the Age of Genocide* (New York: Basic, 2002), chapter 12; and David Gibbs, *First Do No Harm: Humanitarian Intervention and the Destruction of Yugoslavia* (Nashville: Vanderbilt University Press, 2009), chapter 7.

want to appreciate the distinctions he draws. They should then develop a more convincing set of criteria for when such interventions are likely to do more good than harm.

Judging from the actual historical record, Mill makes a reasonable case that nonintervention should be overridden both to prevent the recurrence of aggressive war and to end protracted civil war. Moreover, the interdependencies of globalization make these two reasons even more persuasive than they were in the nineteenth century, if only because of wider consensus on human rights, greater lethality of war, and the ways in which the world economy fuels civil wars by providing a large "sovereignty" premium to whoever wins and encourages armed rebellion through the prospect of international rescue.[3]

But Mill's arguments are not completely coherent. The more extensive list of examples Mill invokes reveals more complexity than he recounts, and in each case that complexity leans against the interventionist conclusions he reaches.

Overriding nonintervention in internationalized civil wars is problematic if only because ideologies tend to display less consistency than would justify intervention in the name of ideological solidarity, as Queen Elizabeth's campaigns for Protestantism and the modern Cold War interventions revealed. Disregarding nonintervention in national liberations and counterinterventions also raises problems and requires clearer doctrines than we now have, including rules for legitimate procedures of self-administration that test whether full independence is indeed morally required.

The case for imperial annexation is made problematic because

3. This includes the ability to borrow on sovereign credit, renegotiate investment and raw-material contracts, and obtain foreign aid, as detailed by Thomas Pogge in *World Poverty and Human Rights* (Cambridge: Polity, 2002). See also my discussion of this topic in Chapter 1.

local anarchy is rooted in ills inflicted as much by previous informal interference as by local "barbarism." But it does raise for us the important questions of what to do about nonsurgical interventions, and the need for a *jus post bellum*, discussed in the previous chapter. Reconstructive occupations raise both material and moral costs that may not be worth incurring unless mediation in protracted civil wars can work by eliciting consent and assisting transformative peacebuilding. That, as I discussed in the previous chapter, depends both on the local balance of forces and well-designed peacebuilding operations. And complexity recommends multilateral authorization as the first step for every intervention.

A NEW WORLD ORDER?

World orders change. Nationalism made imperialism obsolete by making it too costly and too illegitimate.[4] Nuclear weapons reduced the likelihood of world war by lowering the costs of inflicting astounding casualties that would deter rational adversaries.[5] Intervention is now subject to contrary currents. The

---

4. For imperialism and nationalism, see Michael Doyle, *Empires* (Ithaca, NY: Cornell University Press, 1986); Miles Kahler, *Decolonization in Britain and France* (Princeton: Princeton University Press, 1984); Daniel Philpott, *Revolutions in Sovereignty* (Princeton: Princeton University Press, 2001); a valuable account of why counterinsurgency fails more since 1918 than it did before by Paul McDonald, "Retribution Must Succeed Rebellion: The Colonial Origins of Counterinsurgency Failure," *International Organization* 67 (2013), 253–286; and an equally valuable account of how the international system favors self-determination and smaller states by Ryan Griffiths, "Secession and the Invisible Hand of the International System," *Review of International Studies* (2014), 1–23.

5. Kenneth Waltz, "The Spread of Nuclear Weapons: More Would Be Better," *Adelphi Papers*, no. 171 (London: IISS, 1981).

end of Cold War bipolarity made ideological and national security intervention much less likely than when every communist gain was seen as a capitalist, free world loss. Unipolarity of
the 1990s made intervention less costly, and thus more likely.
The Cold War incentive to intervene fell, but the risk of opposition by another great power fell as well.

The pattern of interventions per year in Table 3 reflects some
of those forces at work.[6] The rate of interventions fell from the
Napoleonic Wars (1.71) to the interwar period between World
Wars I and II (0.87), indicating perhaps either the emergence
of the norm of nonintervention or the increased capacity of
formerly weak societies to resist intervention. But the pressures
of war raised the rate of intervention, and Cold War competition drove the rate up again (1.65). Table 4 indicates that nonliberals intervened more than liberals in the nineteenth and
twentieth centuries, with the exception of the immediate pre–
World War I period and near the end of the Cold War. This
may have reflected the greater salience of the nonintervention
norm to liberals. At the end of the Cold War, when liberals
began to intervene (slightly) more, this last change in rates was
perhaps pushed by the commitment to humanitarian protection felt by liberal publics.

Today, despite the end of the Cold War and the beginnings
of a gradual shift toward a multipolar order, trends favor intervention, and thus increase the need for better standards.

Human rights are now global. The rights to equal respect and
autonomy, once barely accorded by Europeans to fellow European nationals, are now global. The two world wars and the
Holocaust brought home even to the richest and most powerful

6. These data are drawn from a study of patterns in intervention that Camille Strauss-Kahn and I are conducting. Data are in Appendix 2.

Table 3

Interventions per Year

			TOTAL	1815–1850	1850–1900	1900–WWI	WWI	WWI–WW2	WW2	WW2–1991	1991–2010
Number of cases per year			1.713	1.714	1.660	1.067	8.000	0.870	7.200	1.652	0.579
Liberal	Success	Empire	0.692	0.343	0.860	0.667	3.500	0.261	3.000	0.630	0.316
		Autocracy	0.549	0.314	0.680	0.667	2.750	0.174	2.600	0.443	0.263
		War	0.374	0.171	0.580	0.600	2.250	0.087	2.200	0.109	0.105
		None	0.067	0.057	0.020	0.000	0.000	0.087	0.000	0.152	0.053
	Failure		0.092	0.086	0.180	0.000	0.000	0.000	0.400	0.087	0.000
			0.097	0.086	0.080	0.067	0.500	0.043	0.400	0.109	0.053
			0.144	0.029	0.180	0.000	0.750	0.087	0.400	0.217	0.053
Nonliberal	Success	Empire	1.021	1.371	0.800	0.400	4.500	0.609	4.200	1.022	0.263
		Autocracy	0.585	0.800	0.480	0.200	2.000	0.391	3.200	0.478	0.211
		War	0.374	0.371	0.300	0.200	2.000	0.304	3.200	0.239	0.000
		None	0.282	0.314	0.140	0.000	1.000	0.261	2.200	0.283	0.158
	Failure		0.185	0.143	0.140	0.133	0.750	0.087	1.400	0.174	0.105
			0.036	0.114	0.040	0.000	0.000	0.000	0.000	0.000	0.053
			0.436	0.571	0.320	0.200	2.500	0.217	1.000	0.543	0.053

Table 4
Trends Controlled for Years and Number of Liberal Regimes

		TOTAL	1815–1850	1850–1900	1900–WW_1	WW_1	WW_1–WW_2	WW_2	WW_2–1991	1991–2010
Number of cases		0.035	0.214	0.128	0.037	0.276	0.030	0.248	0.034	0.012
Liberal										
Success		0.014	0.043	0.066	0.023	0.121	0.009	0.103	0.013	0.006
	Empire	0.011	0.039	0.052	0.023	0.095	0.006	0.090	0.008	0.005
	Oppressive	0.008	0.021	0.045	0.021	0.078	0.003	0.076	0.002	0.002
	War	0.001	0.007	0.002	0.000	0.000	0.003	0.000	0.003	0.001
	None	0.002	0.011	0.014	0.000	0.000	0.000	0.014	0.002	0.000
		0.002	0.011	0.006	0.002	0.017	0.001	0.014	0.002	0.001
Failure		0.003	0.004	0.014	0.000	0.026	0.003	0.014	0.004	0.001
Nonliberal										
Success		0.021	0.171	0.062	0.014	0.155	0.021	0.145	0.021	0.005
	Empire	0.012	0.100	0.037	0.007	0.069	0.013	0.110	0.010	0.004
	Oppressive	0.008	0.046	0.023	0.007	0.069	0.010	0.110	0.005	0.000
	War	0.006	0.039	0.011	0.000	0.034	0.009	0.076	0.006	0.003
	None	0.004	0.018	0.011	0.005	0.026	0.003	0.048	0.004	0.002
		0.001	0.014	0.003	0.000	0.000	0.000	0.000	0.000	0.001
Failure		0.009	0.071	0.025	0.007	0.086	0.007	0.034	0.011	0.001

the experience of devastation that made them realize that all have a stake in a more humane global order. The civil rights movement in the US, the egalitarian thrust of communism, and the rise of the developing world discredited racial and religious bigotry. It made the assertion of racial, religious, or ethnic superiority suspect as a justification to rule, kill, or neglect. The Universal Declaration of Human Rights (1948) began the process that announced a new consensus on human dignity.[7]

Interdependence and globalization also make a noteworthy difference. Globalization has connected the world in both material and ideational ways. Kwame Anthony Appiah retells a powerful modern parable when he recounts an example from Adam Smith, described in the great Scottish political economist's *Theory of Moral Sentiments* (1759).[8] Smith imagines an earthquake in China with enormous loss of life. In 1759, such a "man of humanity in Europe" would have been stirred to reflect on the suffering, and, perhaps, losses to world trade, but he would have returned untroubled to his daily life. But tell that same person that he would suffer the amputation of his little finger the next morning, and he would have experienced a dreadful and sleepless night. "Provided he never saw them," Smith opined, "he will snore with the most profound security over the ruin of a hundred million of his fellow brethren."[9] The message is not just about self-absorption but also shortsightedness. In

---

7. Mary Ann Glendon, *A World Made New: Eleanor Roosevelt and the Universal Declaration of Human Rights* (New York: Random House, 2001); Samuel Moyn, *The Last Utopia: Human Rights in History* (Cambridge: Harvard University Press, 2010); and Stéphane Hessel (adviser to the French delegation at the formulation of the UDHR), *Time for Outrage* (London: Charles Glass, 2011).

8. Kwame Anthony Appiah, *Cosmopolitanism* (New York: Norton, 2006), 156.

9. Adam Smith, *Theory of Moral Sentiments,* ed. Knud Haakonssen (Cambridge: Cambridge University Press, 2002), 157.

today's age, we see on television or on the Internet or hear on the radio the losses of our fellow brethren—and so we feel them. In addition, the world today is informed by an NGO community dedicated to global purposes and prepared to inform, advocate, and organize, even where national interests are opposed or unclear.[10] As Michael Barnett has argued, we have been experiencing an "empire of humanity" managed by an "empire" of humanitarians.[11]

Intervention, moreover, has become much less costly to interveners, at least to the United States (and soon to other advanced economies). Boots on the ground are as costly as they have ever been (perhaps more so with rising military personnel costs).[12] But command of the air, including bombing, coordinated with indigenous ground forces, brought down the Taliban in 2001 and toppled Muammar Qaddafi in 2011. Drone attacks on terrorist leadership targets in Pakistan or Yemen have reduced the costs of military intervention. (Whether these kinds of interventions are effective in the long run is a very different question, discussed in Chapter 5.)

All of this would threaten overintervention or imperialism were it not for other critical developments: nationalism and its concomitant, multilateral authorization. Where nation and territory coincide, nationalism has both greatly raised the human and material costs of conquest and thus reinforced the legal claims of the state to exclusive sovereignty over its territory.

10. Margaret Keck and Kathryn Sikkink, *Activists Beyond Borders* (Ithaca, NY: Cornell University Press, 1998).

11. Michael Barnett, *Empire of Humanity: A History of Humanitarianism* (Ithaca, NY: Cornell University Press, 2011).

12. New York Times editorial, "Putting Military Pay on the Table," *New York Times*, December 1, 2013. Military pay has doubled in the past fifteen years.

Given all the uncertainties and the difficulties of transnational comprehension, the starting point of any intervention must be local.

No intervention should be contemplated unless it is requested by those in most need of it. Victims of genocide or crimes against humanity; citizens held hostage; oppressed minorities; long-suffering factions in a protracted civil war: these are the proper voices to be heard first.[13]

Potential interveners will still need to decide whether the costs are too high or whether allies can be found or other measures can address the legitimate demands for assistance short of armed force. The judgment is rarely straightforward. Difficulties of interpretation will arise and information may be conflicting. Consideration will also need be paid to precedents that will be set.

Respecting national sovereign equality thus also requires multilateralism, because sovereign consent is what underlies the legitimacy and legality of the rules of the UN Charter. Obtaining multilateral authorization not only complies with international law, it also reduces risks of exploitation by requiring deliberation and more impartial authorization.[14] It also improves the prospect of leaving behind a self-sustaining peace that allows genuine self-determination and sovereign capacity to rule. This potentially avoids the three Millian negative con-

13. They also get to veto certain methods of intervention, as the Libyans did when they demanded "no boots on the ground."

14. For background on the value of considering the qualities of the intervener in the decision of whether to authorize, see James Pattison, *Humanitarian Intervention and the Responsibility to Protect: Who Should Intervene* (New York: Oxford University Press, 2010). For cautions regarding the reliability of multilateral authorization during the earlier multilateral interventions in the Cold War, see Anne Orford, *International Authority and the Responsibility to Protect* (New York: Cambridge University Press, 2011).

sequences of military intervention: subsequent civil war, despotism, and imperialism.

Interventions will always be fraught with moral uncertainty. We usually address the problems of *ex ante* uncertainty, incomplete information, and motivated bias in interpretation through *procedural* standards. We subject these judgments to structured deliberation and contestation in the presence of impartial (or at least multiple) decision makers—in the classic phrase, in order to reflect "a decent respect for the opinions of humankind."

On the one hand, under current international law, unilateral intervention is illegal. On the other, multilateral intervention, if designed to prevent an escalating threat to international security, is not only legal but normative: it should also be considered whenever threats arise. The process of multilateral decision making embedded in the UN Security Council by Article 39 of Chapter VII gives the Council the authority to—indeed, requires that the Council "shall"—"determine the existence of *any* threat to the peace, breach of the peace or act of aggression" and take whatever action—including coercive embargoes and forcible measures by land, air, or sea—that the Council sees fit.[15] The Council is specifically empowered not merely to respond to breaches of the peace and acts of aggression that have occurred, but also to address "threats" before they materialize—and not just imminent threats, but "any" threats. Such coercive measures that the Council approves are automatically binding on all UN member states.[16] So anytime a state can get a vote of nine out of fifteen members of the Security Council, including the support (or at least abstention) of the permanent five mem-

15. Charter of the United Nations (San Francisco, 1945), 1 U.N.T.S. XVI, Art. 39 (emphasis added).
16. Ibid., Art. 25.

bers—the United States, Russia, France, the United Kingdom, and China—then fully legal action may be undertaken.[17]

Procedural legitimacy is enhanced by additional multilateral deliberation and by the fact that a national government seeking authorization for intervention must persuade at least eight other states to vote for its cause. The diversity of the other Council member states requires that the arguments for intervention must appeal beyond the narrow confines of interest, ideology, and culture of a single state. At a minimum, the Security Council's Permanent Five includes one hyperpower and four lesser powers; it includes an Asian representative (China) and Western states; it represents Confucian, Orthodox, and Christian religious traditions; and statist (China and Russia), more laissez-faire (United States), and social democratic (France and the United Kingdom) economies. In addition to the Permanent Five, the Security Council includes ten elected and often much less powerful, less wealthy states, which, by tradition, include states from Latin America, Africa, and the remainder of Asia and Europe. Any seven of those ten can block a Security Council authorization.[18]

I do not wish to portray this process as anything close to an "ideal speech situation."[19] The Security Council is an arena for

17. See UN Secretary-General, *Report of the Secretary-General's High-level Panel on Threats, Challenges and Change,* UN Doc. A/59/565 (December 2, 2004), 63–67. The panel included such eminent statespersons as former US national security adviser Brent Scowcroft, former UN high commissioner for refugees Sadako Ogata, and others. The panel reaffirmed traditional just war standards of proportionality and last resort as substantive guidelines.

18. See Thomas Franck, *Fairness in International Law and Institutions* (Oxford: Clarendon, 1995), for a discussion of the "global jury."

19. As, for example, outlined in Jürgen Habermas, *The Theory of Communicative Action,* trans. Thomas McCarthy (Boston: Beacon, 1984), where fair procedure becomes a formal guarantee of fair outcome.

real politics when important issues arise. Pressure in all its varieties is exercised by the powerful states on those less powerful (including, in famous cases, large sums of foreign aid), and some states, most obviously the United States, have "outside options" to act unilaterally (though without legal authorization and multilateral legitimacy) that inherently give additional weight to their preferences.[20] Yet it would be an error to view the Council as a mere servant of US interests. The failure of the United States to secure a second Council vote against Iraq in 2003—one that would have authorized an armed intervention—despite a large investment of positive and negative inducements by the Bush administration, is evidence that the process is no rubber stamp for the United States.

The Security Council process seems a neat and satisfactory solution but for two problems: First, the Council has, in numerous instances in the past, behaved irresponsibly by failing to authorize the use of adequate force when intervention was justified by the evidence of atrocities submitted to it. Second, the Council lacks substantively adequate standards to guide its deliberations concerning when it should authorize force.

With respect to the first problem, I have in mind the failure to act in a timely way to address two humanitarian emergencies, Kosovo and Rwanda, and various lesser decisions.[21] As schol-

---

20. On the hegemonic possibilities of US influence in the UN Security Council, see José E. Alvarez, *International Organizations as Law-makers* (New York: Oxford University Press, 2005), 199–216; and Erik Voeten, "The Strategic Use of Liberal Internationalism: Libya and the U.N. Sanctions, 1992–2003," *International Organization* 59 (2005), 500–503.

21. Lesser decisions include failures to renew the mandated Macedonian peace operation because Macedonia had established relations with Taiwan, leading to Chinese retaliation with a veto. But let me hasten to add that China has cast by far the fewest vetoes between 1946 and 1997 (a total of four). The USSR/Russia and the US lead the league with 116 and 72, respectively. The total is 202 in that period. See Sydney D. Bailey and Sam Daws, *The Procedure*

ars Tom Farer, Robert Keohane, and Allen Buchanan have argued, the Security Council sometimes also fails to take into account the legitimate security needs of states when the Council is stymied by, for example, an irresponsible veto.[22] When should states feel that forcible action is justified *without* Security Council authorization? Procedural standards are not a sufficient answer. In extreme circumstances (when the Security Council should have acted and did not), coalitions of states and even individual states may need to act without multilateral authorization.

With respect to the second problem, rule of law and global public comity require substantive deliberation in the Security Council. The Council itself requires standards for decisions that go beyond any measure that can assemble the requisite nine votes out of fifteen. Not every justification can be deemed legitimate intervention. Similarly, states that decide to bypass the

---

of the U.N. Security Council, 3rd ed. (Oxford: Clarendon, 1998), 231–239. As important, permanent members have threatened to use the veto, and the threat is often enough to derail action on an issue.

22. Farer makes a persuasive case for derogation to regional organization and even individual state action. He adds that in order to avoid exploitative recourses to unjustified force, such derogations should be subject to retroactive judicial assessment by the International Court of Justice. See Tom Farer, "A Paradigm of Legitimate Intervention," in *Enforcing Restraint: Collective Intervention in Internal Conflicts,* ed. Lori Fisler Damrosch (New York: Council on Foreign Relations Press, 1993), 316. Keohane and Buchanan, in addition to deepening Farer's analysis, make a case for derogating such decisions to coalitions of democratic states whose constitutional procedures and democratic principles arguably make them better guarantors of humanitarian principles. See Allen Buchanan and Robert O. Keohane, "The Preventive Use of Force: A Cosmopolitan Institutional Proposal," *Ethics and International Affairs* 18 (2004), 1–22. Cornelius Bjola makes similar arguments, focusing on communicative deliberation. See Cornelius Bjola, "Legitimating the Use of Force in International Politics: A Communicative Action Perspective," *European Journal of International Relations* 11 (2005), 266–303.

Security Council, or take preventive measures without Council authorization, will need to justify those decisions to both international and domestic publics.[23]

There are standards we can derive from this record that suggest how the Security Council should decide whether the next putative emergency justifies armed intervention. Considerable progress has been made in identifying the standards that should trigger a Responsibility to Protect by the Security Council, and in describing considerations that should be taken into account in authorizing forcible measures.[24] Rather than reinvent the standards, our real task is to refine existing standards and show how they apply in contentious cases, judging which cases should serve as positive and negative models for preventive action.[25]

RtoP, with its identification of genocide, crimes against humanity, war crimes, and ethnic cleansing as triggering events for responsibility, has taken a large step in this direction. These norms first of all identify the responsibilities of states to protect their own citizens, thereby affirming legitimate national sovereignty. They add norms of assistance to international politics, including priorities for scarce aid. They also identify norms of legitimate forcible intervention.

23. In *Striking First: Preemption and Prevention in International Conflict* (Princeton: Princeton University Press, 2008), 156–159, I suggest that preventive actions lacking Security Council legal authorization should be subject to review by both domestic commissions and the Security Council (operating with a procedural vote, absent the veto). A similar review should occur for humanitarian and other interventions, lacking Security Council authorization.

24. See GA Res. 60/1, *2005 World Summit Outcome*, UN Doc. A/RES/60/1 at paras. 38–41 (October 24, 2005).

25. For another example of this idea, see Harold Koh's recent refrain on "translation." See http://yaledailynews.com/blog/2013/01/30/koh-shares-state-department-experiences/.

They can be thought of as norms decreed by the entire UN membership for the guidance of the Security Council, instructing the Council how it should interpret "threats to the peace" broadly, with attention to the effects domestic crimes have on international security.

The potentially elastic and expansive character of the RtoP and international security norms are circumscribed by the strict procedural guidelines of Security Council approval. Together, these are both powerful enforcers of basic rights and barriers to imperial exploitation. The practice of UN-authorized peace-building identifies the circumstances that give a reasonable prospect of avoiding a return to civil war and autocratic oppression.

However, the cost is real. Global circumstances favor more intervention. The standards of RtoP have emerged as the new global floor below which states cannot sink with impunity. At the same time, procedural standards require the consensus of the five permanent members of the Security Council and at least four of the elected members. This produces a significant danger of underintervention, illustrated by the current situation in Syria, where 160,000 have died and six million have been displaced. And the UN has yet, as of mid-2014, to sanction any party or exercise concerted pressure to facilitate a negotiated solution to the civil war.

The political contest, balancing ends and means, will continue. If it is done well, lives will be saved; if it is done poorly, nations will be oppressed and innocents will suffer.

APPENDIX 1
John Stuart Mill's
"A Few Words on Non-Intervention"

[111] There is a country in Europe, equal to the greatest in extent of dominion, far exceeding any other in wealth, and in the power that wealth bestows, the declared principle of whose foreign policy is, to let other nations alone. No country apprehends or affects to apprehend from it any aggressive designs. Power, from of old, is wont to encroach upon the weak, and to quarrel for ascendancy with those who are as strong as itself. Not so this nation. It will hold its own, it will not submit to encroachment, but if other nations do not meddle with it, it will not meddle with them. Any attempt it makes to exert influence over them, even by persuasion, is rather in the service of others, than of itself: to mediate in the quarrels which break out between foreign States, to arrest obstinate civil wars, to reconcile belligerents, to intercede for mild treatment of the vanquished, or finally, to procure the abandonment of some national crime and scandal to humanity, such as the slave-trade. Not only does this nation desire no benefit to itself at the expense of others, it desires none in which all others do not as freely participate. It makes no treaties stipulating for separate commercial advantages. If the aggressions of barbarians force it to a successful war, and its victorious arms put it in a position to command liberty of trade, whatever it demands for itself it demands for all mankind. The cost of the war is its own; the fruits it shares in fraternal equality with the whole human

race. Its own ports and commerce are free as the air and the sky: all its neighbours have full liberty to resort to it, paying either no duties, or, if any, generally a mere equivalent for what is paid by its own citizens, nor does it concern itself though they, on their part, keep all to themselves, and persist in the most jealous and narrow-minded exclusion of its merchants and goods.

A nation adopting this policy is a novelty in the world; so much so, it would appear, that many are unable to believe it when they see it. By one of the practical paradoxes which often meet us in human affairs, it is this nation which finds itself, in respect of its foreign policy, held up to obloquy as the type of egoism and selfishness; as a nation which thinks of nothing but of out-witting and out-generalling its neighbours. An enemy, or a self-fancied rival who had been distanced in the race, might be conceived to give vent to such an accusation in a moment of ill-temper. But that it should be accepted by lookers-on, and should pass into a popular doctrine, is enough to surprise even those who have best sounded the depths of human prejudice. Such, however, is the estimate of the [112] foreign policy of England most widely current on the Continent. Let us not flatter ourselves that it is merely the dishonest pretence of enemies, or of those who have their own purposes to serve by exciting odium against us, a class including all the Protectionist writers, and the mouthpieces of all the despots and of the Papacy. The more blameless and laudable our policy might be, the more certainly we might count on its being misrepresented and railed at by these worthies. Unfortunately the belief is not confined to those whom they can influence, but is held with all the tenacity of a prejudice, by innumerable persons free from interested bias. So strong a hold has it on their minds, that when an Englishman attempts to remove it, all their habitual politeness does not enable them to disguise their utter unbelief in his disclaimer. They are firmly persuaded that no word is said, nor act done, by English statesmen in reference to foreign affairs, which has not for its motive principle some peculiarly English interest. Any profession of the contrary appears to them too ludicrously transparent an attempt to impose upon them. Those most friendly to us think they make a great concession in admitting that the fault may possibly be less with the English people, than with the English Government and aristocracy. We do not even receive credit from them for following our own interest with a straightforward recognition of honesty as the best policy. They believe that we have always other objects than those we avow; and the most far-fetched and unplausible suggestion of a selfish purpose appears to them better entitled to credence than anything so utterly incredible as our disinterestedness. Thus, to give one instance among many, when we taxed ourselves twenty millions (a prodigious sum in their estimation) to get rid of negro slavery, and, for the same object, perilled, as everybody thought, destroyed as many thought, the very existence of our West Indian colonies, it was, and still is, believed, that our fine professions were but to delude the world, and that by this self-sacrificing behaviour we were endeavouring to gain some hidden object, which could neither be conceived nor described, in the way of pulling down other nations. The fox who had lost his tail had an intelligible interest in persuading his neighbours to rid themselves of theirs: but we, it is thought by *our* neighbours, cut off our own magnificent brush, the largest and finest of all, in hopes of reaping some inexplicable advantage from inducing others to do the same.

It is foolish attempting to despise all this—persuading ourselves that it is not our fault, and that those who disbelieve *us* would not believe though one should rise from the dead. Na-

tions, like individuals, ought to suspect some fault in themselves when they find they are generally worse thought of than
they think they deserve, and they may well know that they are
somehow in fault when almost everybody but themselves thinks
them crafty and hypocritical. It is not solely because England
[113] has been more successful than other nations in gaining
what they are all aiming at, that they think she must be following after it with a more ceaseless and a more undivided
chase. This indeed is a powerful predisposing cause, inclining
and preparing them for the belief. It is a natural supposition
that those who win the prize have striven for it; that superior
success must be the fruit of more unremitting endeavour; and
where there is an obvious abstinence from the ordinary arts
employed for distancing competitors, and they are distanced
nevertheless, people are fond of believing that the means employed must have been arts still more subtle and profound. This
preconception makes them look out in all quarters for indica-
tions to prop up the selfish explanation of our conduct. If our
ordinary course of action does not favour this interpretation,
they watch for exceptions to our ordinary course, and regard
these as the real index to the purposes within. They moreover
accept literally all the habitual expressions by which we represent ourselves as worse than we are; expressions often heard
from English statesmen, next to never from those of any other
country—partly because Englishmen, beyond all the rest of the
human race, are so shy of professing virtues that they will even
profess vices instead; and partly because almost all English
statesmen, while careless to a degree which no foreigner can
credit, respecting the impression they produce on foreigners,
commit the obtuse blunder of supposing that low objects are the
only ones to which the minds of their non-aristocratic fellow-

countrymen are amenable, and that it is always expedient, if not necessary, to place those objects in the foremost rank.

All, therefore, who either speak or act in the name of England, are bound by the strongest obligations, both of prudence and of duty, to avoid giving either of these handles for misconstruction: to put a severe restraint upon the mania of professing to act from meaner motives than those by which we are really actuated, and to beware of perversely or capriciously singling out some particular instance in which to act on a worse principle than that by which we are ordinarily guided. Both these salutary cautions our practical statesmen are, at the present time, flagrantly disregarding.

We are now in one of those critical moments, which do not occur once in a generation, when the whole turn of European events, and the course of European history for a long time to come, may depend on the conduct and on the estimation of England. At such a moment, it is difficult to say whether by their sins of speech or of action our statesmen are most effectually playing into the hands of our enemies, and giving most colour of justice to injurious misconception of our character and policy as a people.

To take the sins of speech first: What is the sort of language held in every oration which, during the present European crisis, any English minister, or almost any considerable public man, addresses to parliament or to his constituents? The eternal repetition of this shabby *refrain*—"We did not interfere, because no English interest was involved;" "We ought not to interfere where no English [114] interest is concerned." England is thus exhibited as a country whose most distinguished men are not ashamed to profess, as politicians, a rule of action which no one, not utterly base, could endure to be accused of as the maxim by which he guides his private life; not to move a finger for others unless he sees his private advantage in it. There is much to be said for the doctrine that a nation should be willing to assist its neighbours in throwing off oppression and gaining free institutions. Much also may be said by those who maintain that one nation is incompetent to judge and act for another, and that each should be left to help itself, and seek advantage or submit to disadvantage as it can and will. But of all attitudes which a nation can take up on the subject of intervention, the meanest and worst is to profess that it interferes only when it can serve its own objects by it. Every other nation is entitled to say, "It seems, then, that non-interference is not a matter of principle with you. When you abstain from interference, it is not because you think it wrong. You have no objection to interfere, only it must not be for the sake of those you interfere with; they must not suppose that you have any regard for their good. The good of others is not one of the things you care for; but you are willing to meddle, if by meddling you can gain anything for yourselves." Such is the obvious interpretation of the language used.

There is scarcely any necessity to say, writing to Englishmen, that this is not what our rulers and politicians really mean. Their language is not a correct exponent of their thoughts. They mean a part only of what they seem to say. They do mean to disclaim interference for the sake of doing good to foreign nations. They are quite sincere and in earnest in repudiating this. But the other half of what their words express, a willingness to meddle if by doing so they can promote any interest of England, they do not mean. The thought they have in their minds, is not the interest of England, but her security. What they would say, is, that they are ready to act when England's safety is threatened, or any of her interests hostilely or unfairly endangered. This is no more than what all nations, sufficiently powerful for their own protection, do, and no one questions their right to do. It is the common right of self-defence. But if we mean this, why, in Heaven's name, do we take every possible opportunity of saying, instead of this, something exceedingly different? Not self-defence, but aggrandizement, is the sense which foreign listeners put upon our words. Not simply to protect what we have, and that merely against unfair arts, not against fair rivalry; but to add to it more and more without limit, is the purpose for which foreigners think we claim the liberty of intermeddling with them and their affairs. If our actions make it impossible for the most prejudiced observer to believe that we aim at or would accept any sort of mercantile monopolies, this has no effect on their minds but to make them think that we have chosen a more cunning way to the same end. It is a generally [115] accredited opinion among Continental politicians, especially those who think themselves particularly knowing, that the very existence of England depends upon the incessant acquisition of new markets for our manufactures; that the chase after these is an affair of life and death to us; and that we are at all times ready to trample on every obligation of public or international morality, when the alternative would be, pausing for a moment in that race. It would be superfluous to point out what profound ignorance and misconception of all the laws of national wealth, and all the facts of England's commercial condition, this opinion presupposes: but such ignorance and misconception are unhappily very general on the Continent; they are but slowly, if perceptibly, giving way before the advance of reason; and for generations, perhaps, to come, we shall be judged under their influence. Is it requiring too much from our practical politicians to wish that they would sometimes bear these things in mind? Does it answer any good purpose to express ourselves as if we did not scruple to profess that which we not merely scruple to do, but the bare idea of doing which never crosses our minds? Why should we abnegate the character we might with truth lay claim to, of being incomparably the most conscientious of all nations in our national acts? Of all countries which are sufficiently powerful to be capable of being dangerous to their neighbours, we are perhaps the only one whom mere scruples of conscience would suffice to deter from it. We are the only people among whom, by no class whatever of society, is the interest or glory of the nation considered to be any sufficient excuse for an unjust act; the only one which regards with jealousy and suspicion, and a proneness to hostile criticism, precisely those acts of its Government which in other countries are sure to be hailed with applause, those by which territory has been acquired, or political influence extended. Being in reality better than other nations, in at least the negative part of international morality, let us cease, by the language we use, to give ourselves out as worse.

But if we ought to be careful of our language, a thousand times more obligatory is it upon us to be careful of our deeds, and not suffer ourselves to be betrayed by any of our leading men into a line of conduct on some isolated point, utterly opposed to our habitual principles of action—conduct such that if it were a fair specimen of us, it would verify the calumnies of our worst enemies, and justify them in representing not only that we have no regard for the good of other nations, but that we actually think their good and our own incompatible, and will go all lengths to prevent others from realizing even an advantage in which we ourselves are to share. This pernicious, and, one can scarcely help calling it, almost insane blunder, we seem to be committing on the subject of the Suez Canal.

It is the universal belief in France that English influence at Constantinople, strenuously exerted to defeat this project, is the real and only invincible obstacle to its being carried into effect. And unhappily the public declarations of our present Prime Minister not only bear out this persuasion, but warrant the assertion that we [116] oppose the work because, in the opinion of our Government, it would be injurious to the interest of England. If such be the course we are pursuing, and such the motive of it, and if nations have duties, even negative ones, towards the weal of the human race, it is hard to say whether the folly or the immorality of our conduct is the most painfully conspicuous.

Here is a project, the practicability of which is indeed a matter in dispute, but of which no one has attempted to deny that, supposing it realized, it would give a facility to commerce, and consequently a stimulus to production, an encouragement to intercourse, and therefore to civilization, which would entitle it to a high rank among the great industrial improvements of modern times. The contriving of new means of abridging labour and economizing outlay in the operations of industry, is the object to which the larger half of all the inventive ingenuity of mankind is at present given up; and this scheme, if realized, will save, on one of the great highways of the world's traffic, the circumnavigation of a continent. An easy access of commerce is the main source of that material civilization, which, in the more backward regions of the earth, is the necessary condition and indispensable machinery of the moral; and this scheme reduces practically by one half, the distance, commercially speaking, between the self-improving nations of the world and the most important and valuable of the unimproving. The Atlantic Telegraph is esteemed an enterprise of world-wide importance because it abridges the transit of mercantile intelligence merely.

What the Suez Canal would shorten is the transport of the
goods themselves, and this to such an extent as probably to aug-
ment it manifold.

Let us suppose, then—for in the present day the hypothesis
is too un-English to be spoken of as anything more than a
supposition—let us suppose that the English nation saw in this
great benefit to the civilized and uncivilized world a danger
or damage to some peculiar interest of England. Suppose, for
example, that it feared, by shortening the road, to facilitate the
access of foreign navies to its Oriental possessions. The supposition imputes no ordinary degree of cowardice and imbecility
to the national mind; otherwise it could not but reflect that the
same thing which would facilitate the arrival of an enemy, would
facilitate also that of succor; that we have had French fleets in
the Eastern seas before now, and have fought naval battles with
them there, nearly a century ago; that if we ever became unable to defend India against them, we should assuredly have
them there without the aid of any canal; and that our power of
resisting an enemy does not depend upon putting a little more
or less of obstacle in the way of his coming, but upon the
amount of force which we are able to oppose to him when
come. Let us assume, however, that the success of the project
would do more harm to England [117] in some separate capacity, than the good which, as the chief commercial nation, she
would reap from the great increase of commercial intercourse.
Let us grant this: and I now ask, what then? Is there any morality, Christian or secular, which bears out a nation in keeping
all the rest of mankind out of some great advantage, because
the consequences of their obtaining it may be to itself, in some
imaginable contingency, a cause of inconvenience? Is a nation
at liberty to adopt as a practical maxim, that what is good for
the human race is bad for itself, and to withstand it accord-

ingly? What is this but to declare that its interest and that of mankind are incompatible—that, thus far at least, it is the enemy of the human race? And what ground has it of complaint if, in return, the human race determine to be *its* enemies? So wicked a principle, avowed and acted on by a nation, would entitle the rest of the world to unite in a league against it, and never to make peace until they had, if not reduced it to insignificance, at least sufficiently broken its power to disable it from ever again placing its own self-interest before the general prosperity of mankind.

There is no such base feeling in the British people. They are accustomed to see their advantage in forwarding, not in keeping back, the growth in wealth and civilization of the world. The opposition to the Suez Canal has never been a national opposition. With their usual indifference to foreign affairs, the public in general have not thought about it, but have left it, as (unless when particularly excited) they leave all the management of their foreign policy, to those who, from causes and reasons connected only with internal politics, happen for the time to be in office. Whatever has been done in the name of England in the Suez affair has been the act of individuals, mainly, it is probable, of one individual; scarcely any of his countrymen either prompting or sharing his purpose, and most of those who have paid any attention to the subject (unfortunately a very small number) being, to all appearance, opposed to him.

But (it is said) the scheme cannot be executed. If so, why concern ourselves about it? If the project can come to nothing, why profess gratuitous immorality and incur gratuitous odium to prevent it from being tried? Whether it will succeed or fail is a consideration totally irrelevant; except thus far, that if it is sure to fail, there is in our resistance to it the same immorality, and an additional amount of folly; since, on that supposition, we are parading to the world a belief that our interest is inconsistent with its good, while if the failure of the project would really be any benefit to us, we are certain of obtaining that benefit by merely holding our peace.

As a matter of private opinion, the present writer, so far as he has looked into the evidence, inclines to agree with those who think that the scheme cannot be executed, at least by the means and with the funds proposed. But this is a consideration for the shareholders. The British Government does not deem it any part of its business to prevent individuals, even British citizens, from wasting their [118] own money in unsuccessful speculations, though holding out no prospect of great public usefulness in the event of success. And if, though at the cost of their own property, they acted as pioneers to others, and the scheme, though a losing one to those who first undertook it, should, in the same or in other hands, realize the full expected amount of ultimate benefit to the world at large, it would not be the first nor the hundredth time that an unprofitable enterprise has had this for its final result.

There seems to be no little need that the whole doctrine of non-interference with foreign nations should be reconsidered, if it can be said to have as yet been considered as a really moral question at all. We have heard something lately about being willing to go to war for an idea. To go to war for an idea, if the war is aggressive, not defensive, is as criminal as to go to war for territory or revenue; for it is as little justifiable to force our ideas on other people, as to compel them to submit to our will in any other respect. But there assuredly are cases in which it is allowable to go to war, without having been ourselves attacked, or threatened with attack; and it is very important that nations should make up their minds in time, as to what these cases are.

There are few questions which more require to be taken in hand by ethical and political philosophers, with a view to establish some rule or criterion whereby the justifiableness of intervening in the affairs of other countries, and (what is sometimes fully as questionable) the justifiableness of refraining from intervention, may be brought to a definite and rational test. Whoever attempts this, will be led to recognise more than one fundamental distinction, not yet by any means familiar to the public mind, and in general quite lost sight of by those who write in strains of indignant morality on the subject. There is a great difference (for example) between the case in which the nations concerned are of the same, or something like the same, degree of civilization, and that in which one of the parties to the situation is of a high, and the other of a very low, grade of social improvement. To suppose that the same international customs, and the same rules of international morality, can obtain between one civilized nation and another, and between civilized nations and barbarians, is a grave error, and one which no statesman can fall into, however it may be with those who, from a safe and unresponsible position, criticise statesmen. Among many reasons why the same rules cannot be applicable to situations so different, the two following are among the most important. In the first place, the rules of ordinary international morality imply reciprocity. But barbarians will not reciprocate. They cannot be depended on for observing any rules. Their minds are not capable of so great an effort, nor their will sufficiently under the influence of distant motives. In the next place, nations which are still barbarous have not got beyond the period during which it is likely to be for their benefit that they should be conquered and held in subjection by foreigners. Independence and nationality, so essential to the due growth and development of a people further advanced in [119] improvement, are generally impediments to theirs. The sacred duties which civilized nations owe to the independence and nationality of each other, are not binding towards those to whom nationality and independence are either a certain evil, or at best a questionable good. The Romans were not the most clean-handed of conquerors, yet would it have been better for Gaul and Spain, Numidia and Dacia, never to have formed part of the Roman Empire? To characterize any conduct whatever towards a barbarous people as a violation of the law of nations, only shows that he who so speaks has never considered the subject. A violation of great principles of morality it may easily be; but barbarians have no rights as a *nation*, except a right to such treatment as may, at the earliest possible period, fit them for becoming one. The only moral laws for the relation between a civilized and a barbarous government, are the universal rules of morality between man and man.

The criticisms, therefore, which are so often made upon the conduct of the French in Algeria, or of the English in India, proceed, it would seem, mostly on a wrong principle. The true standard by which to judge their proceedings never having been laid down, they escape such comment and censure as might really have an improving effect, while they are tried by a standard which can have no influence on those practically engaged in such transactions, knowing as they do that it cannot, and if it could, ought not to be observed, because no human being would be the better, and many much the worse, for its observance. A civilized government cannot help having barbarous neighbours: when it has, it cannot always content itself with a defensive position, one of mere resistance to aggression. After a longer or shorter interval of forbearance, it either finds itself obliged to conquer them, or to assert so much authority over them, and so break their spirit, that they gradually sink into a state of dependence upon itself, and when that time arrives, they are indeed no longer formidable to it, but it has had so much to do with setting up and pulling down their governments, and they have grown so accustomed to lean on it, that it has become morally responsible for all evil it allows them to do. This is the history of the relations of the British Government with the native States of India. It never was secure in its own Indian possessions until it had reduced the military power of those States to a nullity. But a despotic government only exists by its military power. When we had taken away theirs, we were forced, by the necessity of the case, to offer them ours instead of it. To enable them to dispense with large armies of their own, we bound ourselves to place at their disposal, and they bound themselves to receive, such an amount of military force as made us in fact masters of the country. We engaged that this force should fulfil the purposes of a force, by defending the prince against all foreign and internal enemies. But being thus assured of the protection of a civilized power, and freed from the fear of internal rebellion or foreign conquest, the only checks which either restrain the passions or keep any vigour in the character of an Asiatic despot, the native Governments either became so oppressive and extortionate as to [120] desolate the country, or fell into such a state of nerveless imbecility, that every one, subject to their will, who had not the means of defending himself by his own armed followers, was the prey of anybody who had a band of ruffians in his pay. The British Government felt this deplorable state of things to be its own work; being the direct consequence of the position in which, for its own security, it had placed itself towards the native governments. Had it permitted this to go on indefinitely, it would have deserved to be accounted among the worst political malefactors. In some cases (unhappily not in all) it had endeavoured

to take precaution against these mischiefs by a special article in
the treaty, binding the prince to reform his administration, and
in future to govern in conformity to the advice of the British
Government. Among the treaties in which a provision of this
sort had been inserted, was that with Oude. For fifty years and
more did the British Government allow this engagement to
be treated with entire disregard; not without frequent remon-
strances, and occasionally threats, but without ever carrying
into effect what it threatened. During this period of half a
century, England was morally accountable for a mixture of tyranny and anarchy, the picture of which, by men who knew it
well, is appalling to all who read it. The act by which the Government of British India at last set aside treaties which had
been so pertinaciously violated, and assumed the power of ful-
filling the obligation it had so long before incurred, of giving to
the people of Oude a tolerable government, far from being the
political crime it is so often ignorantly called, was a criminally
tardy discharge of an imperative duty. And the fact, that nothing which had been done in all this century by the East India
Company's Government made it so unpopular in England, is
one of the most striking instances of what was noticed in a
former part of this article—the predisposition of English public opinion to look unfavourably upon every act by which territory or revenue are acquired from foreign States, and to take
part with any government, however unworthy, which can make
out the merest semblance of a case of injustice against our own
country.

But among civilized peoples, members of an equal community of nations, like Christian Europe, the question assumes another aspect, and must be decided on totally different principles.
It would be an affront to the reader to discuss the immorality
of wars of conquest, or of conquest even as the consequence of

lawful [121] war; the annexation of any civilized people to the
dominion of another, unless by their own spontaneous election. Up to this point, there is no difference of opinion among
honest people; nor on the wickedness of commencing an aggressive war for any interest of our own, except when necessary
to avert from ourselves an obviously impending wrong. The
disputed question is that of interfering in the regulation of
another country's internal concerns; the question whether a
nation is justified in taking part, on either side, in the civil
wars or party contests of another: and chiefly, whether it may
justifiably aid the people of another country in struggling for
liberty; or may impose on a country any particular government
or institutions, either as being best for the country itself, or as
necessary for the security of its neighbours.

Of these cases, that of a people in arms for liberty is the
only one of any nicety, or which, theoretically at least, is likely
to present conflicting moral considerations. The other cases
which have been mentioned hardly admit of discussion. Assistance to the government of a country in keeping down the
people, unhappily by far the most frequent case of foreign intervention, no one writing in a free country needs take the
trouble of stigmatizing. A government which needs foreign support to enforce obedience from its own citizens, is one which
ought not to exist; and the assistance given to it by foreigners
is hardly ever anything but the sympathy of one despotism
with another. A case requiring consideration is that of a protracted civil war, in which the contending parties are so equally
balanced that there is no probability of a speedy issue; or if
there is, the victorious side cannot hope to keep down the vanquished but by severities repugnant to humanity, and injurious
to the permanent welfare of the country. In this exceptional
case it seems now to be an admitted doctrine, that the neigh-

bouring nations, or one powerful neighbour with the acquies-
cence of the rest, are warranted in demanding that the contest
shall cease, and a reconciliation take place on equitable terms
of compromise. Intervention of this description has been repeatedly practised during the present generation, with such general
approval, that its legitimacy may be considered to have passed
into a maxim of what is called international law. The interference of the European Powers between Greece and Turkey, and
between Turkey and Egypt, were cases in point. That between
Holland and Belgium was still more so. The intervention of
England in Portugal, a few years ago, which is probably less
remembered than the others, because it took effect without the
employment of actual force, belongs to the same category. At
the time, this interposition had the appearance of a bad and dishonest backing of the government against the people, being so
timed as to hit the exact moment when the popular party had
obtained a marked advantage, and seemed on the eve of over-
throwing the government, or reducing it to terms. But if ever a
political act which looked ill in the commencement could be
justified by the event, this was, for, as the fact turned out, instead of giving ascendancy to a party, it proved a really healing
[122] measure; and the chiefs of the so-called rebellion were,
within a few years, the honoured and successful ministers of
the throne against which they had so lately fought.

With respect to the question, whether one country is justified in helping the people of another in a struggle against their
government for free institutions, the answer will be different,
according as the yoke which the people are attempting to throw
off is that of a purely native government, or of foreigners; considering as one of foreigners, every government which main-
tains itself by foreign support. When the contest is only with
native rulers, and with such native strength as those rulers can

enlist in their defence, the answer I should give to the question of the legitimacy of intervention is, as a general rule, No. The reason is, that there can seldom be anything approaching to assurance that intervention, even if successful, would be for the good of the people themselves. The only test possessing any real value, of a people's having become fit for popular institutions, is that they, or a sufficient portion of them to prevail in the contest, are willing to brave labour and danger for their liberation. I know all that may be said, I know it may be urged that the virtues of freemen cannot be learnt in the school of slavery, and that if a people are not fit for freedom, to have any chance of becoming so they must first be free. And this would be conclusive, if the intervention recommended would really give them freedom. But the evil is, that if they have not sufficient love of liberty to be able to wrest it from merely domestic oppressors, the liberty which is bestowed on them by other hands than their own, will have nothing real, nothing permanent. No people ever was and remained free, but because it was determined to be so; because neither its rulers nor any other party in the nation could compel it to be otherwise. If a people—especially one whose freedom has not yet become prescriptive—does not value it sufficiently to fight for it, and maintain it against any force which can be mustered *within* the country, even by those who have the command of the public revenue, it is only a question in how few years or months that people will be enslaved. Either the government which it has given to itself, or some military leader or knot of conspirators who contrive to subvert the government, will speedily put an end to all popular institutions: unless indeed it suits their convenience better to leave them standing, and be content with reducing them to mere forms; for, unless the spirit of liberty is strong in a people, those who have the executive in their hands

easily work any institutions to the purposes of despotism. There
is no sure guarantee against this deplorable issue, even in a
country which has achieved its own freedom; as may be seen
in the present day by striking examples both in the Old and
New Worlds: but when freedom has been achieved *for* them,
they have little prospect indeed of escaping this fate. When a
[123] people has had the misfortune to be ruled by a government under which the feelings and the virtues needful for maintaining freedom could not develope themselves, it is during an
arduous struggle to become free by their own efforts that these
feelings and virtues have the best chance of springing up. Men
become attached to that which they have long fought for and
made sacrifices for, they learn to appreciate that on which their
thoughts have been much engaged; and a contest in which
many have been called on to devote themselves for their country, is a school in which they learn to value their country's interest above their own.

   It can seldom, therefore—I will not go so far as to say never—
be either judicious or right, in a country which has a free government, to assist, otherwise than by the moral support of its
opinion, the endeavours of another to extort the same blessing
from its native rulers. We must except, of course, any case in
which such assistance is a measure of legitimate self-defence. If
(a contingency by no means unlikely to occur) this country, on
account of its freedom, which is a standing reproach to despotism everywhere, and an encouragement to throw it off, should
find itself menaced with attack by a coalition of Continental
despots, it ought to consider the popular party in every nation
of the Continent as its natural ally, the Liberals should be to
it, what the Protestants of Europe were to the Government of
Queen Elizabeth. So, again, when a nation, in her own defence,
has gone to war with a despot, and has had the rare good for-

tune not only to succeed in her resistance, but to hold the conditions of peace in her own hands, she is entitled to say that she will make no treaty, unless with some other ruler than the one whose existence as such may be a perpetual menace to her safety and freedom. These exceptions do but set in a clearer light the reasons of the rule; because they do not depend on any failure of those reasons, but on considerations paramount to them, and coming under a different principle.

But the case of a people struggling against a foreign yoke, or against a native tyranny upheld by foreign arms, illustrates the reasons for non-intervention in an opposite way; for in this case the reasons themselves do not exist. A people the most attached to freedom, the most capable of defending and of making a good use of free institutions, may be unable to contend successfully for them against the military strength of another nation much more powerful. To assist a people thus kept down, is not to disturb the balance of forces on which the permanent maintenance of freedom in a country depends, but to redress that balance when it is already unfairly and violently disturbed. The doctrine of non-intervention, to be a legitimate principle of morality, must be accepted by all governments. The despots must consent to be bound by it as well as the free States. Unless they do, the profession of it by free countries comes but to this miserable issue, that the wrong side may help the wrong, but the right must not help the right. Intervention to enforce non-intervention is always rightful, always moral, if not always prudent. Though it be a mistake to *give* freedom to a people who do not value the boon, it cannot but be right to insist that if they do value it, they shall not be hindered from [124] the pursuit of it by foreign coercion. It might not have been right for England (even apart from the question of prudence) to have taken part with Hungary in its noble struggle against Austria;

although the Austrian Government in Hungary was in some
sense a foreign yoke. But when, the Hungarians having shown
themselves likely to prevail in this struggle, the Russian despot
interposed, and joining his force to that of Austria, delivered
back the Hungarians, bound hand and foot, to their exasper-
ated oppressors, it would have been an honourable and virtu-
ous act on the part of England to have declared that this
should not be, and that if Russia gave assistance to the wrong
side, England would aid the right. It might not have been consistent with the regard which every nation is bound to pay to
its own safety, for England to have taken up this position single-
handed. But England and France together could have done it;
and if they had, the Russian armed intervention would never
have taken place, or would have been disastrous to Russia alone:
while all that those Powers gained by not doing it, was that
they had to fight Russia five years afterwards, under more difficult circumstances, and without Hungary for an ally. The first
nation which, being powerful enough to make its voice effec-
tual, has the spirit and courage to say that not a gun shall be
fired in Europe by the soldiers of one Power against the re-
volted subjects of another, will be the idol of the friends of freedom throughout Europe. That declaration alone will ensure
the almost immediate emancipation of every people which desires liberty sufficiently to be capable of maintaining it: and the
nation which gives the word will soon find itself at the head
of an alliance of free peoples, so strong as to defy the efforts of
any number of confederated despots to bring it down. The
prize is too glorious not to be snatched sooner or later by some
free country; and the time may not be distant when England,
if she does not take this heroic part because of its heroism, will
be compelled to take it from consideration for her own safety.

APPENDIX 2
List of Interventions 1815–2003
Michael Doyle and Camille Strauss-Kahn

INTERVENER	TARGET	LOCATION	START	END	MILITARY SUCCESS	EMPIRE	AUTOC-RACY	WAR REC	LIBERAL INTERVENER
Britain	France	Guadeloupe	1815	1816	1	1	1	0	0
Britain	Khandian troops	Sri Lanka	1815	1818	1	1	0	1	0
France	Prussia (+Russia, Austria, England)	Belgium	1815	1815	0	0	0	0	0
Maratha chiefs	Britain	India	1817	1818	0	0	0	0	0
Austria	Italian liberals (Carbonari)	Naples	1821	1827	1	0	1	0	0
Austria	Italian liberals (Carbonari)	Sardinia	1821	1821	1	0	1	0	0
Egypt	Greece	Turkey	1825	1829	0	0	0	0	0
Britain, France, Russia	Turkey, Egypt	Turkey	1827	1829	1	0	0	0	0
France	Spanish liberals	Spain	1823	1823	1	0	1	0	0
Britain	Ashanti warriors	Gold Coast	1824	1826	1	1	0	0	0

					Military success	Empire	Autocracy	War Rec	Liberal
Burma	Britain	Bengal	1824	1825	0	0	0	1	0
Britain	Burma	Burma	1825	1826	1	1	0	0	0
Argentina	Brazil	Uruguay	1825	1828	1	0	0	0	0
Persia	Russia	Caucasus	1825	1828	0	1	0	0	0
Britain	Bhurtpore	India	1825	1826	1	1	0	0	0
Honduras	Guatemala	Guatemala	1826	1829	1	0	0	0	0
Laos	Siam	Siam	1826	1828	0	1	0	1	0
Britain	Don Miguel	Portugal	1827	1828	1	0	0	1	0

Coding Notes:

Military success: 1 = successful, 0 = unsuccessful

Empire: 1 = formal annexation; 2 = informal empire (protectorate); 3 = partial territorial annexation

Autocracy: 0 = successor regime not conclusively more autocratic; 1 = successor more autocratic

War Rec assesses war recurrence within two years of intervention: 0 = no recurrence; 1 = conflict between same two parties in same territory; 2 = conflict between the same parties in different territory.

Liberal: 0 = nonliberal intervener; 1 = liberal intervener

This list is an ongoing project. An updated list can be found at camillesk.com. We welcome suggestions for and corrections to our coding, which can be sent to Michael Doyle at md2221@columbia.edu.

INTERVENER	TARGET	LOCATION	START	END	MILITARY SUCCESS	EMPIRE	AUTOC-RACY	WAR REC	LIBERAL INTERVENER
Peru	Colombia	Colombia	1828	1829	0	0	0	0	0
Russia	Turkey	Balkans, Anatolia	1828	1829	1	1	0	0	0
Spain	Mexico	Mexico	1829	1829	0	0	0	0	0
Netherlands	Belgium	Belgium	1831	1831	1	1	1	1	0
France	Netherlands	Belgium	1832	1833	1	0	0	0	1
France	Algeria	Algeria	1830	1870	1	1	0	1	1
Egypt	Turkey	Syria	1831	1833	1	1	0	0	0
France, Austria	Italian liberals (Garibaldi)	Papal states, Parma, Modena	1831	1834	1	0	1	0	0
Siam	Vietnam	Cambodia	1831	1834	1	2	0	1	0
Britain, France	Carlists	Spain	1835	1837	1	0	0	0	1
Xhosa tribes	Britain	South Africa	1834	1834	0	0	0	1	0

Intervener	Target	Location						
Xhosa tribes	Britain	South Africa	1835	1835	0	0	0	0	0
Vietnam	Siam	Cambodia	1834	1841	2	0	0	0	0
Persia	Afghanistan	Afghanistan	1836	1838	1	0	0	0	0
Chile	Peru, Bolivia	Peru	1836	1839	0	0	0	1	0
Mexico	Texan state	Texas	1837	1845	0	0	0	1	0
Dutch	Zulu tribes	South Africa	1838	1838	1	0	0	0	0
France	Mexico	Mexico	1838	1838	0	1	1	0	0
Britain	Afghanistan	Afghanistan	1839	1842	3	0	0	1	1
Britain	China	China	1839	1842	1	0	0	1	1
Russia	Kazakhstan, Uzbekistan, Turkmenistan	Central Asia	1839	1839	0	0	0	0	0
Turkey, Austria, Britain	Egypt	Syria	1839	1841	1	0	0	0	0
Brazil	Uruguayan liberals	Uruguay	1845	1851	0	0	0	0	0

INTERVENER	TARGET	LOCATION	START	END	MILITARY SUCCESS	EMPIRE	AUTOC-RACY	WAR REC	LIBERAL INTERVENER
Paraguay	Uruguayan liberals	Uruguay	1845	1851	0	0	0	0	0
Britain, France	Uruguayan conservatives	Uruguay	1845	1851	1	0	0	0	1
Guatemala	Honduras	Guatemala	1840	1842	1	0	1	0	0
Bolivia	Peru	Peru	1841	1842	0	0	0	0	0
Siam	Vietnam	Cambodia	1841	1845	1	2	0	0	0
Britain	Gwalior state	India	1843	1844	1	1	0	0	1
Sikh army	Britain	Punjab	1845	1845	0	0	0	1	0
Britain	Sikh army	Punjab	1845	1846	1	1	0	1	1
Britain	Xhosa tribes	South Africa	1847	1847	0	0	0	1	1
Britain, Spain	Septembrist liberals	Portugal	1847	1847	1	0	1	1	1
United States	Mexico	Texas	1846	1848	1	1	0	0	1

Russia	Kazakhstan, Uzbekistan, Turkmenistan	Central Asia	1847	1847	0	0	0	0	0
Austria	Sardinia	Sardinia	1848	1849	1	1	0	0	0
Prussia	Denmark	Denmark	1848	1849	0	0	0	0	0
Sweden	Insurrectionists	Denmark	1848	1849	1	0	0	0	0
Russia	Hungarian revolutionaries	Hungary	1849	1849	1	1	0	0	0
France, Austria, Spain	Roman Republic	Italy	1849	1849	1	1	0	0	0
Austria	Italian revolutionaries	Naples, Venice	1849	1849	1	1	0	0	0
Haiti	Dominican Republic	Dominican Republic	1849	1849	0	0	0	0	0
Guatemala	Salvador, Honduras, Nicaragua	Central America	1850	1851	1	1	0	1	0
Britain	Xhosa tribes	South Africa	1850	1853	1	0	1	0	1

INTERVENER	TARGET	LOCATION	START	END	MILITARY SUCCESS	EMPIRE	AUTOC- RACY	WAR REC	LIBERAL INTERVENER
Brazil	Argentina	Argentina, Uruguay	1851	1852	1	3	0	2	0
Britain	Basuto	Basutoland	1852	1865	0	0	0	0	1
Britain	Basuto	Basutoland	1857	1857	0	0	0	1	1
Netherlands (Boers)	Basuto	Basutoland	1858	1858	0	0	0	1	0
Netherlands (Boers)	Basuto	Basutoland	1865	1868	0	1	0	1	0
Britain	Basuto	Basutoland	1880	1881	1	1	0	0	1
Britain	Burma	Burma	1852	1852	1	1	0	0	1
Guatemala	Honduras	Honduras	1853	1853	1	0	1	0	0
Haiti	Dominican Republic	Dominican Republic	1854	1856	0	0	0	0	0
Persia	Afghanistan	Afghanistan	1855	1855	0	1	0	1	0
Britain	Persia	Afghanistan	1856	1857	1	0	0	0	1

Actor	Target							
Britain, France	China	1856	1860	1	1	0	1	0	1
Netherlands	Indonesia	Bali	1849	1856	1	1	0	1	1
France	Vietnam	Vietnam	1858	1862	1	1	0	1	0
Austria	Sardinia	Piedmont	1859	1859	0	0	0	0	0
France	Austria	Piedmont, Lombardy	1859	1859	1	1	0	1	0
Spain	Morocco	Tetuan	1859	1860	1	1	0	1	0
France	Mexico	Mexico	1862	1864	1	1	0	1	0
United States	France	Mexico	1855	1857	1	0	0	0	1
Guatemala, Nicaragua	Honduras, El Salvador	Central America	1863	1863	1	0	1	1	0
Ecuador	Colombia	Colombia	1863	1863	0	0	0	0	0
Spain	Dominican Republic	Dominican Republic	1863	1865	0	0	0	1	0
Paraguay	Brazil, Argentina, Uruguay	Rio de la Plata	1864	1870	0	0	0	0	0

INTERVENER	TARGET	LOCATION	START	END	MILITARY SUCCESS	EMPIRE	AUTOC- RACY	WAR REC	LIBERAL INTERVENER
Russia	Kazakhstan, Uzbekistan	Central Asia	1864	1876	1	1	0	0	0
Prussia, Austria	Denmark	Denmark	1864	1864	1	1	0	0	0
Prussia	Austria	Bohemia, Germany	1866	1866	1	1	0	0	0
Italy	Austria	Venetia, Tyrol	1866	1866	1	1	1	1	1
France	Italy	Papal states	1867	1870	1	0	1	1	0
Prussia	France	France	1871	1873	1	1	0	0	0
Honduras	Salvador	Salvador	1871	1871	1	0	1	1	0
Guatemala, Salvador	Honduras	Honduras	1872	1872	1	0	1	0	0
Netherlands	Kingdom of Aceh	Sumatra	1873	1874	1	1	0	1	1
Ashanti tribes	Britain	Gold coast	1873	1873	0	0	0	1	0
Britain	Ashanti tribes	Ashantiland	1874	1896	1	1	0	0	1

Country	Target							
France	Vietnam	Tonkin	1873	1874	0	0	0	0	1
Guatemala	Honduras	Honduras	1876	1876	1	0	0	0	0
Belgium	Congo tribes	Congo	1876	1884	1	1	0	0	1
Britain	Xhosa tribes	South Africa	1877	1878	1	1	0	0	1
Russia	Turkey	Romania	1877	1878	1	0	0	0	0
Egypt	Russia	Balkans	1877	1878	0	0	0	0	0
Russia	Turkmenistan	Central Asia	1878	1878	0	1	0	1	0
Britain	Afghanistan	Afghanistan	1878	1881	1	2	0	0	1
Egypt	Sudan, Uganda	Sudan, Uganda	1870	1872	1	1	0	0	0
Chile	Peru, Bolivia	Atacama Desert	1879	1884	1	1	0	0	0
Russia	Turkmenistan	Central Asia	1880	1881	1	1	0	0	0
Mahdist army	Egypt	Sudan	1881	1883	1	1	0	1	0
Britain	Mahdist troops	Sudan	1883	1885	0	0	0	0	1
France	Western Sudan	Mali	1881	1898	1	1	0	0	1

INTERVENER	TARGET	LOCATION	START	END	MILITARY SUCCESS	EMPIRE	AUTOC- RACY	WAR REC	LIBERAL INTERVENER
France	Tunisia	Tunisia	1881	1956	1	1	0	0	1
Britain	Egypt	Egypt	1882	1882	1	1	0	0	1
France	Mandingo tribes	Mali, Senegal	1882	1886	1	1	0	0	1
France	Vietnam	Tonkin	1882	1883	1	1	0	0	1
China	France	Tonkin	1883	1884	0	0	0	1	0
Russia	Afghanistan	Afghanistan	1884	1885	1	1	0	0	0
Guatemala	Salvador (+Costa Rica, Nicaragua)	Salvador	1885	1885	0	0	0	0	0
Serbia	Bulgaria	Bulgaria	1885	1885	0	0	0	0	0
Britain	Burma	Burma	1885	1886	1	1	0	0	1
Italy	Abyssinia	Eritrea	1882	1885	1	1	0	1	1
Italy	Abyssinia	Ethiopia	1887	1887	0	0	0	0	1
Guatemala	Salvador	Salvador	1890	1890	1	0	1	0	0
France	Dahomey tribes	Benin	1892	1892	1	1	0	1	1

Country		Location						
France	Dahomey tribes	Benin	1893	1899	1	1	0	1
France, Britain	Mandingo tribes	Mali, Senegal	1893	1898	1	1	0	1
France	Siam	Siam	1893	1893	1	1	0	1
Mahdist state	Italy	Sudan	1893	1894	0	0	0	0
Britain	Ndebele tribes	Zambia (Matabeleland)	1893	1894	1	1	0	1
Netherlands	Indonesia	Lombok	1894	1894	1	1	0	1
Japan	China	Korea	1894	1895	1	1	0	0
Greece	Turkey	Crete	1895	1896	0	0	0	1
Britain, France, Russia	Insurrectionists & Turkey	Crete	1895	1897	0	0	0	1
Italy	Abyssinia	Ethiopia	1895	1896	0	0	0	1
Britain	Mahdist state	Sudan	1896	1899	1	1	0	1
Britain	Kingdom of Benin	Benin	1897	1897	1	1	0	1
France	Chad	Chad	1899	1901	1	1	1	1

INTERVENER	TARGET	LOCATION	START	END	MILITARY SUCCESS	EMPIRE	AUTOC-RACY	WAR REC	LIBERAL INTERVENER
Greece	Turkey	Crete	1897	1897	0	0	1	0	1
US, Britain	Kingdom of Samoa	Samoan Islands	1898	1899	0	0	0	0	1
United States	Spain	Puerto Rico	1898	1898	1	2	0	0	1
United States	Cuba	Cuba	1899	1901	1	2	0	1	1
Britain, Italy	Somalia	Somalia	1901	1904	0	0	0	1	1
Britain	Somalia	Somalia	1920	1920	1	0	0	0	1
Boers Republics	Britain	South Africa	1899	1902	0	1	0	1	0
United States	China	China	1900	1901	1	0	0	0	1
Britain	Kingdom of Kano	Nigeria	1903	1903	1	1	0	0	1
France	Morocco	Morocco	1903	1914	1	1	0	0	1
Britain	Tibet	Tibet	1903	1904	1	2	0	0	1
United States	Colombia	Panama	1903	1903	1	2	0	0	1

Intervener	Against	Location							
Japan	Russia	Manchuria, Korea	1904	1905	1	1	0	0	0
Salvador	Guatemala	Guatemala	1906	1906	0	0	0	0	0
United States	Cuba	Cuba	1906	1906	1	2	0	0	1
Nicaragua	Honduras, El Salvador	Honduras	1907	1907	0	0	0	0	0
United States	Nicaragua	Nicaragua	1909	1909	1	3	0	0	1
Russia	Persia	Persia	1909	1909	1	2	0	1	0
United States	Mexican nationalists	Mexico	1914	1914	1	2	0	0	1
Italy	Turkey	Libya	1911	1912	1	1	0	0	1
Russia	Persia	Persia	1911	1911	1	2	0	1	0
Bulgaria	Serbia, Greece, Turkey	Balkans	1913	1913	0	0	0	0	0
United States	Haiti	Haiti	1914	1915	1	3	0	0	1
Austria (+Bulgaria)	Serbia, Montenegro	Salonika Front (Serbia, Montenegro)	1914	1915	1	1	1	1	0

INTERVENER	TARGET	LOCATION	START	END	MILITARY SUCCESS	EMPIRE	AUTOC- RACY	WAR REC	LIBERAL INTERVENER
France, Britain	Austria	Salonika Front (Serbia)	1915	1915	0	0	0	1	1
Germany	France, Britain	Western Front (France)	1914	1918	0	0	1	0	0
Germany	Belgium	Western Front (Belgium)	1914	1914	1	1	1	1	0
United States	Germany	Western Front (France)	1917	1918	1	4	0	0	1
Germany, Austria	Poland	Eastern Front (Poland)	1914	1916	1	1	1	0	0
Britain	Germany	Western Front (France)	1914	1918	1	0	0	0	1

United States, France, Britain	Germany	Western Front (Belgium)	1918	1918	1	4	0	0	1
Russia	Germany	Eastern Front (East Prussia, Carpathians)	1914	1917	0	0	0	0	0
Russia	Austria	Eastern Front (Galicia)	1914	1917	0	0	0	0	0
Russia	Austria, Germany	Eastern Front (Poland)	1914	1915	0	1	1	0	0
Britain	Germany	South Africa	1914	1915	1	1	0	0	1
France, Belgium	Germany	Cameroon	1914	1916	1	1	0	0	1
France, Britain	Germany	Togo	1914	1914	1	1	0	0	1
Britain	Germany	East Africa	1914	1918	1	1	0	0	1
Japan (+Britain)	Germany	Tsingtao (China)	1914	1914	1	2	0	0	0
Britain	Turkey	Mesopotamia	1914	1916	0	0	1	1	1
Britain	Turkey	Mesopotamia	1916	1918	1	1	0	0	1

INTERVENER	TARGET	LOCATION	START	END	MILITARY SUCCESS	EMPIRE	AUTOC-RACY	WAR REC	LIBERAL INTERVENER
Britain	Turkey	Gallipoli, Dardanelles	1915	1915	0	0	0	0	1
Bulgaria (+Germany)	France, Britain	Salonika Front (Greece)	1916	1916	0	0	0	1	0
France, Britain	Bulgaria	Salonika Front (Greece, Serbia)	1916	1918	1	1	0	0	1
Britain	Turkey, Germany	Palestine Front (Syria)	1918	1918	1	1	0	0	1
Turkey, Germany	Britain	Palestine Front (Egypt)	1916	1918	0	0	0	1	0
Turkey	Britain	Palestine Front (Egypt)	1915	1915	0	0	0	1	0
Russia	Turkey	Caucasus Front	1914	1917	1	1	0	1	0

Turkey	Russia	Caucasus Front	1918	1918	1	1	0	0	o
Austria	Italy	Italian Front	1916	1918	o	0	0	1	o
Italy	Austria	Italian Front	1915	1916	0	0	0	1	o
France, Britain	Austria, Germany	Italian Front	1917	1918	1	o	0	0	1
Romania	Austria	Hungary	1916	1916	0	0	0	1	o
Austria, Germany	Romania	Romania	1916	1917	1	1	1	0	o
United States	Dominican Republic	Dominican Republic	1916	1920	1	3	1	0	1
Italy	Austria	Salonika Front (Albania)	1916	1920	1	2	0	0	o
United States	Russia	Russia	1917	1920	0	0	0	0	1
France, Britain	Russia	Russia	1917	1920	0	0	0	0	1
Japan	Russia	Russia	1917	1920	0	0	0	0	o

INTERVENER	TARGET	LOCATION	START	END	MILITARY SUCCESS	EMPIRE	AUTOC-RACY	WAR REC	LIBERAL INTERVENER
Russia	Hungary	Hungary	1919	1919	1	2	1	1	0
Hungary	Czechoslovakia, Romania	Czechoslova-kia, Romania	1919	1919	0	0	0	0	0
Romania	Hungary	Hungary	1919	1919	1	2	1	0	0
USSR, Ukraine	Poland	Poland	1920	1921	1	1	0	0	0
Britain	Afghanistan	Afghanistan	1919	1919	1	0	0	0	1
USSR	Mongolia	Mongolia	1920	1921	1	1	1	0	0
Britain	Kurds	Kurdistan	1920	1922	1	0	1	0	1
United States	Sandinista rebels	Nicaragua	1927	1933	1	2	0	0	1
Japan	China	Manchuria	1931	1933	1	3	1	1	0
Bolivia	Paraguay	Chaco	1932	1935	0	0	0	0	0
Italy	Ethiopia	Ethiopia	1935	1936	1	1	0	0	0
USSR	Spain	Spain	1936	1938	0	0	1	0	0

Germany (+Italy, Portugal)	Spain	Spain	1936	1939	1	0	1	0	0
Japan	China	China	1932	1945	0	0	0	0	0
Italia	Albania	Albania	1939	1939	1	1	0	0	0
Germany	Poland	Eastern Front (Poland)	1939	1939	1	1	1	1	0
Germany	France, Belgium, Netherlands	Western Front (Belgium, Netherlands, France)	1939	1940	1	1	1	1	0
Britain	Germany	Western Front (France)	1940	1940	0	0	0	1	1
Italy	France	Western Front (France)	1940	1940	0	0	0	0	0

INTERVENER	TARGET	LOCATION	START	END	MILITARY SUCCESS	EMPIRE	AUTOC- RACY	WAR REC	LIBERAL INTERVENER
Germany	USSR	Eastern Front (USSR, Crimea, Ukraine)	1941	1944	0	0	0	1	0
USSR	Germany	Eastern Front (Ukraine, Poland, Bulgaria, Romania)	1941	1945	1	1	1	0	0
USSR	Finland	Finland	1939	1940	1	1	1	0	0
Japan	United States, Britain	Pacific Front (Hong Kong, Malaysia, Singapore)	1941	1942	0	1	1	1	0
United States	Japan	Pacific Front (Philippines)	1944	1945	1	2	0	0	1

United States (+Britain)	Germany	France, Germany	1944	1945	I	O	O	O	I
United States	Japan	Pacific Front (Japan)	1945	1945	I	O	O	O	I
Germany	Denmark, Norway	Denmark, Norway	1940	1940	I	I	I	O	O
Britain	Norway	Norway	1940	1940	O	O	O	I	I
Italy	Britain	North African Front (Egypt)	1940	1940	I	I	O	I	I
Britain	Italy	North African Front (Egypt, Libya)	1940	1941	I	I	I	I	O
Germany	Britain	North African Front (Libya)	1941	1941	I	I	O	I	O
Britain	Germany	North African Front (Libya)	1942	1943	I	I	O	O	I

INTERVENER	TARGET	LOCATION	START	END	MILITARY SUCCESS	EMPIRE	AUTOC-RACY	WAR REC	LIBERAL INTERVENER
United States	Germany (+Vichy French)	North African Front (Morocco, Algeria)	1942	1942	1	1	0	0	1
United States (+Britain)	Germany	North African Front (Tunisia)	1942	1943	1	1	0	1	1
Italy	Britain	East African Front (Sudan, Kenya)	1940	1940	0	2	0	1	0
Britain	Italy	East African Front (Ethiopia, Eritrea)	1940	1941	1	1	0	0	1
Britain	Germany, Italy	Malta	1940	1942	1	3	0	0	1
Britain (+Free French)	Germany	West African Front (Senegal, Gabon)	1940	1940	1	1	0	0	1

Germany	Yugoslavia	Balkan Front (Yugoslavia)	1941	1941	I	I	I	o	o
Germany	Britain	Balkan Front (Greece)	1941	1941	I	I	I	o	o
Italy	Greece	Balkan Front (Albania, Greece)	1940	1940	o	o	o	I	o
Germany (+Italy)	Greece	Balkan Front (Macedonia, Albania, Greece)	1940	1941	I	I	I	o	o
Japan	France	Indochina	1940	1945	I	o	I	o	o
Thailand	France	Indochina	1941	1941	I	I	o	o	o
Japan	Britain	Pacific Front (Burma)	1941	1943	I	I	I	I	o
Britain (+USSR)	Iran	Iran, Iraq, Syria	1941	1943	I	o	o	o	I
United States (+Britain)	Italy	Italy	1943	1945	I	I	o	o	I

INTERVENER	TARGET	LOCATION	START	END	MILITARY SUCCESS	EMPIRE	AUTOC-RACY	WAR REC	LIBERAL INTERVENER
Britain	Japan	Pacific Front (Burma)	1944	1945	1	2	0	0	1
USSR	Bulgaria	Bulgaria	1944	1944	1	1	0	0	0
Germany	Hungary	Hungary	1944	1945	1	1	1	1	0
USSR	Romania	Romania	1944	1944	1	1	0	0	0
United States	China	China	1947	1949	0	0	1	0	1
USSR	Hungary	Hungary	1945	1945	1	1	0	0	0
USSR	Czechoslovakia	Eastern Front (Czechoslovakia)	1945	1945	1	1	0	0	0
Israel	Palestinians (+Syria, Sudan, Lebanon, Iraq)	Palestine	1948	1949	1	1	0	0	0
Egypt	Israel	Israel	1948	1949	0	0	0	0	0
Pakistan	India	Kashmir	1947	1949	1	1	0	0	0

India	Hyderabad	Hyderabad	1948	1948	1	1	0	0	1
China	Tibet	Tibet	1950	1951	1	1	0	0	0
North Korea	South Korea	Korea	1950	1953	0	0	0	0	0
United States	North Korea	Korea	1950	1953	1	0	0	0	1
China (+USSR)	South Korea	Korea	1950	1953	1	0	1	0	0
United States, Britain	Iran	Iran	1953	1953	1	0	1	0	1
USSR	East Germany	East Germany	1953	1953	1	0	1	0	0
United States	Guatemala	Guatemala	1954	1954	1	0	1	0	1
USSR	Hungary	Hungary	1956	1956	1	1	1	0	0
Israel	Egypt	Egypt	1956	1957	0	0	0	2	1
France, Britain	Egypt	Egypt	1956	1956	0	0	0	0	1
Britain	Oman	Oman	1957	1959	1	1	1	0	1
United States	Lebanon	Lebanon	1958	1958	1	0	0	0	1
United States	Laos	Laos	1962	1973	0	0	0	0	1

INTERVENER	TARGET	LOCATION	START	END	MILITARY SUCCESS	EMPIRE	AUTOC- RACY	WAR REC	LIBERAL INTERVENER
North Vietnam	Laos	Laos	1969	1973	0	0	0	0	0
United States (+Korea, Australia, New Zealand, Thailand)	Vietnam	Vietnam	1965	1975	0	0	0	1	1
China (+North Korea)	Vietnam	Vietnam	1965	1970	1	0	1	1	0
USSR (+Cuba)	Vietnam	Vietnam	1965	1974	1	0	1	1	0
United States	Cuba	Bay of Pigs	1961	1961	0	0	0	0	1
India	Portugal	Goa	1961	1961	1	1	0	0	1
United Nations	DRC	Katanga	1961	1963	0	0	0	1	1
Indonesia	Britain	Borneo	1963	1966	0	0	0	0	0
France	Gabon	Gabon	1964	1964	1	0	1	0	1
Yemen	Oman	Oman	1965	1976	0	0	0	0	0

Intervener	Target	Location							
Iran (+Britain, Jordan)	Oman	Oman	1972	1976	1	0	1	0	0
United States	Dominican Republic	Dominican Republic	1965	1965	1	0	1	0	1
Pakistan	India	Kashmir	1965	1965	0	0	0	0	0
Israel	Egypt	Golan, Gaza, West Bank	1967	2013	1	1	0	1	1
USSR	Czechoslovakia	Czechoslovakia	1958	1958	1	1	1	0	0
France	Chadian rebels	Chad	1966	1978	1	0	1	1	1
Salvador	Honduras	Honduras	1969	1969	1	1	0	0	0
Egypt	Israel	Suez	1969	1970	0	0	0	1	0
United States	Cambodia	Cambodia	1970	1975	0	0	0	1	1
North Vietnam	Cambodia	Cambodia	1970	1975	1	0	1	1	0
Portugal	Guinea	Guinea	1970	1970	1	2	0	0	0
Syria	Jordan	Jordan	1970	1970	0	0	1	0	0
India	Pakistan	Bangladesh	1971	1971	1	0	0	0	1

INTERVENER	TARGET	LOCATION	START	END	MILITARY SUCCESS	EMPIRE	AUTOC-RACY	WAR REC	LIBERAL INTERVENER
Turkey	Greece	Cyprus	1974	1974	1	3	1	0	0
USSR	Eritrea	Eritrea	1974	1989	1	1	0	1	0
South Africa	MPLA	Angola	1975	1988	0	0	0	1	0
USSR, Cuba	FNLA-UNITA	Angola	1975	1989	0	0	0	1	0
Syria	Lebanon	Lebanon	1975	1976	1	0	1	1	0
Indonesia	Timor	East Timor	1975	1999	0	0	0	0	0
Rhodesia, South Africa	Mozambique	Mozambique	1976	1982	0	0	0	1	0
Zimbabwe, Zambia, Tanzania	Mozambique rebels	Mozambique	1976	1982	0	0	0	1	0
Morocco	DRC	Katanga	1977	1977	1	0	1	1	0
Somalia	Ethiopia	Ethiopia	1977	1978	0	0	0	1	0
South Africa	Namibia	Namibia	1978	1988	0	0	0	0	0
Vietnam	Cambodia	Cambodia	1979	1988	0	0	0	1	0

Israel	Lebanon	Lebanon	1978	1978	I	C	O	I	I
France, Belgium	DRC	Katanga	1978	1978	I	C	I	O	I
Morocco	DRC	Katanga	1979	1979	I	O	I	O	O
USSR	Afghanistan	Afghanistan	1979	1989	C	O	O	I	O
Uganda	Tanzania	Tanzania	1978	1978	O	O	O	I	O
Tanzania	Uganda	Uganda	1978	1979	I	O	O	I	O
Libya	Tanzania	Tanzania	1979	1979	O	O	O	I	O
Libya	Chad	Chad	1979	1990	O	O	O	O	O
United States	Salvador	Salvador	1981	1990	I	O	O	O	I
China	Vietnam	Vietnam	1979	1979	O	O	O	I	O
Iraq	Iran	Iran	1980	1988	O	O	O	O	O
Iran	Iraq	Iran, Iraq, Kurdistan	1981	1988	O	O	O	O	O
United States	Nicaragua	Nicaragua	1981	1988	C	O	O	O	I
Argentina	Britain	Falkland	1982	1982	C	O	O	O	O
Israel	Lebanon	Lebanon	1982	1982	I	O	O	I	I

INTERVENER	TARGET	LOCATION	START	END	MILITARY SUCCESS	EMPIRE	AUTOC-RACY	WAR REC	LIBERAL INTERVENER
Syria	Israel	Lebanon	1982	1982	0	0	0	1	0
United States	Lebanon	Lebanon	1983	1984	0	0	0	1	1
United States	Grenada	Grenada	1983	1983	1	0	0	0	1
Nigeria, Ghana, Guinea, Sierra Leone	Liberia	Liberia	1989	1994	1	0	1	1	0
United States	Panama	Panama	1989	1989	1	2	0	0	1
Iraq	Kuwait	Kuwait	1990	1990	1	1	0	0	0
United States (+)	Iraq	Saudi Arabia, Kuwait	1990	1991	1	3	0	0	1
Nigeria, Ghana, Guinea, Sierra Leone	Sierra Leone	Sierra Leone	1996	1998	1	0	1	1	0
NATO	Bosnia	Bosnia	1992	1995	1	0	0	0	1
United States	Somalia	Somalia	1992	1994	0	0	0	1	1

United States	Haiti	Haiti	1994	1994	1	3	1	0	1
Angola	Congo-Brazza-ville	Congo-Braz-zaville	1997	1997	1	0	1	0	0
NATO	Serbia	Kosovo	1998	1999	1	2	0	0	1
Uganda, Rwanda	DRC	Congo	1998	1999	0	0	1	1	0
Zimbabwe, Chad, Namibia, Angola	Uganda, Rwanda	Congo	1998	1999	1	0	1	1	0
Nigeria, Ghana, Guinea, Sierra Leone	Liberia	Liberia	1999	2003	1	0	0	0	0
United States (+)	Afghanistan	Afghanistan	2001	—	1	0	0	—	1
United States (+)	Iraq	Iraq	2003	—	1	0	0	—	1

INDEX

Page numbers followed by *t* indicate tables. Page number followed by *f* indicates a figure.